SECOND CLASS

Discrimination Against Palestinian Arab Children in Israel's Schools

Human Rights Watch
New York • Washington • London • Brussels

ISBN: 1-56432-266-1
Library of Congress Control Number: 2001095949

Cover photo: Copyright © 2001 Zama Coursen-Neff/Human Rights Watch
A severely rusted school building, still in use, stands in mud and water at an Arab primary school in Israel.
Cover design by Rafael Jiménez

Addresses for Human Rights Watch
350 Fifth Avenue, 34th Floor, New York, NY 10118-3299
Tel: (212) 290-4700, Fax: (212) 736-1300, E-mail: hrwnyc@hrw.org

1630 Connecticut Avenue, N.W., Suite 500, Washington, DC 20009
Tel: (202) 612-4321, Fax: (202) 612-4333, E-mail: hrwdc@hrw.org

33 Islington High Street, N1 9LH London, UK
Tel: (171) 713-1995, Fax: (171) 713-1800, E-mail: hrwatchuk@gn.apc.org

15 Rue Van Campenhout, 1000 Brussels, Belgium
Tel: (2) 732-2009, Fax: (2) 732-0471, E-mail:hrwatcheu@skynet.be

Web Site Address: http://www.hrw.org

Listserv address: To subscribe to the Human Rights Watch news e-mail list, send a blank e-mail message to subscribe@igc.topica.com.

Human Rights Watch is dedicated to
protecting the human rights of people around the world.

We stand with victims and activists to prevent
discrimination, to uphold political freedom, to protect people from inhumane
conduct in wartime, and to bring offenders to justice.

We investigate and expose
human rights violations and hold abusers accountable.

We challenge governments and those who hold power to end abusive practices
and respect international human rights law.

We enlist the public and the international
community to support the cause of human rights for all.

HUMAN RIGHTS WATCH

Human Rights Watch conducts regular, systematic investigations of human rights abuses in some seventy countries around the world. Our reputation for timely, reliable disclosures has made us an essential source of information for those concerned with human rights. We address the human rights practices of governments of all political stripes, of all geopolitical alignments, and of all ethnic and religious persuasions. Human Rights Watch defends freedom of thought and expression, due process and equal protection of the law, and a vigorous civil society; we document and denounce murders, disappearances, torture, arbitrary imprisonment, discrimination, and other abuses of internationally recognized human rights. Our goal is to hold governments accountable if they transgress the rights of their people.

Human Rights Watch began in 1978 with the founding of its Europe and Central Asia division (then known as Helsinki Watch). Today, it also includes divisions covering Africa, the Americas, Asia, and the Middle East. In addition, it includes three thematic divisions on arms, children's rights, and women's rights. It maintains offices in New York, Washington, Los Angeles, London, Brussels, Moscow, Dushanbe, and Bangkok. Human Rights Watch is an independent, nongovernmental organization, supported by contributions from private individuals and foundations worldwide. It accepts no government funds, directly or indirectly.

The staff includes Kenneth Roth, executive director; Michele Alexander, development director; Reed Brody, advocacy director; Carroll Bogert, communications director; Barbara Guglielmo, finance director; Jeri Laber special advisor; Lotte Leicht, Brussels office director; Michael McClintock, deputy program director; Patrick Minges, publications director; Maria Pignataro Nielsen, human resources director; Jemera Rone, counsel; Malcolm Smart, program director; Wilder Tayler, general counsel; and Joanna Weschler, United Nations representative. Jonathan Fanton is the chair of the board. Robert L. Bernstein is the founding chair.

The regional directors of Human Rights Watch are Peter Takirambudde, Africa; José Miguel Vivanco, Americas; Sidney Jones, Asia; Holly Cartner, Europe and Central Asia; and Hanny Megally, Middle East and North Africa. The thematic division directors are Joost R. Hiltermann, arms; Lois Whitman, children's; and Regan Ralph, women's.

The members of the board of directors are Jonathan Fanton, chair; Lisa Anderson, Robert L. Bernstein, David M. Brown, William Carmichael, Dorothy Cullman, Gina Despres, Irene Diamond, Adrian W. DeWind, Fiona Druckenmiller, Edith Everett, Michael E. Gellert, Vartan Gregorian, Alice H. Henkin, James F. Hoge, Stephen L. Kass, Marina Pinto Kaufman, Bruce Klatsky, Joanne Leedom-Ackerman, Josh Mailman, Yolanda T. Moses, Samuel K. Murumba, Andrew Nathan, Jane Olson, Peter Osnos, Kathleen Peratis, Bruce Rabb, Sigrid Rausing, Orville Schell, Sid Sheinberg, Gary G. Sick, Malcolm Smith, Domna Stanton, John J. Studzinski, and Maya Wiley. Robert L. Bernstein is the founding chair of Human Rights Watch.

ACKNOWLEDGEMENTS

This report was based on information gathered in Israel in November and December 2000 by Zama Coursen-Neff and Yodon Thonden, both counsel to the Children's Rights Division of Human Rights Watch, and written by Zama Coursen-Neff. Yodon Thonden wrote the chapter on curricula. Raheek Rinawi, Beth Packman, Noam Lupu, and Juliette Abu-Iyun provided additional research assistance.

Lois Whitman, executive director of the Children's Rights Division; Clarissa Bencomo, researcher at Human Rights Watch; Michael McClintock, deputy program director of Human Rights Watch; and Wilder Tayler, legal and policy director, edited the report. Hanny Megally, Isis Nusair, Joe Stork, and Saman Zia-Zarifi also reviewed and commented on the manuscript. Dana Sommers, Fitzroy Hepkins, Veronica Matushaj, and Patrick Minges provided production assistance.

Human Rights Watch is indebted to numerous nongovernmental organizations and individuals who generously assisted us in the course of our field research. We would especially like to thank: the Adva Center, Adalah (the Legal Center for Arab Minority Rights in Israel), the Arab Association for Human Rights (HRA), the Arab Children Friends Association, the Al-Tufula Pedagogical Center, the Center for Bedouin Studies and Development, the Follow-Up Committee for Arab Education, Daphna Golan, Ittijah, Yousef Taiseer Jabareen, Andre Elias Mazawi, Mossawa, Shatil, Maya Steinitz, and Tali Yariv-Mashal. Human Rights Watch would also like to thank the Israeli officials who agreed to be interviewed for this report and who facilitated access to schools.

Most of all, we would like to acknowledge the many students, teachers, and school administrators, both Palestinian Arab and Jewish, who spoke with us and opened their schools to us. Without them this report would not have been possible.

TABLE OF CONTENTS

LIST OF TABLES

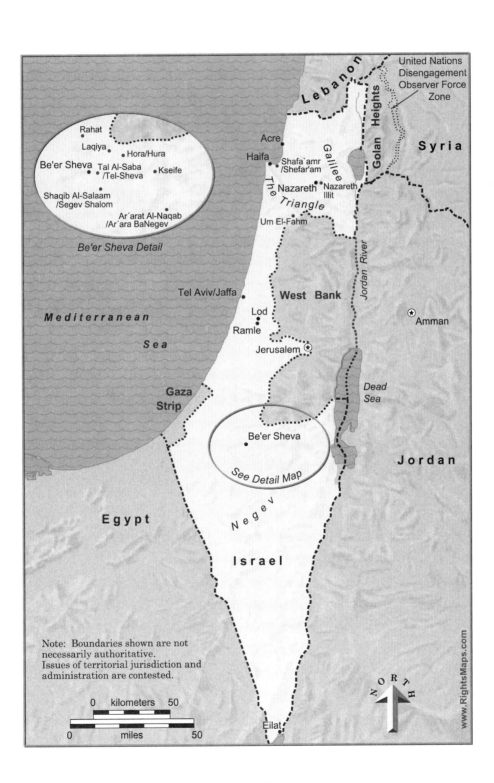

Rahat
Laqiya
Be'er Sheva
Hora/Hura
Tal Al-Saba
/Tel-Sheva
Kseife
Shaqib Al-Salaam
/Segev Shalom
Ar´arat Al-Naqab
/Ar´ara BaNegev

Be'er Sheva Detail

Lebanon
Acre
Haifa
Galilee
Golan Heights
Syria
United Nations
Disengagement
Observer Force
Zone

Shafa`amr
/Shefar'am
Nazareth
Nazareth
Illit
The
Triangle
Um El-Fahm

Mediterranean

Sea

Tel Aviv/Jaffa
Lod
Ramle
Jerusalem

West Bank

Jordan River

Amman

Gaza
Strip

Be'er Sheva

See Detail Map

Dead
Sea

Jordan

Egypt

Negev

Israel

Note: Boundaries shown are not
necessarily authoritative.
Issues of territorial jurisdiction and
administration are contested.

0   kilometers   50

0   miles   50

Eilat

NORTH

www.RightsMaps.com

I. SUMMARY

Nearly one in four of Israel's 1.6 million schoolchildren are educated in a public school system wholly separate from the majority. The children in this parallel school system are Israeli citizens of Palestinian Arab origin. Their schools are a world apart in quality from the public schools serving Israel's majority Jewish population. Often overcrowded and understaffed, poorly built, badly maintained, or simply unavailable, schools for Palestinian Arab children offer fewer facilities and educational opportunities than are offered other Israeli children. This report is about Israel's discrimination against its Palestinian Arab children in guaranteeing the right to education.

The Israeli government operates two separate school systems, one for Jewish children and one for Palestinian Arab children. Discrimination against Palestinian Arab children colors every aspect of the two systems. Education Ministry authorities have acknowledged that the ministry spends less per student in the Arab system than in the Jewish school system. The majority's schools also receive additional state and state-sponsored private funding for school construction and special programs through other government agencies. The gap is enormous–on every criterion measured by Israeli authorities.

The disparities between the two systems examined in this report are identified in part through a review of official statistics. These findings are tested and complemented by the findings of Human Rights Watch's on-site visits to twenty-six schools in the two systems and our interviews with students, parents, teachers, administrators, and national education authorities.

Palestinian Arab children attend schools with larger classes and fewer teachers than do those in the Jewish school system, with some children having to travel long distances to reach the nearest school. Arab schools also contrast dramatically with the larger system in their frequent lack of basic learning facilities like libraries, computers, science laboratories, and even recreation space. In no Arab school did we see specialized facilities, such as film editing studios or theater rooms that we saw as a sign of excellence in some of the Jewish schools we visited. Palestinian Arab children with disabilities are particularly marginalized, with special education teachers and facilities often unavailable in the system, despite the highly developed special education programs of the Jewish school system.

The unavailability of schools for three and four-year-old children in many communities, despite legislation making such schools–and attendance–obligatory, is matched by inadequate kindergarten construction for Palestinian Arab children throughout much of the country, particularly in the Negev. A Bedouin man in a recognized Bedouin town told us, "I have a daughter five years old. I thought last year with [former Education Minister] Yosi Sarid's promise she would go to [a government] preschool, but there were none there."[1]

A bar on school construction in some Palestinian Arab communities, in line with government policies pressing Palestinian Arab populations to move out of some areas, imposes enormous hardship on families with children and denies many children their right to an education. Poor school facilities and schools requiring travel over long distances result in children dropping out of the education system altogether at a very high rate.

The educational system has given a low priority to teacher training for the Arab school system and provides less "in-service" training to Palestinian Arab teachers already within the system than is routine within the majority system. Palestinian Arab teachers on average have lower qualifications and receive lower salaries than non-Palestinian Arab teachers. Financial incentives for teachers assigned in particularly deprived areas like parts of the Negev are lower than those made available to teachers in Jewish schools identified as hardship postings. Training in special education for teachers in the Arab school system has been largely insufficient.

Despite higher rates of disability among Palestinian Arabs, in the area of special education the Ministry of Education spends less proportionately on integration ("mainstreaming"), special education services, and special schools for Palestinian Arab children than it does for Jewish children. "We have been asking for special support for many years," the father of a disabled boy explained. "Usually we go to the Ministry of Education, and they tell us to go to the local municipality, and we go and are denied."[2] Arab special education schools suffer from a scarcity of trained professionals, such as psychologists and speech therapists. Palestinian Arab children who cannot attend a regular school have only a tiny handful of schools to choose from, and there is often only one Arab school in the country for children with a particular disability. Many of these children must travel long distances daily or attend a Jewish school if one happens to be available. But Jewish special education schools are not designed for Palestinian Arab pupils. For example, speech therapists in some schools with both Jewish and Palestinian Arab hearing impaired students do not speak Arabic. For some families, the only option is keep their disabled children at home.

Palestinian Arab students study from a government-prescribed Arabic curriculum that is adapted second hand from the Hebrew curriculum: common

---

[1] Human Rights Watch interview, Laqiya (recognized Bedouin locality), December 14, 2000.
[2] Human Rights Watch interview, village in the Triangle region, December 6, 2000.

subjects are developed with little or no Palestinian Arab participation and translated years after the Hebrew language material is published. The government devotes inadequate resources to developing the subjects unique to Arab education. No curricula in Arabic for special education existed until 2000, and it was not available in any of the Arab special education schools that Human Rights Watch visited. "We adapt curriculum from regular schools and try to make it easier," a school speech therapist explained.[3] Palestinian Arab teachers have considerably less choice in textbooks and teaching material than do Jewish teachers.

The curricula's content often alienates students and teachers alike. For example, in Hebrew language class, Palestinian Arab students are required to study Jewish religious texts including Tanach (Jewish bible) and Jewish Talmudic scholars. This material is included in the mandatory subjects in the matriculation exams (*bagrut*) taken at the end of high school. A Hebrew language teacher in an Arab high school described her pupils' reaction: "Some children see it as imposed on them. It makes it hard for the teacher to motivate students to study. It doesn't relate to Arab children as a whole. . . but because of the *bagrut* we have to cover the material."[4] Palestinian Arab students and teachers also expressed a desire to study more works of Palestinian writers and more about Palestinian history. The Ministry of Education has recently made some positive reforms in Arabic curricula, including in history, geography, and civics. However, many of these changes have not been fully implemented because textbooks and other teaching materials are lacking.

Discrimination at every level of the education system winnows out a progressively larger proportion of Palestinian Arab children as they progress through the school system–or channels those who persevere away from the opportunities of higher education. The hurdles Palestinian Arab students face from kindergarten to university function like a series of sieves with sequentially finer holes. At each stage, the education system filters out a higher proportion of Palestinian Arab students than Jewish students. Children denied access to kindergarten do less well in primary school. Children in dilapidated, distant, under-resourced schools have a far higher drop-out rate. Children who opt for vocational programs are often limited to preparation for work as "carpenters, machinists, or mechanics in a garage," as one school director told Human Rights Watch.[5]

---

[3] Human Rights Watch interview, Israel, December 11, 2000.
[4] Human Rights Watch interview, Nazareth, December 8, 2000.
[5] Human Rights Watch interview, Israel, December 9, 2000.

Many Palestinian Arab students who might otherwise have academic or professional aspirations are barred from higher education by an examination system established firstly for the Jewish majority's school system—the point at which the two unequal systems converge. Palestinian Arab students who stay in school perform less well on national examinations, especially the matriculation examinations (*bagrut*)–the prerequisite for a high school diploma and university application Others are weeded out by a required "psychometric" examination–generally described as an aptitude test–which Palestinian Arab educators describe as culturally weighted, a translation of the test given students of the Jewish school system.   A consequence is that Palestinian Arabs seeking admission to university are rejected at a far higher rate than are Jewish applicants. All but 5.7 percent of the students receiving their first university degree in the 1998-1999 school year were Jewish.

The Israeli government has offered various other explanations for the gaps between Jewish and Palestinian Arab students' performance.   These include poverty and cultural attitudes, especially regarding girls. Human Rights Watch found that in light of clear examples of state discrimination, neither poverty nor cultural attitudes adequately explained the existing gap.   Indeed, in many instances, the data run directly contrary to the claim that these factors, and not discrimination, are at the root of the problem. Moreover, discrimination in education is cyclical and cumulative.   When one generation has fewer educational opportunities of poorer quality, their children grow up in families with lower incomes and learn from less well-educated teachers.

Although low income Jewish students–especially new immigrant, Sephardic, or Mizrahi students[6]–face some of the same challenges related to poverty that Palestinian Arab students do, the government provides disadvantaged Jewish students with a battery of resources designed to improve academic performance and to keep them from dropping out. The remedial and enrichment resources made available for Jewish schools include extra school hours and remedial and enrichment programs, offered both during school hours and after school, as well as truant officers, counseling, and the opportunity for vocational education.

For Palestinian Arab students, the Ministry of Education uses a different instrument to measure disadvantage than it does for Jewish students and measures their need only against other Palestinian Arab students, not against Jewish students.   Some Palestinian Arab students receive some enrichment and

---

[6] Ashkenazi Jews are of Eastern European origin: Sephardic Jews are descendants of Jews expelled from Spain and Portugal in the fifteenth and sixteenth centuries who resettled in the Mediterranean region, the Balkans, and elsewhere; Mizrahi Jews are, literally, Eastern Jews, or Jews from the Middle East.

remedial programs, but Jewish students receive a proportionately much greater share despite Palestinian Arab students' greater need: a 2000 study by professors at Hebrew University found that Jewish students receive five times the amount of remedial instruction that Palestinian Arab students receive.[7] Thus, while the Israeli government states that it has a kind of an affirmative action policy for needy students, this policy excludes and discriminates against Palestinian Arab students.

The Israeli government has, to a certain extent, acknowledged that its Arab education system is inferior to its Jewish education system. For example, it reported to the United Nations Committee on the Rights of the Child in 2001:

> There is a great deal of variance in the resources allocated the education in the Arab versus the Jewish sector. These discrepancies are reflected in various aspects of education in the Arab sector, such as physical infrastructure, the average number of students per class, the number of enrichment hours, the extent of support services, and the level of education of professional staff.[8]

It also reported that in 1991, government investment per Palestinian Arab pupil was about 60 percent of its investment per Jewish pupil. In the last decade the government has appointed various committees to look at problematic aspects of education, such as education for Bedouin in the Negev and special education. These committees have found striking gaps in the way the government treats Jewish and Palestinian Arab students and made recommendations for fixing the problem. The Ministry of Education's Committee for Closing the Gap also pointed out the stark differences to the ministry's leadership in December 2000, although its principle mandate concerned the gaps among Jewish students.

Despite this compelling evidence, the government has failed to change the discriminatory way in which its education system operates. Instead, in the last decade, the government has promised lump sums of money, insufficient to equalize the two systems, and then largely failed to keep these promises. Funding for Arab education in most areas still does not even reflect Palestinian Arabs' representation in the population, much less begin to correct for years of past discrimination.

---

[7] Sorrell Kahen and Yakov Yeleneck, Hebrew University, "Discrimination Against the Non-Jewish Sector in the Allocation of Resources for Educational Development (Hebrew)," 2000.

[8] State of Israel Ministry of Justice, Ministry of Foreign Affairs, *Initial Periodic Report of the State of Israel Concerning the Implementation of the Convention on the Rights of the Child (CRC)*, February 20, 2001, p. 307.

This neglect reflects the very low priority given Palestinian Arab students by the Israeli government–even by those responsible for the Arab education system. The system itself appears almost as an afterthought in the public statements of top education officials. The new education minister Limor Livnat, for example, appears to have completely overlooked her Palestinian Arab charges when she stated that she would like to see that "there is not a single child in Israel who doesn't learn the basics of Jewish and Zionist knowledge and values." She later explained that she was not referring to Palestinian Arab children.[9]

Worse, other Israeli education officials have been criticized in the news media for frankly racist statements. The head of the Educational Authority for Bedouins, Moshe Shohat, said in an interview with *Jewish Week* that Bedouin who complain about poor living conditions are "blood-thirsty Bedouins who commit polygamy, have 30 children and continue to expand their illegal settlements, taking over state land." When questioned about providing indoor plumbing in Bedouin schools, he responded: "In their culture they take care of their needs outdoors. They don't even know how to flush a toilet."[10]

Some Israeli government officials pointed out to Human Rights Watch the improvements in Arab education in the fifty-three year period since Israel's statehood.[11] Yair Levin, the deputy director-general, head of international relations of the Ministry of Education, told Human Rights Watch: "For me there is no doubt that both gaps–Ashkenazi and Sephardic, and Jewish and Arab–will be closed in thirty to forty years. Thirty to forty years for history is nothing."[12]

The children who will pass through Israel's school system in the next forty years require more than this, as does international human rights law. At the present rate, Israel will not close the gap between Jewish and Arab education, even if it were to allocate equally annual allowances to schools. "If everyone gets more or less the same share in society and the gap is ignored, we will never

---

[9] Allyn Fisher-Ilan, "Livnat's Lessons," *Jerusalem Post*, June 19, 2001.

[10] Robby Berman, "Israeli Official Slurs Bedouins" *Jewish Week*, July 20, 2001. Shohat later apologized and stated that he used "blood-thirsty" to refer to only a small group of Bedouin. Relly Sa'ar, "Bedouin Schools Chief Apologizes for Racial Slur," *Ha'aretz Daily Newspaper (English Edition)* (Israel), August 17, 2001.

[11] See, for example, U.N. Human Rights Committee, *Initial Report of States Parties Due in 1993: Israel,* paras. 788-791, 843, U.N. Doc. CCPR/C/81/Add.13 (April 9, 1998). As a party to the International Covenant on Civil and Political Rights, Israel was obligated to submit this report to the U.N. Human Rights Committee, which is responsible for receiving and commenting on state party reports and for interpreting the covenant.

[12] Human Rights Watch interview with Yair Levin, Deputy Director-General, Head of International Relations of the Ministry of Education, Jerusalem, December 19, 2000.

close it when it comes to physical conditions of schools, the number of kids in class, and teachers' skills and training," Dr. Daphna Golan, the chair of the Committee for Closing the Gap in the Education Ministry's Pedagogical Secretariat, told Human Rights Watch.[13] When Human Rights Watch asked Dalia Sprinzak, of the Education Ministry's Economics and Budgeting Administration, if she thought the gap between Jewish and Arab education would ever be closed, she answered, "It is very difficult. No, I don't think so. . . . But it is the right direction. Our expectations are too high that we can advance very quickly in this direction."[14]

Addressing the cumulative effect of generations of educational disadvantage upon Israel's Palestinian Arab citizens requires major new initiatives by the government of Israel. One-time influxes of funds are only a band-aid measure, not a cure. Parity in funding levels alone, even should this be provided, would not itself be enough to overcome the legacy of past failure to provide facilities conducive to learning. Closing the gap requires funding–and also political will. Israel should commit to equalizing every aspect of education, make the structural changes necessary to implement this commitment, and monitor the educational system to ensure that it is done. In short, it should institutionalize equality.

As long as the gap exists, Palestinian Arabs are not likely to feel like full citizens of Israel. An eleventh-grade high school student told Human Rights Watch, "There is no balance between what is given to [Jewish students] and what is given to us. I wrote one sentence in a letter to my friend in Gaza: 'In order to dream and to work, we have to pay. It's difficult to fulfill our dreams in this country. It's not considered our country. We're like guests. And we're not welcomed guests.'"[15]

Palestinian Arabs are a significant minority of Israel's citizens. They make up 18.7 percent of the country's population and almost one-quarter of school-

---

[13] Human Rights Watch interview with Daphna Golan, Chair, Committee for Closing the Gap, Pedagogical Secretariat, Ministry of Education, Jerusalem, December 20, 2000. The Ministry of Education created the Committee for Closing the Gap in late 1999 to look primarily at gaps within the Jewish population. Dr. Golan left the ministry in the spring of 2001, and the committee was not functioning at the time of writing.

[14] However, Sprinzak noted that, "[i]t is important for the state to say that it [closing the gaps] is important to us." Human Rights Watch interview with Dalia Sprinzak, Economics and Budgeting Administration, Ministry of Education, Jerusalem, December 19, 2000.

[15] Human Rights Watch interview, Nazareth, December 6, 2000.

aged children.[16] Of these, about 80 percent are Muslim, including the Bedouin and a small number of Circassians,[17] about one-tenth are Christian, and slightly fewer are Druze, adherents of a monotheistic religion that originated in the late tenth and early eleventh century.[18]

Israel's Obligations under International and National Law

The right to education is universally recognized under international law. The International Covenant on Economic, Social and Cultural Rights and the Convention on the Rights of the Child, to which Israel is a party, guarantee a right to education. The Universal Declaration of Human Rights also enshrines such a right. According to these international legal standards, the right to education must be enjoyed without discrimination on the basis of race, color, sex, language, religion, national or social origin, property, or birth. The Convention against Discrimination in Education, to which ninety countries are parties and which Israel ratified in 1961, requires that if Israel maintains separate systems for Jews and Palestinian Arabs, the two systems must provide the same standard of education in equivalent conditions.

Although Israel's constitutional law does not explicitly recognize the right to education, its ordinary statutes effectively provide such a right.[19] However, these laws, which prohibit discrimination by individual schools, do not specifically prohibit discrimination by the national government. And Israel's

---

[16] At the beginning of 2001, 18.7 percent of Israel's population, including East Jerusalem, was Palestinian ("Arab"). State of Israel Central Bureau of Statistics (CBS), "Table B/1.–Population, By Population Group," Monthly Bulletin of Statistics, vol. 52, April 2001. At the end of 1998, the most recent year for which data on population by age is available, 24.1 percent of children ages three to seventeen were Palestinian. State of Israel Central Bureau of Statistics (CBS), Statistical Abstract of Israel 2000, no. 51, tables 2.1, 2.18. In the 2000-2001 school year, 1,606,000 kindergarten through twelfth grade students were enrolled in the Israeli education system; 356,000 were enrolled in the Arab education system and 1,250,000 were enrolled in the Jewish education system. Ministry of Education, "Students Enrolled in Jewish Education and Arab Education 2000/01."

[17] There are only about 3,000 Circassians in Israel, and their children attend both Jewish and Arab schools.

[18] CBS, Statistical Abstract of Israel 2000, table 2.1.

[19] Although Israel has no formal constitution, a series of Basic Laws, together with the decisions of the Israeli High Court, form a kind of unwritten constitution and are considered constitutional law. Israel's education laws include the State Education Law (1953), the Compulsory Education Law (1949), the Pupils' Rights Law (2000), and the Special Education Law (1988).

courts have yet to use either these laws or more general principles of equality to protect Palestinian Arab children from discrimination in education.

In this report, the word "child" refers to anyone under the age of eighteen. Article 1 of the Convention on the Rights of the Child defines as a child "every human being under the age of eighteen years unless, under the law applicable to the child, majority is attained earlier." Consistent with international law, Israeli law defines the period of minority as ending at age eighteen.[20]

Methodology and Scope

This report is based on research conducted in Israel in November and December 2000.[21] During this period, Human Rights Watch visited twenty-six schools: Jewish and Arab; kindergarten, primary, and secondary; mainstream academic, vocational, and special education. The schools were almost all government schools, but we also visited several quasi-private schools in areas where such schools played an important role in educating Palestinian Arabs.[22] We went to schools in urban and rural areas; schools in cities with mixed Palestinian Arab and Jewish populations; schools in cities that were primarily Jewish or Palestinian Arab; schools for Bedouin, which are part of the Arab education system, in northern and southern Israel, and in recognized and unrecognized communities; and Jewish schools in development towns with large immigrant populations.

At these schools we interviewed students, teachers (including teachers of Arabic, Hebrew, English, special education, geography, history, and vocational subjects), principals, coaches, speech therapists, reading specialists, psychologists, and social workers. We interviewed both girls and boys, among whom were student council presidents, musicians, and disabled students. We looked at classrooms, staff rooms, offices, bathrooms, and where they existed– libraries, playgrounds, gymnasiums, science and computer laboratories, art and drama rooms, and production studios. We also interviewed parents, teachers,

---

[20] Guardianship and Legal Capacity Law, sec. 3 (1962).

[21] Shortly before Human Rights Watch began its investigations, demonstrations took place within Israel in which Israeli police killed thirteen Palestinian Arab citizens. See Human Rights Watch, "Investigation into Unlawful Use of Force in the West Bank, Gaza Strip, and Northern Israel: October 4 through October 11," *A Human Rights Watch Report,* vol. 12, no. 3(E), October 2000. Schools within Israel closed briefly. When Human Rights Watch conducted its research in November and December, schools were back in session.

[22] Various Christian churches run schools that receive most of their funding from the Ministry of Education. The ministry categorizes these as missionary schools, as well as some ultra-orthodox Jewish schools, as "recognized but unofficial."

and students outside of the school setting, and we interviewed Bedouin university students about their pre-university education.

The names of all students have been changed to protect their privacy. Most teachers and administrators also requested confidentiality, and the principals of the Arab schools that we visited asked that we not name their schools.

Within the Education Ministry, we interviewed persons responsible for Arab education, including the head of the Arab education department, the director of Arab curriculum, and the inspectors for the subjects unique to Arab education, including Arab history and Arabic language and literature. We also spoke with persons in the ministry's Economics and Budget Administration, and the Pedagogical Secretariat, with the heads of the Haifa and Nazareth district offices, and, in Be'er Sheva, with the municipal official responsible for education. In addition, we met with education researchers at Israel's Central Bureau of Statistics[23] and with both Palestinian Arab and Jewish staff of various nongovernmental organizations.

In the 1999-2000 school year, there were 3,407 primary and secondary schools in Israel.[24] The twenty-six schools we visited were not a scientific sample, although we strove to visit schools in diverse areas and at different levels. Accordingly, wherever possible we have supplemented information from our firsthand observation and direct interviews with statistical data, primarily from the Ministry of Education and the Central Bureau of Statistics, for information on a national scale. Where there was conflict between data from various sources, this is indicated in the notes. Human Rights Watch has used the most recent data available at the time of writing. In some instances the statistical data includes schools in East Jerusalem supervised by the Ministry of Education and run by the United Nations Relief and Works Agency for Palestine Refugees in the Near East (UNRWA); where data clearly excludes East Jerusalem, this is also indicated in a footnote.[25]

---

[23] The Central Bureau of Statistics is a central government body charged with collecting, processing, and publicizing statistical information on the Israeli population, economy, and society.

[24] CBS, *Statistical Abstract of Israel 2000*, table 22.7. This figure includes East Jerusalem schools that are run by the Israeli government and by the United Nations Relief and Works Agency for Palestine Refugees in the Near East (UNRWA).

[25] According to the Ministry of Education, there were 4,100 seventeen-year-olds in East Jerusalem in the 1999-2000 school year. However, the ministry also reported that "0.00" percent were enrolled in twelfth grade. Ministry of Education, "Statistics of the Matriculation Examination (*Bagrut*) 2000 Report," http://www.netvision.net.il/bagrut /netunim2000.htm (accessed on May 10, 2001), p. 5.

Out of all those in Arab schools, Bedouin who live in the Negev region, especially those in unrecognized villages, fare far worse by every measurement detailed in the report.[26] Because of their small numbers–fewer than 2,100 per grade[27]–their situation is hidden in data about the Palestinian Arab population as a whole. Accordingly, wherever data about the Negev Bedouin was available, it is highlighted in this report.

This report does not address discrimination against Sephardic, Mizrahi, or Ethiopian Jews. Nor does it address discrimination at the university level or aspects of discrimination that are particular to East Jerusalem.[28]

Terminology

Terminology regarding Israel's Arab citizens is highly politicized. Increasingly, individuals are rejecting the term "Israeli Arab," which is used by the Israeli government, in favor of "Palestinian Arab."[29] Many, but not all, Druze and Bedouin in Israel also identify themselves as Palestinian Arab or a variation of the term.[30] When referring to people, this report uses "Palestinian Arab citizens of Israel" or "Palestinian Arabs" because that is how most people we interviewed defined themselves. However, it should be noted that not everyone of Arab origin we interviewed identified herself or himself as Palestinian, and a few rejected the term altogether.

---

[26] Although some Bedouin also live in northern Israel, most statistical data relating to education is available for Negev Bedouin only.

[27] Ministry of Education, "Statistics of the Matriculation Examination (*Bagrut*) 2000 Report," p. 5.

[28] The Ministry of Education's Arab schools in East Jerusalem are overcrowded and do not have space for all Palestinian Arab children who need them. Jerusalem city counselor Joseph Alalu, from the Meretz party, has stated that there are four to five thousand children ages five through eighteen who neither can be accommodated in government schools nor can afford private school tuition and who do not attend school at all. Allyn Fisher-Illan, "East Jerusalem Arab Children Seek Admission into City Schools," *Jerusalem Post*, July 2, 2001.

[29] For example, a 1999 survey of the adult Palestinian Arab population by the Institute for Peace Research at Givat Haviva found that 32.8 percent of respondents said that the description "Israeli" was "appropriate to their self-identity." Givat Haviva, "2001 Survey–Attitudes of the Arabs to the State of Israel," http://www.dialogate.org.il/peace /publications.asp#academic (accessed on May 30, 2001).

[30] In a 1998 survey, 33 percent of Negev Bedouin tenth and eleventh graders described themselves as "Palestinian Arab," 26 percent as "Israeli Arab," 15 percent as "Arab," 14 percent as "Palestinian Israeli," 7 percent as "Palestinian," and 6 percent as "Israeli." Center for Bedouin Studies and Development, *Newsletter*, vol. 2, Winter 1999, p. 1.

Schools in this report are referred to as "Jewish" and "Arab." These terms correspond with what all government English publications and many other sources call "Hebrew schools" and "Arab schools." Human Rights Watch has used "Jewish" both because it is one translation of the Hebrew word that is used for these schools and because it is parallel with "Arab." We use "Arab schools" and "Arab education" because this is the term that everyone, both Palestinian Arab and Jewish, used when we interviewed them.

II. RECOMMENDATIONS

- The Israeli government should recognize that discrimination against Palestinian Arab citizens has been, and continues to be, a major social and political problem in the Israeli education system. The government should measurably improve Palestinian Arab participation in all aspect of decision-making about education policies and resources.

To the Knesset
- Amend Part II, 3B(a) of the Compulsory Education Law and article 5(a) of the Pupils' Rights Law to prohibit discrimination by the national government, as well as by local education authorities and institutions.
- Fully fund in the annual Budget Law current plans address inadequacies in Arab education. Where deficiencies in the current plans are found, allocate additional funds to correct these.

To the Ministry of Education
- Adopt and make public a written policy of equality that explicitly prohibits discrimination on the basis of religion, race, ethnicity, or gender. The policy should require all Ministry of Education programs and funds to be allocated to all schools, Jewish and Arab, on the basis of a criteria that does not discriminate and, where appropriate, seeks to correct past discrimination. Implement the policy immediately, rather than gradually.
- Restructure the Ministry of Education's current resource allocation (including funds for teaching, and enrichment and remedial programs) so that Jewish and Arab schools are funded on a non-discriminatory basis. Where funds are allocated for all children, Palestinian children should, at minimum, receive funds proportionate to their representation in the population.
- Equalize the average class size and teacher-to-student ratio in Jewish and Arab schools.
- Allocate additional funding to close the gaps between Jewish and Arab education in all areas, including the physical condition of school buildings; the existence of libraries, laboratories, and recreation facilities; and the availability of kindergartens, vocational education, special education, and teacher training.
- In collaboration with Israel's Central Bureau of Statistics, collect and publish data on total spending for Jewish and for Arab education by sector, as well as spending on individual aspects of education by sector, so that equality in resource distribution may be accurately assessed and monitored.

- Increase the Arab education system's autonomy, along the lines of that granted to state religious, ultra-orthodox, and kibbutz education.
- Promptly increase Palestinian Arabs' representation and participation in all aspects of the Ministry of Education, in particular at the highest levels.
- Respond to the request from the Director General of UNESCO regarding Israel's implementation of the Convention against Discrimination in Education.
- Invite the U.N. Special Rapporteur on the Right to Education, K. Tomaševski, to Israel to assess the realization of the right to education and, specifically, discrimination against Palestinian Arab citizens.

Needs-Based Spending

- Assess Jewish and Palestinian Arab children's needs, as well as Jewish and Arab schools' needs, on the same scale, and end the use of measurements that are weighted against Palestinian Arab communities, such as the national priority list, to distribute education resources.
- Minimize discretion in the allocation of supplementary programs and increase oversight to ensure that all programs are distributed equally, with full participation by Palestinian Arab educators. In particular, provide enrichment and remedial programs–such as preparation for the matriculation and psychometric exams and programs to prevent dropping out–on an equal basis to Jewish and Arab schools.

Physical Facilities

- Construct all needed classrooms, including the 2,500 classrooms that the Follow-Up Committee on Arab Education estimates are needed in Arab education. Move classes out of rented rooms and buildings. Replace or repair buildings that are dangerous to students.
- Devise and implement a plan to assess and construct each year the classrooms needed in Arab schools, according to standards used for Jewish schools. This plan should include regular classes as well as those for special education.
- Construct new schools in areas where children currently travel long distances to reach the nearest school, regardless of the government's position on the legal status of the parents' residences.
- Construct auxiliary facilities, including libraries, science and computer labs, and sports facilities, in Arab schools so that they reach the same level as Jewish schools. Mandate and ensure that these facilities' quality, including library books, and science and sports equipment, be adequate and

equivalent. After Arab schools reach the same level as Jewish schools, allocate all new maintenance and construction funds equally among Arab and Jewish schools.

In-School Social Services
- Provide social services, including counseling, special education services, medical care, and truant officers in Arab schools on an equal basis with Jewish schools.
- Where there are shortages of trained Arabic-speaking professionals, such as psychologists and speech therapists, make available and publicize opportunities for additional training and education.

Vocational/Technological Education
- Adapt all existing schools, both Jewish and Arab, to offer advanced technological education in addition to traditional vocational classes.
- Require private organizations with which the ministry contracts to provide Palestinian Arab and Jewish students with equal access vocational and technological education. Collect and publish data on their compliance.

Curricula
- Insure that both the curricula and the materials needed to teach them are available in Arabic for all subjects and at every level, including for special education.
- Equalize resources for curriculum development for Arab and Jewish schools.
- Actively seek increased Palestinian Arab participation in the development of curricula for all subjects, including common curricula.
- Develop new curricula contemporaneously in Hebrew and in Arabic, and implement the curricula at the same pace, so that Palestinian Arab students are not left behind.
- Eliminate stereotypes and negative representation of Palestinian Arabs from all curricula.
- Include in all curricula more material on the history and cultural identity of the Palestinian Arab people.

Kindergartens
- Build preschools in all Palestinian Arab communities that lack them, including in unrecognized villages.

- Specifically, change the order of implementation of free and compulsory kindergarten for three and four-year-olds to include Palestinian Arab localities equally, taking into consideration the lower attendance rates among Palestinian Arab children and that proportionately fewer Palestinian Arab communities than Jewish communities have kindergartens. All seven recognized Bedouin towns in the Negev should immediately be added to the list.
- Increase the opportunities for teacher training for Palestinian Arab kindergarten teachers.

Special Education
- Provide resources and funding for integration ("mainstreaming") to Arab and Jewish education proportionate to the rate of disability in the sectors. Ensure that all children who need special education services receive them.
- Establish additional Arab special education classes or schools where they are needed.
- Adapt Jewish special education schools for the Palestinian Arab children who attend them, with the full participation of Palestinian Arab educators, parents, and students to make this happen.
- Train additional Palestinian Arab speech therapists.

Teacher Training
- Allocate additional resources for in-service training for Palestinian Arab teachers.
- Hold more teacher training courses in or near Arab schools in consultation with teachers' associations and with Palestinian Arab participation.
- Specifically, offer more training on teaching methods.
- Provide incentives equally to Jewish and Palestinian Arab teachers who teach in areas where the ministry wishes to attract more teachers, such as national priority areas and Negev Bedouin communities.

To Local Governments
- Spend all the monies from the Ministry of Education for education as designated.
- Prioritize the construction of preschools.

To the General Conference of the United Nations Educational, Scientific and Cultural Organization (UNESCO)

- Set a schedule for states parties to the Convention against Discrimination in Education to submit periodic reports, as provided in article 7 of the convention.
- Issue recommendations, as prescribed in article 6 of the Convention against Discrimination in Education, "defining the measures to be taken against the different forms of discrimination in education and for the purpose of ensuring equality of opportunity and treatment in education."

III. SEPARATE SYSTEMS

From their first day in kindergarten until they reach university, Palestinian Arab and Jewish children almost always attend separate schools. Palestinian Arab children are taught in Arabic, Jewish children in Hebrew. The two systems' curricula are similar but not identical. For example, Hebrew is taught as a second language in Arab schools, while Jewish students are not required to study Arabic.

There is little support in Israel for integrating Jewish and Arab schools.[31] Although there are a few well-known exceptions, including several mixed kindergartens and private experiments with peace education, even these efforts are experiencing great strain since the confrontations in October 2000 in which Israeli police killed thirteen Palestinian Arab citizens. No one Human Rights Watch interviewed, either Jewish or Palestinian Arab, expressed a desire for integration, although Palestinian Arab students were often quite enthusiastic about school-related exchange programs with Jewish children. Rather than seeking integration, many Palestinian Arab citizens are asking for autonomy over their education system.[32]

The law does not prohibit Palestinian Arab parents from enrolling their children in Jewish schools, but in practice, very few Palestinian Arab parents

---

[31] "There are no records of any serious attempts on the part of the state, nor records of any requests from the Arab side, to merge the Jewish and Arab school systems under one 'Israeli' roof . . . . There are individual cases of Arab pupils who study in Jewish schools, but no cases of Jews who study in Arab schools. The two national communities remain educationally separated. In Israel, the discourse of integration refers only to Jews of different origins." Shlomo Swirski, *Politics and Education in Israel: Comparisons with the United States* (New York: Falmer Press, 1999), p.118. For a discussion of the advantages and costs of segregation in the Israeli education system, see Stephen Goldstein, "Multiculturalism, Parental Choice and Traditional Values," in *Children's Rights and Traditional Values*, eds. Gillian Douglas and Leslie Sebba (Brookfield: Ashgate Pub. Co., 1998).

[32] University researchers who studied the underlying circumstances of the October 2000 demonstrations, in which Israeli army and police shot and killed thirteen Palestinian Arab citizens, rejected full integration on the grounds that it would injure the group identities of both Palestinian Arabs and Jews, that the different starting points of the two groups would perpetuate inequality, and that segregated residences make full integration impossible. Instead, the researchers called for a separate administration for Arab education which would operate within the Ministry of Education's framework but which would maintain absolute autonomy over management and curriculum content. Majid Al-Haj, Ismael Abu-Sa'ad, Yossi Yona, "Schooling and Further Education," in *After the Rift: New Directions for Government Policy towards the Arab Population in Israel*, eds. Dan Rabinowitz, As'ad Ghanem, Oren Yiftachel, November 2000.

send their children to Jewish schools.[33] Enrollment is based on residence; thus, enrollment in a Jewish school is only a real choice in mixed cities like Jaffa and Haifa; even in these, neighborhoods are mostly segregated, and there are separate schools for Palestinian Arabs and Jews. The vast majority of Palestinian Arabs live in towns and villages where the only option is an Arab school.

Moreover, Palestinian Arab children who attend Jewish schools must be able to study in Hebrew from a curriculum designed for Jewish children. Human Rights Watch interviewed Deneis A., a parent who sent her daughter to Jewish preschools and primary schools:

> I was living near the Jewish nursery and there wasn't a good Arab nursery. I wasn't aware of issues of identity and culture and how language and culture are influenced. I wanted to feel Israeli, and I didn't have a problem with this. I grew up in Haifa. I married at twenty-two and worked as a practical engineer in a hospital. I was dreaming and talking in Hebrew. . . . I visited several [private Arab] kindergartens in Haifa and Jerusalem. I didn't want Christianity imposed. Then when my daughter was three, I took her to the kibbutz. It was like a dream–a big place, freedom, near the beach. But through this experience I became more aware of her identity and my identity. . . . The history was the history of the Jewish people. The school was a good experience, but it became harder to deal with the Zionist part. I can see that my youngest child is not getting the education she got there. . . . With the youngest I wanted to send him [to the Jewish school] but he didn't want to go. He wanted to go to an Arab school and wanted to speak Arabic."[34]

Even the few integrated kindergartens tend to teach mainly in Hebrew with an emphasis on Jewish culture. The Arabic teacher at an integrated kindergarten in Kibbutz Shoval observed: "In Arab kindergartens, the emphasis is mainly on Bedouin tradition, customs, and heritage. The children can't get all this in an integrated kindergarten. The parents have to make it up at home."[35]

---

[33] According to Israel's Central Bureau of Statistics, "[a]mong pupils in Hebrew education there is also a small number of Moslem, Christian, Druze and other pupils, as well as non-Jewish immigrant pupils who study in schools of the Hebrew education [sic]." CBS, *Statistical Abstract of Israel 2000*, p. (106).

[34] Human Rights Watch interview, Haifa, December 6, 2000.

[35] Aliza Arbeli, "Bedouin and Jews: The Right Connection," *Ha'aretz Daily Newspaper (English Edition)* (Israel), August 14, 1998.

For many Palestinian Arabs, school integration is, in fact, assimilation into the majority's Jewish education at the expense of Arabic language and their own cultures and religions. Accordingly, the primary education issue for Palestinian Arabs in Israel is not access to Jewish schools but rather equalizing the Arab system with the Jewish system.

International law permits the maintenance of separate educational systems for religious or linguistic reasons as long as participation in such systems is optional and "if the education provided conforms to such standards as may be laid down or approved by the competent authorities, in particular for education of the same level."[36]

Historical Context

Ethnicity, language, and religion have long played a role in education in the region.[37] Under the Ottoman Empire, which ruled Palestine for four centuries, religious-based schools functioned independently.[38] Traditional Muslim schools *(kuttabs)* and schools run by missions of various European Christian churches taught primarily in Arabic, although the missionary schools also emphasized the sponsoring European church's language. Both Arab Muslim and Arab Christian children attended the missionary schools, as they do today. Jewish residents also ran schools, and beginning in the late nineteenth century, settlers established various networks of Jewish communal schools, many with Hebrew as the language of instruction. The Ottoman empire, after assuming responsibility in 1846 for educational services in the area, established in 1869 its own system of primary and secondary public schools based on the French system. However, the level of education that Ottoman schools offered was relatively low and, with Turkish as the language of instruction, the schools did not attract much of the Arab population.

From the end of World War I until the state of Israel was established in 1948, Britain ruled Palestine under a mandatory administration. The British

---

[36] Convention against Discrimination in Education, art. 2(b), *adopted* December 14, 1960, General Conference of the United Nations Educational, Scientific and Cultural Organization (UNESCO), 429 U.N.T.S. 93 (entered into force May 22, 1962, and ratified by Israel September 22, 1961). The full text of this convention is reprinted in the appendix.

[37] Information in this section was taken from: Swirski, *Politics and Education in Israel*; Majid Al-Haj, *Education, Empowerment, and Control: The Case of the Arabs in Israel* (Albany: State University of New York Press, 1995); Sami Khalil Mar'i, *Arab Education in Israel* (Syracuse: Syracuse University Press, 1978).

[38] The Ottoman legal system allowed religious minorities recognized by the sultan to have a certain cultural autonomy under a practice known as the *millet* system.

Mandatory Government took over many *kuttabs* and expanded the Ottoman school system; however, the 1937 Palestine Royal Commission (known as the "Peel Commission") found that the government system was "able to satisfy no more than half the Arab demand for education."[39]   In addition, almost all government schools were primary level only.   The British Mandatory Government administered the government school system directly; Palestinian Arabs had little input or control.   In addition to government schools, private Muslim schools (although decreased in number from the Ottoman period) and missionary schools together educated about a third of Palestinian Arab students. Jewish schools–both religious and secular, and most under the Zionist school network–continued to operate independently.[40]

After the war in 1948 following Israel's establishment as a state, the Israeli Ministry of Education took over most schools, maintaining separate systems for religious Jews, secular Jews, and Palestinian Arabs.   The vast majority of Palestinian Arabs lived in three rural areas: the Galilee region to the north, the Triangle region south-east of Haifa, and the Negev desert in the south. These areas were separated from Jewish localities and were kept under a military government until 1966.

As it did under the British Mandatory Government, the quality of the Jewish and Arab systems differed markedly. The Compulsory Education Law's passage in 1949 increased enrollment substantially in the Arab system in the north, and there were not enough classrooms and qualified teachers for students. Educational authorities rented rooms, established a shift system for students, and appointed many uncertified teachers.

Until Israeli military rule was ended in 1966, Palestinian Arabs could not travel from their residences without a permit from authorities, which severely limited their ability to seek education. They were excluded from high level positions in the Ministry of Education, and the security services screened applicants for teaching and administrative positions and influenced appointments, a practice that continues today.[41] There were no Palestinian Arab

---

[39] *Report of the Palestine Royal Commission,* Cmd 5479 (London: HMSO, 1937), p. 339.
[40] The Zionist school network allowed religious and secular schools to be institutionally separate but to both fall under the Zionist movement's political and financial roof. Swirski, *Politics and Education in Israel,* pp. 47-48.
[41] Human Rights Watch received numerous reports of the security services' continued involvement in Arab education. Several sources described incidents in which Palestinian Arab teachers were not hired for or were dismissed from teaching positions because of their political activity. Adalah (The Legal Center for Minority Rights in Israel) has also reported recent cases of Arab teachers being denied teaching positions for alleged

teacher, parent, or student organizations during this period. Only in the 1970s, after the cessation of the military government and the rise of a small middle class, did community organizations begin to emerge. These later established a Follow-Up Committee on Arab Education "which has since acted as the main Israeli Palestinian spokesperson on educational matters."[42] However, there are still far fewer community organizations than in the Jewish system, where they play a significant role in education.

Bedouin and Residents of Unrecognized Villages

Although the Negev Bedouin fall under the Arab education system, the Israeli government has, since statehood, provided them with even fewer educational services than other Palestinian Arabs.[43] The Bedouin were historically organized in nomadic or semi-nomadic tribes that raised sheep, goats, and camels and engaged in seasonal agriculture. The Bedouin constitute most of the Palestinian Arab population of the Negev region of southern Israel, and about 10 percent of the country's total Palestinian Arab population. Roughly 110,000 Bedouin live in the Negev around the city of Be'er Sheva; about 50,000 to 60,000 live elsewhere, primarily in the Galilee region of northern Israel.[44]

---

security reasons. See Adalah, "Adalah Successfully Pressures the Ministry of Education to Hire a Shfaram Teacher after Nine Years of Refusing Him Based on Discriminatory Policies," September 6, 2000, http://www.adalah.org/news32000.html#9 (accessed on May 31, 2001).

[42] Swirski, *Politics and Education in Israel*, p. 79.

[43] Except where otherwise indicated, background information about the Bedouin is taken from Penny Maddrell, "The Beduin of the Negev," *Minority Rights Group Report*, no. 81, January 1990; Salim Abu-Rabiyya, et. al, "Survey of Bedouin Schools in the Negev," *Israel Equality Monitor*, no. 5, March 1996, pp. 1-8; Ismael Abu-Saad, "The Education of Israel's Negev Beduin: Background and Prospects," *Israel Studies*, vol. 2, no. 2, 1997; Ismael Abu-Saad, "Bedouin Arab Education in the Context of Radical Social Change: What is the Future?," *Compare*, vol. 25, no. 2, 1999, pp. 149-160; and U.N. Human Rights Committee, *Initial Report of States Parties Due in 1993: Israel*, paras. 853, 857.

[44] The Negev Bedouin population is estimated from data in the *Statistical Yearbook of the Negev Bedouin*, according to which there were 61,000 Bedouin living in the seven recognized localities in 1996, and 48,975 Bedouin living in unrecognized localities in 1998. Center for Bedouin Studies and Development, and the Negev Center for Regional Development, *Statistical Yearbook of the Negev Bedouin*, no. 1 (Be'er Sheva: Ben-Gurion University of the Negev, December 1999), pp. 29-30. Others have estimated that about 10,000 Bedouin live in the central region and about 50,000 live in the north. Yosef Ben-David, "The Bedouin in Israel," July 1999, Ministry of Foreign Affairs website, http://www.israel-mfa.gov.il/mfa/go.asp?MFAH0fg30 (accessed on June 5, 2001).

In 1948, the government moved the Bedouin who remained in the Negev to a restricted military zone around Be'er Sheva, and they lost access to the limited schooling that was available before 1948. Under the military rule, the government provided only minimal education services: most schools had only four grades, and attendance rates were very low, especially among girls. [45] Before 1969, when the first high school for Negev Bedouin was established, those who wished to study beyond the primary level had to obtain a permit to study in schools in northern Arab villages and be able to afford the expense of traveling and boarding outside of their homes.

Since the late 1960s and early 1970s, the Israeli government has been trying to pressure the Bedouin in the Negev to leave their villages and resettle in seven urban localities: Tal Al-Saba/Tel-Sheva, Rahat, Ar'ara Al-Naqab/Ar'ara BaNegev, Kseife, Shaqib Al-Salaam/Segev Shalom, Hora/Hura, and Laqiya. These towns rank at the bottom of the government's socio-economic index, making them the poorest in Israel, and lack many basic services.[46] The Bedouin have been reluctant to abandon their traditional lands, and in 1996, it was estimated that only about 56 percent of Bedouin in the Negev lived in the seven officially recognized localities.[47]

The government considers the Bedouin, as well as other Palestinian Arabs who live outside of localities approved by the Israeli government, to be living in

However, the Israeli government reported to the Human Rights Committee in 1998 that there were 100,000 Bedouins in the Negev and roughly 38,000 in the Galilee. U.N. Human Rights Committee, *Initial Report of States Parties Due in 1993: Israel*, para. 851. The Bedouin who live in the northern part of the country have a somewhat different history and are less isolated than Bedouin in the Negev. See Maddrell, "The Beduin of the Negev."

[45] See Abu-Saad, "The Education of Israel's Negev Beduin"; and Maddrell, "The Beduin of the Negev."

[46] In 1999, out of 203 local authorities in Israel, Rahat, Ar'ara Al-Naqab/Ar'ara BaNegev, Tal Al-Saba/Tel-Sheva, and Kseife ranked one through four, respectively, one being the lowest ranking. Shaqib Al-Salaam/Segev Shalom ranked sixth, Laqiya seventh, and Hora/Hura seventeenth. CBS, *Characterization and Ranking of Local Authorities, According to the Population's Socio-Economic Level in 1999, Based on the 1995 Census of Population and Housing*, no. S.P. 1118, 1999, table 2. In 1998, only three of the seven communities had municipal libraries, three had community centers, two had police stations in the community, and one had an ambulance and fire department in the community. While all had health clinics, only Rahat had a night clinic. Ibid., pp. 67-69.

[47] Center for Bedouin Studies and Development, *Statistical Yearbook of the Negev Bedouin*, p. (20).

illegal villages, known as "unrecognized villages."[48] These villages fare much worse than those the government recognizes. They are not marked on government maps, lack recognized local governing bodies, and receive limited or no government services such as schools, running water, electricity, or sewage and garbage collection."[49] Where there are schools in unrecognized villages, they generally are in poor repair, and some of their students travel long distances to reach them.

Since the 1960s, literacy rates among all Palestinian Arabs have risen and participation in higher education has increased.[50] The number of schools has increased significantly, particularly for Negev Bedouin. Despite these improvements, the gaps between Jewish and Arab education in the quality of education and in students' academic success remain dramatic.

Structure of the Israeli School System

Israel heavily finances and regulates the education of almost all children in Israel. Under Israel's Compulsory Education Law, the state is responsible for providing free education and bears joint responsibility with state and local authorities for maintaining school buildings.[51] The Ministry of Education develops curricula and educational standards, supervises teachers, and constructs school buildings. Local authorities maintain the buildings and provide equipment and supplies, in some cases with support from the ministry. The ministry directly employs and pays kindergarten and primary school teachers, and provides the funds for secondary school teachers' salaries to local authorities who employ them directly.[52] The ministry also provides additional educational funding to local authorities and in 1998 allocated 20.8 percent of its

---

[48] Estimates of the total number of unrecognized villages in Israeli vary, ranging from around seventy to over one hundred. The Regional Council of Unrecognized Villages in the Negev, a nongovernmental organization, has mapped forty-five unrecognized villages in the northern Negev. Regional Council of Unrecognized Villages in the Negev, "Map of the Unrecognized Villages in the Northern Negev," 2001, http://www.arabhra.org/rcuv/map.htm (accessed on July 5, 2001).

[49] Article 157A of the Planning and Construction Law (1981) forbids water, electricity, or telephone networks from connecting to unlicensed buildings.

[50] In 1961, 63.4 percent of the Palestinian population had attended four or fewer years of school, and 1.5 percent had post-secondary education. In 1998, these numbers were 12.5 percent and 19.7 percent, respectively. CBS, *Statistical Abstract of Israel 2000*, table 22.1.

[51] Compulsory Education Law, part III, 7A, B (1949).

[52] Ministry of Foreign Affairs, "Facts About Israel: Education," http://www.israel.org/mfa/go.asp?MFAH00110, 1999 (accessed on May 30, 2001).

budget–NIS 3,903,666 ($975,916.50)–to local authorities for educational and cultural services.[53]

Other government ministries fund and supervise particular educational facilities and programs. For example, the Ministry of Labor and Social Affairs operates vocational schools, called `Amal schools. The Ministry of Defense runs programs in schools to prepare students for military service. The Ministry of Immigrant Absorption provides assistance to immigrant students. The Ministry of Religious Affairs funds religious schools, and the Ministry of Health is involved in special education schools and health education.[54]

Until 1987, there was a separate department for Arab education within the Education Ministry. When the department was dissolved in 1987, its employees were spread out among the ministry's various branches. While most divisions typically have a single Palestinian Arab representative, there are small departments for Arab education and Druze education within the ministry's Pedagogical Secretariat.

Despite this reorganization, Palestinian Arabs continue to be significantly under-represented in the ministry. At the time of writing, none of the top positions in the Ministry of Education were held by Palestinian Arabs. Altogether only 127 (4.8 percent) of the 2,662 employees of the Ministry of Education (excluding teachers) were Palestinian Arab in the 2000-2001 school year.[55] Thirty-seven of these 127 were women.[56]

The highest ranked Palestinian Arab in the education system is Ali Assadi, the head of the Arab education department, a department of the Pedagogical Secretariat.[57] He oversees a team of inspectors who monitor Arab schools, including inspectors for subjects unique to Arab schools: Arabic, Arab history,

---

[53] Economics and Budgeting Administration, Ministry of Education, *Facts and Figures About Education and Culture in Israel* (Jerusalem: Ministry of Education, 1998), p. 49. "NIS" stands for new Israeli shekels. An exchange rate of NIS 4 to U.S.$1 is used throughout this report.

[54] Ibid., pp. 38-39.

[55] Ali Haider, "Arab Citizens in the Civil Service," *Sikkuy's Report on Equality and Integration of the Arab Citizens in Israel 2000-2001*, Spring 2001, table 5. This data includes "autonomous affiliates." Ibid. The Israeli government reported to the Human Rights Committee in 1998 that the Ministry of Education employed 101 non-Jewish employees, not including teachers, principals, and educational inspectors. U.N. Human Rights Committee, *Initial Report of States Parties Due in 1993: Israel*, para. 870.

[56] Haider, "Arab Citizens in the Civil Service," table 7.

[57] Above the director of the Arab education department is the chair of the Pedagogical Secretariat, one of many positions reporting to the Director General, who reports to the Minister of Education.

and Hebrew as a second language.[58]   Suliman Al-Sheikh heads a similar department for Druze. A small department–six full-time positions–develops curricula for Arab schools.[59] Curricula for Druze are also developed separately.

Because Palestinian Arabs have not been represented at the Ministry of Education's highest levels, their voices are often not heard. For example, Minister of Education, Limor Livnat, stated in June 2001 that she would like to see that "there is not a single child in Israel" who did not learn "Jewish and Zionist knowledge and values," but then explained that she did not include Palestinian Arab students in this statement.[60] In the same year, the head of the Educational Authority for Bedouins, Moshe Shohat, who is Jewish, spoke of "blood-thirsty Bedouins who commit polygamy, have 30 children and continue to expand their illegal settlements, taking over state land." When questioned about providing indoor plumbing in Bedouin schools, he responded: "In their culture they take care of their needs outdoors. They don't even know how to flush a toilet."[61] Shohat later apologized for his statements.[62]

Palestinian Arabs have the right to fair representation in the education system under international and domestic law. Article 2(3) of the 1992 General Assembly Declaration on the Rights of Persons Belonging to National or Ethnic, Religious or Linguistic Minorities provides: "Persons belonging to minorities have the right to participate effectively in decisions on the national and, where appropriate, regional level concerning the minority to which they belong[.]"[63] The Israeli High Court of Justice ruled on July 9, 2001, in a decision regarding the Israel Lands Administration Board, that Palestinian Arab citizens are entitled to fair representation in public bodies, especially those vested with decision-making powers, and stated that affirmative action was required. However, the

---

[58] Human Rights Watch interview with Ali Assadi, Director of Arab Education in Israel, Vice Chief of the Pedagogical Secretariat, Ministry of Education, Dier El Asad, December 2, 2000.

[59] Human Rights Watch interview with Khawla Saadi, Director of Curriculum for Israeli Arab Schools, Ministry of Education, Jerusalem, December 20, 2000.

[60] Allyn Fisher-Ilan, "Livnat's Lessons," *Jerusalem Post*, June 19, 2001.

[61] Berman, "Israeli Official Slurs Bedouins." See also Aliza Arbeli, "Bedouin Leaders to Sue Education Boss over Racist Slurs," *Ha'aretz Daily Newspaper (English Edition)* (Israel), July 30, 2001. Shohat later stated: "I meant only a group of Bedouins who were at a tour in the Unrecognized Villages in the Negev with representatives of 'the Jewish Week.'" *Kul Al-Arab*, July 27, 2001 (English translation from Arab Association of Human Rights, *Weekly Review of the Arab Press in Israel*, no. 40, July 24-30, 2001).

[62] Sa'ar, "Bedouin Schools Chief Apologizes for Racial Slur."

[63] Declaration on the Rights of Persons Belonging to National or Ethnic, Religious or Linguistic Minorities, art. 4(4), *adopted* December 18, 1992. G.A. Res. 47/135. This declaration is not binding but provides authoritative guidance to states.

Court also stated that "fair representation" did not necessarily mean one-fifth, (the percentage of Palestinian Arabs in the Israeli population), and the Court did not require the government to implement the ruling immediately.[64]

The Ministry of Education heavily finances almost all schools in Israel, both its own and those run by other organizations. Government-run schools are divided into state secular and state religious schools.[65] Arab state schools fall under the state secular framework; there are no state religious schools for Palestinian Arab children. Most children, Jewish or Palestinian Arab, attend state schools within this framework. However, private associations consisting primarily of ultra-orthodox Jewish groups and, for Palestinian Arabs, Christian churches, also run schools that are considered "recognized but unofficial schools."[66] The Ministry of Education regulates and provides most of the funding for these schools, which, in turn, are supposed to use the ministry's prescribed curricula.[67] Only a very few students, mostly "ultra-ultra orthodox" Jewish students, attend completely private schools in the sense that they receive no government funding. Even these are still legally subject to the Ministry of Education's supervision.[68]

Classes are divided into kindergarten (pre-primary), primary, secondary, and post-secondary levels. From ages two to five, children attend kindergarten, which, as explained below, is becoming mandatory from age three. Primary education consists of grades one through eight, and secondary education of grades nine through twelve. In some schools, grades seven through nine are separated into intermediate (or lower secondary) schools, mostly in the Jewish system.

The secondary level is designed to prepare students for the matriculation examinations (*bagrut*), a series of exams usually taken at the end of the twelfth grade, which entitle those who pass to a matriculation certificate (high school

---

[64] See Moshe Reinfeld, "Court: State Must Ensure Affirmative Action for Arab Citizens," *Ha'aretz Daily Newspaper (English Edition)* (Israel), July 10, 2001.

[65] State Education Law, art. 1 (1953).

[66] In the 1999-2000 school year, 20 percent of Jewish primary students and 12.2 percent of Jewish secondary students attended an ultra-orthodox school. CBS, *Statistical Abstract of Israel 2000*, table 22.16. Private associations ran 5 percent of Arab schools. Ministry of Justice, *Initial Periodic Report*, p. 304. (While Israel submitted its report in 2001, it does not come before the Committee until September/October 2002.) Parents, students, and teachers told us that missionary schools, which charge tuition, play an important role in cities like Haifa, where the state system for Palestinians is particularly weak.

[67] Human Rights Watch interview with Inspector Mattar, Inspector of Arab Private Schools, Ministry of Education, Nazareth, December 7, 2000.

[68] Schools Control Law (1969).

diploma).[69] Students may elect academic or vocational tracks, the latter falling under the supervision of the Ministry of Labor and Social Affairs. Matriculation exams and certificates are available for both tracks.

Post-secondary education includes thirteenth and fourteenth grades for vocational training, technical training institutes, colleges (including teacher training colleges), and universities. Some colleges are accredited to award academic degrees. To attend a university, students must take prescribed secondary school classes, pass the requisite matriculation exams, and achieve a specified score on an educational aptitude test known as the psychometric exam.

---

[69] A small number of students take matriculation exams for other systems such as the Jordanian or French system.

IV. CONSEQUENCES OF DISCRIMINATION

Compared with Jewish students, Palestinian Arab students are more likely to drop out of school, less likely to pass the matriculation examinations (*bagrut*), and less likely to qualify for university admission if they do pass. Among Palestinian Arabs, these differences are much greater for Negev Bedouin.

Human Rights Watch recognizes that what determines a child's educational achievement is complex, and this report does not attempt to tackle every factor or to identify all causes of poor performance. In addition to discrimination documented by this report, factors within the Palestinian Arab community[70] as well as lower returns on, or benefits from, education for Palestinian Arabs also play a role.[71] However, these factors, too, are arguably indirect consequences of a legacy of discrimination. For example, students who benefit less from academic credentials have less incentive to acquire them.

Nevertheless, that discrimination affects academic performance is indisputable.[72] The link is particularly evident when programs designed to improve performance and decrease dropping out are implemented in a discriminatory manner. The government has used low academic performance among certain groups of Jewish children to justify additional programs and

---

[70] For a detailed analysis of internal factors that affect Palestinian Arabs' performance, see Khalil Rinnawi, "Structural Obstacles to Education amongst the Palestinian Minority in Israel," *Israel Equality Monitor*, no. 6, March 1996. Rinnawi concludes that along with discrimination, factors within the Palestinian Arab community that affect achievement include: teacher's status; teaching methods; relations among the school, the municipality, and the Ministry of Education; parental attitudes toward education; and, especially, tracking. Ibid. Among Negev Bedouin, low parental involvement, low economic status, the marginality of Bedouin society in Israel, lack of Bedouin representation at high levels in the Ministry of Education, and "the absence of any official encouragement" contribute to high drop-out rates. Abu-Rabiyya, "Survey of Bedouin Schools in the Negev," pp. 7-8.

[71] Swirski, *Politics and Education in Israel*, p. 220 (discussing low returns on education for Palestinian Arabs); Human Rights Watch interview with Andre Elias Mazawi, senior lecturer and head of the Sociology of Education Program, School of Education, Tel Aviv University, Tel Aviv, November 30, 2000.

[72] See, for example, Victor Lavy, "Disparities between Arabs and Jews in School Resources and Students' Achievement in Israel," *Economic Development and Cultural Change*, vol. 47, no. 1, October 1998 (finding that the gaps between resources allocated by the central government to Jewish and Arab schools "is a major cause for the poor performance of Arab primary school children in cognitive achievement tests in arithmetics [sic] and reading comprehension relative to the performance of Jewish school children. The gap in resources is augmented by a much lower socioeconomic status of the Arab population[.]").

resources for those students without providing equal assistance to Palestinian Arab students similarly or worse situated.

Dropping Out of School
Palestinian Arabs drop out of school at a younger average age and at a much higher rate than Jewish students. The Convention on the Rights of the Child, which Israel has ratified, obligates states to "take measures to encourage regular attendance and the reduction of drop-out rates."[73] As described below, the measures that Israel has taken, such as providing truant officers, counseling, and vocational education, have been on average less available to Palestinian Arab students than to Jewish students.

In the 1998-1999 school year, the most recent year for which complete figures are available,10.4 percent of Jewish seventeen-year-olds had dropped out of school. In contrast, 31.7 percent of seventeen-year-old Palestinian Arabs had dropped out.[74]

Table 1: Drop-Out Rates 1998-1999

	Jewish students	Palestinian Arab students
By age 14	0.3%	7.4%
By age 15	5.8%	20.6%
By age 17	10.4%	31.7%

Source: CBS, *Statistical Abstract of Israel 2000*, no. 51, table 22.12.

For example, by age fourteen, usually the first year of high school, 7.4 percent of Palestinian Arabs had dropped out, compared with 0.3 percent of Jewish students. Of students in the ninth through twelfth grades from the 1998-1999 to 1999-2000 school years, 11.8 percent of Palestinian Arab students dropped out,

---

[73] Convention on the Rights of the Child, art. 28(1)(d), (e), *adopted* November 20, 1989, G.A. Res. 44/55, U.N. Doc. A/RES/44/25 (entered into force September 2, 1990, and ratified by Israel October 3, 1991).
[74] Data exclude East Jerusalem. CBS, *Statistical Abstract of Israel 2000*, table 22.12. Attendance rates include students at all grade levels. For example, five out of every 1,000 Jewish seventeen-year-olds and six out of every 1,000 Palestinian Arab seventeen-year-olds were enrolled in primary education in 1998-1999. Ibid. The Ministry of Education reported that in the 1999-2000 school year, 83.0 percent of Jewish seventeen-year-olds and 71.2 percent of Palestinian Arab seventeen-year-olds (excluding East Jerusalem seventeen-year-olds) were enrolled in the twelfth grade. It did not report how many seventeen-year-olds were enrolled in other grades. Ministry of Education, "Statistics of the Matriculation Examination (*Bagrut*) 2000 Report," p. 5.

including 24.8 percent of ninth grade Palestinian Arab boys. In contrast, 4.8 percent of Jewish students, including 8.1 percent of ninth grade boys, dropped out during the same period.[75] Education is compulsory in Israel through grade ten (age fifteen).

Performance on National Examinations

Palestinian Arab students also score lower, on average, on national examinations. Fourth, sixth, and eighth grade students take national examinations in math, English, and science. In each of these areas, Jewish pupils average higher scores than Palestinian Arab pupils.[76] This is true even when scores are assessed in accordance with the government's own index of educational disadvantage (see below).[77]

The most important series of tests, however, are the matriculation examinations (*bagrut*), which students must pass to receive an academic or vocational certificate (high school diploma), or to attend a university. Although fewer Palestinian Arab students make it to the twelfth grade, those who do make it take the matriculation examinations at roughly the same rate as Jewish students. However, Palestinian Arab examinees are more likely to fail the examinations and, even if they pass, are less likely to meet the standards for university admittance.[78]

---

[75] CBS, *Statistical Abstract of Israel 2000*, tables 22.19, 22.20.

[76] See Daphna Golan, Chair, Committee for Closing the Gap, Pedagogical Secretariat, Ministry of Education, *Closing the Gaps in Arab Education in Israel: Data About Hebrew-Arab Education; Recommendations of the Committee for Closing the Gap; Protocol of the Meeting of the Directorship, December 13, 2000*, December 2000, p. 5.

[77] Ibid.

[78] Ministry of Education, "Statistics of the Matriculation Examination (*Bagrut*) 2000 Report," pp. 5, 7, 45. Data exclude East Jerusalem.

Table 2:   Performance on the Matriculation Examinations (*Bagrut*) 1999-2000

	Jewish students	Palestinian Arab students
Pass rate among all seventeen-year-olds	45.6%	27.5%
Pass rate among examinees	63.0%	43.4%
Passing students who also qualified for university admission	88.6%	66.9%
Qualification rate for university admission among all seventeen-year-olds	40.4%	18.4%

Source: Ministry of Education, "Statistics of the Matriculation Examination (*Bagrut*) 2000 Report," http://www.netvision.net.il/bagrut/netunim2000.htm (accessed on May 10, 2001), pp. 5, 7, 45.[79]

For example, 43.4 percent of Palestinian Arab students who took the matriculation exams passed, compared with 63.0 percent of Jewish students. Of those passing students, 66.9 percent of Palestinian Arab students achieved the minimum scores needed for university admission, compared with 88.6 percent of Jewish students. This left only 18.4 percent of Palestinian Arab seventeen-year-olds, compared with 40.4 percent of Jewish seventeen-year-olds, eligible to attend a university in 2000. And of those with minimum passing scores, Jewish students averaged higher scores.[80]   Matriculation exam scores determine a student's eligibility to major (specialize) in particular subjects at university, such as law, engineering, or medicine. Thus, Jewish students were, on average, eligible for more majors than Palestinian Arab students were.

Over 40 percent of all students fail because they are missing a mandatory subject. Over half of Palestinian Arab students who fail because they lack one subject fail because they lack English.[81] Kamal G., a recent university graduate and Negev Bedouin, told Human Rights Watch:

> Many subjects I had to do the *bagrut* in I didn't have in school, so I had to go home and study at home so I would be able to have an

---

[79] Data exclude East Jerusalem.

[80] Ministry of Education, "Statistics of the Matriculation Examination (*Bagrut*) 2000 Report." Data exclude East Jerusalem.

[81] Ibid., p. 41. Data exclude East Jerusalem.

academic education. For example, my school taught three units of English but the university required four, so I had to complete one unit by myself. I stayed home for one year to study for the fourth unit.[82]

Palestinian Arab students learn English as a third language after Arabic and Hebrew, while Jewish students learn it as a second language.

The differences in performance on the matriculation examinations were reflected in Human Rights Watch's interviews at schools. Expectations at government-run Arab schools were generally low. The director of an Arab vocational school told us that very few of his students would take the exams. Out of about 800 students, the school had set a goal that the top sixty would take the exams, and he expected ten to fifteen students to pass, that is, 17 to 25 percent of expected examinees, and less than 2 percent of all 800 students.[83]

In contrast, the principal of a Jewish secondary school with a high immigrant population told Human Rights Watch that he hoped that 60 to 70 percent of his students would pass in 2001, although he later said that this was a high estimate. "We know the strengths and weaknesses of each student, and we give them help," he explained. "School is open in the afternoon, and we work with pupils."[84]

Recognized but unofficial secondary schools run by Christian religious organizations are perceived to offer a better quality of education to Palestinian Arabs in cities such as Haifa and Nazareth. Indeed, the principal of a missionary high school in Nazareth told Human Rights Watch that 116 out of 118 students who took the matriculation examinations the previous year passed them.[85] However, these schools do not exist in all areas with significant Palestinian Arab populations, particularly the Triangle region and the Negev in southern Israel, and educate only about 5 percent of all Palestinian Arab students.[86] Manal M., from a village in the Triangle region, told us that she had tried sending her younger daughter to a missionary high school in Nazareth. "She had to get up at 5:30 in the morning and returned at 5:30 at night and then had to do her homework," she said. "We decided that she would come back and learn near our house."[87]

---

[82] Human Rights Watch interview, Be'er Sheva, December 16, 2000.

[83] Human Rights Watch interview, Israel, December 9, 2000.

[84] Human Rights Watch interview with Israel Vargist, principal, Alon High School, Nazareth Ilit, December 13, 2000.

[85] Human Rights Watch interview, Nazareth, December 7, 2000.

[86] Ministry of Justice, *Initial Periodic Report,* p. 304.

[87] Human Rights Watch interview, village in the Triangle region, December 6, 2000.

Many Palestinian Arab students and teachers told us they saw the psychometric exam, an aptitude test that is required to apply to university, even more than the *bagrut*, as a barrier to attending university or to majoring in the most rewarding or prestigious subjects. A Bedouin university student explained, "I wanted to study law but my psychometric exam score was too low. This was the barrier. I really admire lawyers."[88] Instead, he majored in psychology and sociology.

Several university students also complained about the exam's translation from Hebrew to Arabic.[89] A tenth-grade girl told us that she saw the exam as an "obstacle," and that she believed that she would encounter problems in the exam's translation to Arabic.[90] An English teacher who was also the parent of three high school students explained:

> The students are not sufficiently prepared, especially for the psychometric. It is translated from Hebrew and sometimes the translation is wrong. Sometimes the words are unknown to the pupils. Many of them fail and can't go to university. They have the ability and the *bagrut*, but this test makes them fail. The ministry puts it as a stone in front of students and denies some a chance to learn in the university.[91]

Nabil R., a university student, told us:

> I specialized in computers [in high school] and wanted to do it in university, but my score on the psychometric exam was insufficient. My *bagrut* score was fine–the psychometric exam was the barrier. This serves as the main barrier. The exam is translated to Arabic and the translation, especially for reading comprehension, is not so good. I see a big difference between Jewish and Arab schools.[92]

Nadia S., an eleventh-grade student, told us that while she hoped to attend a university,

> I don't know what subjects [I will study] because I know that there are difficulties for Arabs. For example, the psychometric exam is so

---

[88] Human Rights Watch interview, Be'er Sheva, December 17, 2000.
[89] Ibid.
[90] Human Rights Watch interview, Nazareth, December 8, 2000.
[91] Human Rights Watch interview, village in the Triangle region, December 6, 2000.
[92] Human Rights Watch interview, Be'er Sheva, December 17, 2000.

difficult–the reason is to decrease the numbers of Arab students. I hear it is so difficult–the way they ask us is the Jewish way. I am doing a preparation course after school, but I don't think it is enough. I go for four to five hours one day a week. We do practice questions, and they show us the quick and easy way.[93]

At the time of writing, the Knesset Education Committee was considering proposals to eliminate or provide alternatives to the psychometric exam.[94]

Access to Higher Education

Overall, Palestinian Arab students are less likely than Jewish students to continue with post-secondary education of any kind and, in particular, to study at a university. Out of a group of 1990-1991 high school graduates followed by the Central Bureau for Statistics until 1997-1998, 45.8 percent of Jews began some form of post-secondary education, compared with 26.0 percent of non-Jews.[95] Post secondary education includes a thirteenth and fourteenth grade, technological training institutes, teacher training colleges, academic colleges, and universities.[96]

As explained in the previous section, Palestinian Arabs are less likely to obtain the minimum score on the matriculation examinations needed to apply to a university. However, even achieving the minimum qualifying score does not guarantee university admission. Rather, the student's secondary school classes and scores on the matriculation and psychometric exams are all factors in whether a student will be admitted. Palestinian Arab applicants are rejected at more than twice the rate of Jewish applicants.

---

[93] Human Rights Watch interview, Nazareth, December 9, 2000.

[94] Relly Sa'ar, "Psychometric Exams Placed on Chopping Block," *Ha'aretz Daily Newspaper (English Edition)* (Israel), June 28, 2001.

[95] CBS, *Statistical Abstract of Israel 2000*, table 22.26.

[96] Ibid., "Introduction to 'Education and Culture,'" p. (106).

Table 3: University Admission 1998-1999

	Jewish students	Non-Jewish students[97]
Students who applied to university who were rejected[98]	16.7%	44.7%
Students who applied to university and were accepted but who are not studying	18.2%	14.2%
Students who applied to university who were accepted and who are studying	65.1%	41.2%

Source: CBS, *Statistical Abstract of Israel 2000*, no. 51, table 22.37.

While 44.7 percent of non-Jewish applicants who applied to university were rejected and 41.2 percent were accepted and went on to study, o16.7 percent of Jewish applicants were rejected and 65.1 percent went on to study.

In the 1998-1999 school year, fewer than 9 percent of university students seeking a first degree were not Jewish and only 5.7 percent of degree recipients were not Jewish.[99]

---

[97] Data from the Central Bureau of Statistics distinguished between Jewish and non-Jewish students, rather than Jewish and Arab students.

[98] CBS, *Statistical Abstract of Israel 2000*, table 22.37. The applications were for the first year of studies for a first (undergraduate) degree only. These data are derived from percentages given in table 22.37. The same table also states that 7,537 applicants our of 35,040 were rejected, of whom 70.6 percent were Jewish and 29.4 percent were "other religions." By these figures, 17.6 percent of Jewish applicants were rejected and 46.8 percent of non-Jewish applicants were rejected.

[99] CBS, *Statistical Abstract of Israel 2000*, table 22.34. Only 3.5 percent of students seeking a second (graduate) degree and only 2.4 percent of second degree recipients were non-Jewish in 1998-1999. Ibid., tables 22.34, 22.39.

Table 4: University Attendance 1998-1999

	Jewish students	Non-Jewish students[100]
University students studying for first (undergraduate) academic degree	91.3%	8.7%
University students receiving a first academic degree[101]	94.3%	5.7%

Source: CBS, *Statistical Abstract of Israel 2000*, no. 51, tables 22.34, 22.39.

It should be noted that other factors outside of this report's scope, especially advantages for military service such as grants for higher education or, in some cases, partial or total exemptions from university tuition, affect university attendance and academic performance there.[102] While Jewish students typically begin mandatory military service after twelfth grade, most Palestinian Arab students do not serve in the military.[103] In addition, fewer than 1 percent of lecturers at Israeli universities are Arab.[104]

One generation's failure to obtain higher education also negatively affects the next generation's education by depressing the family's socio-economic status and by limiting their teachers' educational qualifications.

---

[100] Data from the Central Bureau of Statistics distinguished between Jewish and non-Jewish students, rather than Jewish and Arab students.

[101] In 1994-1995, non-Jewish students represented 5.1 percent of first degree recipients; in 1984-1985, they represented 4.7 percent. Ibid., table 22.39.

[102] The Released Soldiers Absorption Law (1994) provides for various education benefits upon their release to soldiers and persons who perform National Service.

[103] Jewish men and women, and Druze and Circassian men are subject to compulsory military service, and some Bedouin also serve. Persons studying in religious institutions can receive a deferment from military service, and Jewish orthodox woman can receive an exemption. All other Palestinian Arab citizens have been exempted since Israel's establishment as a state.

[104] Vered Levy-Barzilai, "Know thy neighbor – but don't hire him," *Ha'aretz Magazine* (Israel), July 12, 2001. Ten of 1,500 lecturers at Tel Aviv University are Arab; at Bar-Ilan University, three of 1,300 lecturers are Arab; at Ben-Gurion University of the Negev, there are ten Arab lecturers; at the University of Haifa, it is estimated that about fifteen to twenty lecturers are Arab; and at Hebrew University, the faculty estimates the number to be less than ten. Ibid.

Access to Employment

[M]any human rights can only be accessed through education, particularly rights associated with employment and social security. Without education, people are impeded from access to employment. Lower educational accomplishment routinely prejudices their career advancement. Lower salaries negatively affect their old-age security.

–K. Tomaševski, U.N. Special Rapporteur on the Right to Education[105]

Discrimination in education hurts students' abilities to get rewarding and well-paying jobs. Unemployment is greater among Palestinian Arabs than it is among Jews. Overall, according to Israel's Central Bureau of Statistics, the unemployment rate in 1999 was 11.4 percent for Palestinian Arabs and 8.5 percent for Jews.[106] However, the Central Bureau of Statistics' definition of "unemployed" arguably underestimates the unemployment rate among Palestinian Arabs.[107] More accurate may be data on persons who "do not work" and "do not study." In 1999, about 42 percent of Palestinian Arabs ages twenty-five to thirty-four did not work and did not study, compared with about 24 percent of Jews of the same age; for persons ages fifteen to seventeen, 14.3 percent of Palestinian Arabs and 5.5 percent of Jews did not work or study.[108]

---

[105] K. Tomaševski, "Removing Obstacles in the Way of the Right to Education," *Right to Education Primers*, no. 1., 2001, p. 9.

[106] CBS, *Statistical Abstract of Israel 2000*, table 12.20.

[107] Unemployed persons are defined as those ages fifteen and over who "did not work at all during the determinant week (even for a single hour), and actively sought work during the preceding four weeks by registering at the Labor Exchanges of the Employment Service . . . and would have been available to start work during the determinate week." Those over fifteen-years-old who do not work but do not meet the above definition are not considered part of the civilian labor force and, therefore, are not counted as unemployed. Ibid., p. 69. The Central Bureau of Statistics counts 42.5 percent of the non-Jewish population, compared with 53.8 percent of the total population of Israel, as part of the civilian labor force. Ibid., table 12.1. Moreover, soldiers doing compulsory military service or in the permanent army and students are not considered part of the civilian labor force. Ibid., p. 69. If persons in the army, who are almost entirely Jewish, were counted, there would be an even greater difference between the percent of the Jewish population counted as part of the civilian labor force, compared with the Palestinian Arab population. Accordingly, it may be argued the 11.4 percent figure underestimates the unemployment rate among Palestinian Arabs.

[108] Of Palestinian Arabs ages twenty-five to twenty-nine, 43.0 percent did not work or study in 1999, compared with 22.9 percent of Jews. Of Palestinian Arabs ages thirty to

Of persons ages eighteen to twenty-four, the age at which most Jews and a few Palestinian Arabs complete military service, 42.1 percent of Palestinian Arabs did not work or study, compared with 43.6 percent of Jews.[109] However, soldiers on compulsory military service or in the permanent army are included in those not working or studying.[110]

In addition, returns on education–benefits from academic credentials–affect students' incentive and motivation to pursue education. One return on education is employment. Job opportunities for educated Palestinian Arabs in Israel are more limited due to employment discrimination and the fact that certain labor markets, such as the military-industrial complex and many government jobs, are closed to them.[111] In January and February 2001, 30 percent (3,895) of Palestinian Arabs registered at employment service offices as unemployed professional and academic job seekers held advanced degrees.[112] The director of an Arab vocational school told Human Rights Watch: "The Arab sector is not really open–there aren't really job opportunities–so Arab students choose to get practical jobs like in a garage rather than in art or cinema." The school's graduates, he said, tend to work as "carpenters, machinists, or mechanics in a garage."[113]

Special Issues for Girls

Some argue that one reason for Palestinian Arabs' lower academic performance is that their culture does not value educating girls. In the past, this has been an issue, and by many reports it is still an issue among Bedouin, particularly for higher education. However, cultural attitudes cannot shoulder much of the blame. If this were still the case, Palestinian Arab girls should be performing at lower rates than boys, driving down the average. They are not. Palestinian Arab girls on average outperform boys on the matriculation

---

thirty-four, 42.4 percent did not work or study in 1999, compared with 24.5 percent of Jews. Ibid., table 12.17.

[109] Ibid.

[110] Ibid., p. 69.

[111] Swirski, *Politics and Education in Israel*, p. 220 (discussing low returns on education for Palestinian Arabs); Human Rights Watch interview with Andre Elias Mazawi, senior lecturer and head of the Sociology of Education Program, School of Education, Tel Aviv University, Tel Aviv, November 30, 2000.

[112] Haider, "Arab Citizens in the Civil Service."

[113] Human Rights Watch interview, Israel, December 9, 2000.

examinations. In 1999, 56.9 percent of Palestinian Arab girls who took the exams passed them, compared with 46.4 percent of boys.[114]

Nationally, Palestinian Arab girls are also less likely than boys to drop out. Between the 1998-1999 and 1999-2000 school years, 53.1 percent of Palestinian Arab twelfth graders were girls.[115] And in every grade, nine through twelve, Palestinian Arab boys dropped out at higher rates than girls.[116] However, during the same period, only 47.7 percent of Palestinian Arab ninth graders were girls,[117] suggesting that while girls are slightly less likely to make the transition to high school, those who do are more likely than boys to stay in. This is true for Bedouin girls, as well as Palestinian Arab girls nationally.[118]

One possible explanation for this fact is that there are fewer high schools and, thus, students are more likely to have to travel farther to reach them. Travel distance appears to disproportionately cause girls to drop out. A Bedouin teacher who recently graduated from university told us that he has six brothers and one sister. All the brothers finished high school, but the sister did not: "The long distance between home and school makes it difficult for a girl to walk alone in the desert. She preferred to stay at home after eighth grade. She is eighteen years old now."[119] As explained below in the section on school buildings, many Bedouin living in unrecognized villages in the Negev must travel long distances even to reach a primary school, and attendance rates among Bedouin are lower for girls.[120] According to a study of Bedouin mothers' attitudes towards their children's education, Bedouin girls and women "were (and continue to be) considered the 'bearers of the family honor,' and thus, their families preferred not to risk their reputations by allowing girls to travel among and mix with males from other tribes. Therefore, there has been much more reluctance among the Bedouin over sending their daughters to school than over sending their sons to school, especially when schools were far away."[121] Of 305 women surveyed

---

[114] CBS, *Statistical Abstract of Israel 2000*, table 22.22. In 1998. more girls than boys took the matriculation exams. Ibid., table 22.21,

[115] Ibid., table 22.20.

[116] Ibid.

[117] Ibid. In 1998, 51.1 percent of all Palestinian Arab fourteen-year-olds and 51.2 percent of all seventeen-year-olds were girls. Ibid., table 2.18.

[118] Abu-Saad. "Bedouin Arab Education in the Context of Radical Social Change." p. 157.

[119] Human Rights Watch interview, Be'er Sheva, December 16, 2000.

[120] In 1998-1999, in both recognized and unrecognized Bedouin localities in the Negev, less than half of the students in grades one through nine were girls. Center for Bedouin Studies and Development, *Statistical Yearbook of the Negev Bedouin*, pp. 76, 80.

[121] Ismael Abu-Saad. Kathleen Abu-Saad, Gillian Lewando-Hundt, Michele R. Forman, Ilana Belmaker, Heinz W. Berendes, and David Chang, "Bedouin Arab Mothers'

from 1991-1992 about their daughters finishing high school, 80.7 percent wanted their daughters to finish, although of those surveyed, 24.9 percent stated that financial barriers, the fact that their extended families did not allow girls to finish high school, and the fact that schools were too far away would prevent their daughters from finishing.[122]

International law affords special protection for women and girls against discrimination in education.[123]

Negev Bedouin

> Every time we meet professors or are invited to meet family, everyone is shocked at how we can get an education while coming from such a bad economic situation.
>
> –Nawal A., Bedouin university student, Be'er Sheva, December 17, 2000

Aspirations for Their Children's Education in the Context of Radical Social Change," *International Journal of Educational Development*, vol. 18, no. 4, 1998, p. 351 (internal citations omitted).

[122] Ibid., pp. 353, 355, table 2. It should be noted that there was no difference in responses from mothers who lived in recognized and unrecognized settlements. The authors conclude that the data do not support the hypothesis "that the planned towns would lead to a social change in relation to girls' education, given the easier access to schools." Ibid., p. 357.

[123] The Convention on the Elimination of All Forms of Discrimination against Women (CEDAW) obligates states to:

> take all appropriate measures to eliminate discrimination against women in order to ensure them equal rights with men in the field of education and in particular to ensure, on the basis of equality of men and women: (a) The same conditions . . . for access to studies and for the achievement of diplomas in educational establishments of all categories in rural as well as in urban areas; this equality shall be ensured in preschool, general, technical, professional and higher technical education, as well as in all types of vocational training; . . . (f) the reduction of female student drop-out rates[.]

Convention on the Elimination of All Forms of Discrimination against Women (CEDAW), art. 10, *adopted* December 18, 1979, G.A. Res. 34/180, U.N. Doc. A/34/46 (entered into force September 3, 1981, and ratified by Israel October 3, 1991). The Convention on the Rights of the Child and the International Covenant on Economic, Social and Cultural Rights each provide for a right to education and specify that this right must be enjoyed without discrimination on the basis of gender. Convention on the Rights of the Child, arts. 2, 28; International Covenant on Economic, Social and Cultural Rights (ICESCR), arts. 2, 13, *adopted* December 16, 1966, G.A. Res. 2200A (XXI), 993 U.N.T.S. 3 (entered into force January 2, 1976, and ratified by Israel October 3, 1991).

I went to university and was exposed to Jewish people. I saw huge
gap between Bedouin and Jewish families. This exposure to the
other side made me realize something should be done.

> –Anwar B., Bedouin university
> student, Be'er Sheva, December 17,
> 2000

Negev Bedouin drop out of school at higher rates than Palestinian Arabs.
If they make it to the twelfth grade, they are less likely to pass the matriculation
exam and, if they do pass, to qualify for university admission: in 2000, only 6.4
percent of Bedouin students who took the exam had *bagrut* scores that met
minimum university requirements for admission. Of the Bedouin students who
have met minimum university requirements, only a tiny handful have actually
attended and graduated.

The majority of Bedouin students who go to university attend Ben Gurion
University of the Negev in Be'er Sheva.[124] In 2000-2001, 344 Bedouin students
total were enrolled at Ben Gurion University, of whom 120 were women, and
twenty-two were graduate students. In 2001, forty-seven Bedouin students,
including fourteen women, graduated–the most of any year at the university.[125]

Table 5: Educational Performance of Negev Bedouin 2000

	Jewish students	All Palestinian Arab students	Negev Bedouin students
Seventeen-year-olds enrolled in 12th grade	83.0%	71.2%	62.8%
Seventeen-year-olds who passed the matriculation exams (*bagrut*)	45.6%	27.5%	16.8%
Passing students who also qualified for university admission	88.6%	66.9%	38.4%
Seventeen-year-olds who qualified for university admission	40.4%	18.4%	6.4%

[124] Ismael Abu-Saad, e-mail to Human Rights Watch, July 13, 2001.
[125] Ibid.

Source: Ministry of Education, "Statistics of the Matriculation Examination (*Bagrut*) 2000 Report," http://www.netvision.net.il/bagrut/netunim2000.htm (accessed on May 10, 2001), pp. 5, 7, 45.

Performance and Social Class

It is sometimes argued that the differences between Jewish and Palestinian Arab students' performance is more a function of family income than discrimination. For example, the Israeli government reported to the Committee on the Rights of the Child in 2001 that "the socio-economic differences among sectors, coupled with the relative homogeneity of schools, has led to gaps in achievements among different groups."[126]   Dalia Sprinzak, of the Education Ministry's Economics and Budgeting Administration, explained that she thought that poverty would always be a barrier to closing the gap. "It is a big problem because the Arabs are poor," she said. "This is also an issue in the Jewish sector."[127]

Clearly economic class affects educational performance. Low income Jewish children, particularly those in outlying areas, experience some of the same performance problems as Palestinian Arab children. However, the Israeli government has directed more resources to low income and low performing Jewish children than it has to similarly situated Palestinian Arab children.[128] Indeed, the argument is circular in that discrimination perpetuates class differences.

The strongest evidence against the claim that income, exclusive of discrimination, is at play is that when Jewish and Palestinian Arab children of the same economic level are compared, the Jewish children appear to out-perform the Palestinian Arab children. Although the data that Human Rights Watch was able to gather are incomplete, it appears that Jewish children on average still drop out at lower rates and perform better on national examinations than Palestinian Arab children at the same economic level.[129] For example,

---

[126] Ministry of Justice, *Initial Periodic Report*, pp. 270, 303.

[127] Although Sprinzak did not state that poverty was the only cause of the current gaps between Jewish and Palestinian Arab students, she did say that she thought it was an important one. Human Rights Watch interview with Dalia Sprinzak, Economics and Budgeting Administration, Ministry of Education, Jerusalem, December 19, 2000.

[128] See, for example, Swirski, *Politics and Education in Israel*, pp. 158, 164; and the chapter on school buildings below.

[129] See Ministry of Justice, *Initial Periodic Report,* p. 266 (reporting that in 1993, 81 percent of "lower class" and 99 percent of "middle and upper class" Jewish students ages fifteen to eighteen attended school, compared with 59 percent of lower class and 81 percent of middle and upper class Palestinian Arabs and 31 percent of lower class Bedouin); Golan, *Closing the Gaps in Arab Education in Israel*, p. 5 (results of national

[129 (cont.)] math, English, and science exams in the fourth, sixth, and eighth grades by sector and economic level); and CBS, *Statistical Abstract of Israel 2000*, table 22.21 (matriculation exam results by sector and socio-economic cluster of locality of residence; however, 10.6 percent of Jewish twelfth graders and 8.4 percent of Palestinian Arab twelfth graders are not classified).

A study of 1999 *bagrut* pass rates in localities with more than 10,000 residents found that:

> In all but two (Kafr Qari' and 'Ar'ara) of the Arab localities, the percentage of students passing the exams was *lower than the national average*. The lowest percentage was in Umm el Fahm [14%]. In 'Ar'ara, the level was 42% of the age cohort (in other words, only slightly above the national average). In 15 of the 21 Jewish development towns included in Table 1, the rate of success in the age cohort was *lower than the national average*. In only six of the development towns–Yavne, Yokne'am 'Illit, Carmiel, Netivot, Afula and Arad–was the success rate higher.

Shlomo Swirski, Adva Center, "Students Passing Matriculation Exams in 1999," May 2000 (emphasis in original). But see Andre Elias Mazawi, "Region, Locality Characteristics, High School Tracking and Equality in Access to Educational Credentials: the Case of Palestinian Arab Communities in Israel," *Educational Studies*, vol. 24, no. 2, 1998, pp. 223-240 (discussing importance of socio-economic status and locality of residence in relation to education).

according to news reports, between 1991 and 1998, 13 percent of students in development towns who passed the matriculation examinations went on to university, compared with 5 percent of students in Palestinian Arab localities.[130]

---

[130] Hana Kim, "The Demon World of Sharon and Livnat," *Ha'aretz Daily Newspaper (English Edition)* (Israel), March 13, 2001.

V. DISCRIMINATION IN BUDGET ALLOCATIONS

The funding for state education comes from four sources: the central government, local councils or municipalities, private organizations, and parents. Arab schools on average receive proportionately less money than Jewish schools from each of these sources.

The greatest source, by far, is the central government, which is legally responsible for providing free education to children ages three to seventeen.[131] Through the Ministry of Education, the government accredits schools, determines curricula and approves textbooks; certifies, hires, supervises, and pays teachers; administers the matriculation examinations and awards diplomas; and finances about three quarters of the total cost of education.[132] Local governments are responsible for setting up and maintaining educational facilities, and providing administrative staff. Their funding comes from local taxes and transfers from the central government, including the Ministry of Education. Organizations such as the Jewish Agency, which is privately funded but which fulfills certain basic government functions, have historically funded only Jewish education, but their role has decreased in recent years. Supplements to the basic school day, funded by parents and known as "gray education," have increased in importance as real funding from the government has decreased.

International law requires states to provide education "without discrimination of any kind irrespective of the child's race, colour, sex, language, religion, political or other opinion, national ethnic or social origin, property, disability, birth or other status."[133] As a party to the Convention against Discrimination in Education, Israel must not allow "in any form of assistance granted by the public authorities to educational institutions, any restrictions or preference based solely on the ground that pupils belong to a particular group."[134]

---

[131] Compulsory Education Law, part III (1949).

[132] Surie Ackerman, "The Cost of 'Free Education,'" *Jerusalem Post*, August 30, 1991. See Ministry of Foreign Affairs, "Facts About Israel: Education," (stating that the "government finances 72 percent of education, while the rest comes from local authorities and other sources"). In 1996, the latest year for which the Central Bureau of Statistics published data, the government financed 73 percent of the total national expenditure on education, local authorities financed 7 percent, and households financed 20 percent. However, this data includes post-secondary and higher education, in which non-government financing plays a larger role. CBS, *Statistical Abstract of Israel 2000*, table 22.5.

[133] Convention on the Rights of the Child, arts. 28(1), 2(1).

[134] Convention against Discrimination in Education, art. 3(d).

Government Acknowledgement of the Problem

For at least the last ten years, Israeli government bodies have acknowledged that the government spends more on Jewish students than on Palestinian Arab students.[135] The State Comptroller documented this gap in several annual reports in the 1990s. In February 2001, the Israeli government reported to the Committee on the Rights of the Child that:

> in 1991, the total investment in education per pupil in Arab municipalities was approximately one-third of the investment per pupil in Jewish municipalities. Government investment per Arab pupil was approximately 60% of the investment per Jewish pupil.[136]

In the last decade, the government has attempted to correct, at least in part, for certain inequalities in government funding to Palestinian Arabs by allocating lump sums of money through what it has called "five-year plans." In plans passed in 1991 and 1998, allocations were made for Arab education, but these plans have been implemented only in part.[137] In July 1999, the Ministry of Education announced that it was activating a five-year plan to allocate NIS 250 million ($62.5 million)–NIS 50 million ($12.5 million) annually–to correct imbalances in education. Following demonstrations in early October 2000 in which thirteen Palestinian Arab citizens were killed, the Prime Minister's office on October 22, 2000, ratified a plan to allocate NIS 4 billion ($1 billion) over four years to seventy-four Arab localities that included some funding for Arab education.[138] Because the funds for these plans are not separately designated, it is impossible to determine whether they were allocated in the 2001 budget.[139]

Even if all aspects of the 1991, 1998, 1999, and 2000 plans were to be fully implemented, the monies allocated are insufficient to equalize the two systems

---

[135] See, for example, U.N. Human Rights Committee, *Initial Report of States Parties Due in 1993: Israel* (also pointing to "impressive advances towards equality").

[136] Ministry of Justice, *Initial Periodic Report*, p. 303.

[137] Ibid., p. 307.

[138] The October 2000 plan promised funds for classroom construction, teaching programs, and inaugurating curricular programs in technology. "Multiannual Plan for Development of Arab Sector Localities," Government Resolution 2476, cited in Shlomo Swirski, et al., *Looking at the Budget of the State of Israel 2001*, Adva Center, November 2000.

[139] See Ministry of Education, *Proposed Budget for the Ministry of Education 2001 and Explanations as Presented to the Fifteenth Knesset*, no. 11, October 2000; and Swirski, *Looking at the Budget of the State of Israel 2001*.

or correct past discrimination against Palestinian Arab students.[140]   Most
importantly, none of the plans address the most significant structural problems
in the Arab educational system. For example, the education provisions of the
1999 plan consist of supplementary programs for only a limited number of
schools, implemented by private contractors, not by the education system itself.
The plan does not address schools' physical conditions and focuses on only a
small minority of Palestinian Arab students. The Adva Center, a nonprofit
policy analysis and advocacy organization, concluded that "the Ministry of
Education's decision to focus in its five-year plan on the advancement of a
minority of Arab pupils is misguided. . . . [T]his decision was evidently meant
to assure fast results; since a small percentage of Arab high schoolers qualify for
matriculation certificates, even a small increase in their numbers would probably
raise the overall proportion considerably."[141] More generally, the 1999 five-year
plan fails to change the way the education system works:

> Apparently the Ministry of Education would like to attain this worthy
> goal at minimum cost, without undertaking to improve the Arab
> education system on a permanent basis. If the Ministry outsources
> the program, the funds earmarked for it will not be added to the
> budget base of the Arab education system. In other words, the
> privatization of the five-year plan makes this allocation a
> nonrecurrent and replaceable item that, in all probability, will not
> have a sustained effect. Furthermore, the project will not enhance
> the capabilities of Arab teachers, because most of the contractors will
> probably be Jewish agencies that have already participated in similar
> projects for the Education Ministry. As privatization continues
> apace, the Ministry and the contractors become interdependent. As
> the contractors prosper, gather strength, and become permanent

---

[140] For additional information, see Wadi'a Awauda, "Five-Year Plan for Improving Arab
Education: How It's Holding Up in Reality," *Sikkuy's Report on Equality and
Integration of the Arab Citizens in Israel 2000-2001*, Spring 2001.
[141] Adva Center, "Education Ministry Privatizes Arab-Sector Five-Year Plan," August
2000. See also Swirski, *Looking at the Budget of the State of Israel 2001* (stating that the
supplemental allocation for education in the 2001 budget does not improve schools but
only reinforces "prospective graduates at the eleventh hour before their matriculation
exams. These programs, however worthy they may be, cannot be expected to cope with
education disparities between working-class neighborhoods, development towns, and
Arab localities, on the one hand, and affluent localities, on the other hand. Furthermore,
the budget proposal does nothing to confront the large inter-school disparities in financial
and human resources.").

fixtures, the Ministry accustoms itself to tackling education problems not by making substantive and long-term change but by putting out fires by means of private firefighters.[142]

The 1999 plan began operating in early 2001, and not all targeted schools had the programs at the time of writing.[143]

Funding from the Ministry of Education
The Ministry of Education provides several kinds of funding to schools. The largest amount goes to teachers' salaries and related expenses such as in-service teacher training. The second type funds a great variety of supplemental programs, both enrichment and remedial, that play a critical role in the Israeli education system. Some of this funding is purportedly allocated on the basis of need, although even the least needy schools depend heavily on this funding. The ministry also finances school construction.

Despite its acknowledgement of past disparities in its report to the Committee on the Rights of the Child, the Israeli government does not officially release data on how much it spends total per Palestinian Arab child compared with how much it spends per Jewish child. There are no separate lines in the budget for Arab education,[144] and when Human Rights Watch requested this information, the Deputy Director General, Head, Economics and Budgeting Administration, in Ministry of Education, on behalf of the ministry's director general, responded: "On the Ministry level (headquarters and districts), the administration, operation and inspection are common to both Hebrew and Arab education. Similarly, there is no budgetary separation. Therefore, I regret that it is not possible for us to determine the exact amount spent on Arab education."[145]

The government's continued failure to make public such basic data further indicates the weakness of its commitment to real improvements in the Arab education system. As a party to the International Covenant on Economic, Social and Cultural Rights, Israel is required to monitor educational programs and spending patterns, to disaggregate educational data "by the prohibited grounds

---

[142] Swirski, *Looking at the Budget of the State of Israel 2001.*

[143] During the 2000-2001 school year, 238 schools were selected, but not all selected schools had the programs by the end of the year. Awauda, "Five-Year Plan for Improving Arab Education."

[144] See, for example, Ministry of Education, *Budget Instructions for 2000,* no. 11, January 2000; and Ministry of Education, *Proposed Budget for the Ministry of Education 2001.*

[145] Ady Hershcovitsh, Deputy Director General, Head, Economics and Budgeting Administration, Ministry of Education, letter to Human Rights Watch, August 19, 2001.

of discrimination," and to use this information "to identify and take measures to redress any de facto discrimination."[146]

The government allocates much, but not all, funding in terms of "teaching hours," one teaching hour being a unit that represents a particular sum of money. The Ministry of Education referred Human Rights Watch to the 1990/2000 distribution of teaching hours when we requested information about how much it spends per Palestinian Arab student and per Jewish student.[147] According to the ministry, "[t]he schools' main resource of that of teaching positions, 72% of the total budget in 2001."[148] Because not all teaching hours are worth the same amount and vary in value from year to year, it is difficult to convert the allocation of teaching hours into exact sums of money.[149] Nonetheless, comparison of how teaching hours are distributed between Jewish and Arab education does show how resources are apportioned.

At every grade level, Arab education receives proportionately fewer teaching hours than Jewish education. In 1999-2000, although 21.4 percent of children in kindergarten through secondary schools were Palestinian Arab, only 18.4 percent total teaching hours were allocated to Arab education.[150]

[146] *General Comment 13, The Right to Education*, Committee on Economic, Social and Cultural Rights, 21st sess., U.N. Doc. E/C.12/1999/10 (December 8, 1999), para. 37. The committees established by human rights treaties–including the Committee on Economic, Social and Cultural Rights, the Committee on the Rights of the Child, and the Human Rights Committee–issue General Comments that are not addressed to any particular government. These bodies use the General Comments to interpret and clarify the treaties' meaning and content. The General Comments are also a useful means of establishing jurisprudence and are agreed by consensus by the members of the monitoring bodies.
[147] Ady Hershcovitsh, Deputy Director General, Head, Economics and Budgeting Administration, Ministry of Education, letter to Human Rights Watch, August 19, 2001.
[148] Ibid.
[149] See Swirski, *Looking at the Budget of the State of Israel 2001.*
[150] CBS, *Statistical Abstract of Israel 2000*, table 22.27; Ministry of Education, *Proposed Budget for the Ministry of Education 2001*, p. 144.

Table 6: Distribution of Teaching Hours by Grade Level 1999-2000[151]

	Jewish schools	Arab schools
Total	81.6%	18.4%
Kindergarten (official)	88.5%	11.5%
Primary	78.3%	21.7%
Intermediate	81.0%	19.0%
Secondary	84.7%	15.3%

Sources: CBS, *Statistical Abstract of Israel 2000*, no. 51, table 22.27; and Ministry of Education, *Proposed Budget for the Ministry of Education 2001 and Explanations as Presented to the Fifteenth Knesset*, no. 11, October 2000, p. 144.

For example, Arab official (government-run) kindergartens received 11.5 percent of the teaching hours for kindergarten education, while Jewish official kindergartens received the remaining 88.5 percent. Arab primary schools received 21.7 percent of the teaching hours for primary education, and Arab secondary schools received 15.3 percent of the teaching hours for secondary education.

Per student, in 1999-2000, Jewish students received an average of 1.84 teaching hours per week, and Palestinian Arab students received an average of 1.51 teaching hours per week. The differences were greatest at the kindergarten through intermediate levels and smaller at the secondary level.

---

[151] At the primary level, the data reflect financing from the Ministry of Education only. CBS, *Statistical Abstract of Israel 2000*, p. (104). At the intermediate and secondary levels, the data reflect funding from parents and local authorities in addition to ministry funding. Yosef Gidanian, Central Bureau of Statistics, e-mail to Human Rights Watch, June 18, 2001.

Table 7:   Distribution of Teaching Hours–Weekly Hours/Student 1999-2000[152]

	Jewish students	Palestinian Arab students
Total	1.84	1.51
Kindergarten (official)	1.51	0.76
Primary	1.81	1.55
Intermediate	1.78	1.46
Secondary	2.18	2.11

Sources: CBS, *Statistical Abstract of Israel 2000*, no. 51, table 22.27; and Ministry of Education, *Proposed Budget for the Ministry of Education 2001 and Explanations as Presented to the Fifteenth Knesset*, no. 11, October 2000, p. 144.

Although data by sector was not available for 2000-2001, the average number of teaching hours per student, Jewish and Palestinian Arab, was virtually unchanged from 1999-2000.[153]   In 2000-2001, 22.2 percent of kindergarten through secondary level students were Palestinian Arab.

The Committee for Closing the Gap, a division of the Education Ministry's Pedagogical Secretariat that was created primarily to examine gaps within the Jewish sector, also estimated total resource allocation in 1999-2000 to Jewish and Arab primary education. Using internal ministry sources, the Committee looked specifically at the Northern District, which contains approximately equal numbers of Jewish and Palestinian Arab students, and found that the ministry distributed teaching hours as follows:

Table 8: Distribution of Teaching Hours–Primary Schools in the Northern District 1999-2000

	Jewish schools		Arab schools		
	state secular	state religious	Arab	Druze	Bedouin
Hours/child	1.98	2.15	1.42	1.7	1.61

---

[152] See the appendix for a chart of how these data were calculated.

[153] In 1999-2000, the average teaching hours per student in primary, intermediate, and secondary education were, respectively, 1.75, 1.71, and 2.17. In 2000-2001, the average teaching hours were 1.75, 1.72, and 2.16. Ministry of Education, *Proposed Budget for the Ministry of Education 2001*, pp. 157, 168, 179.

Source: Daphna Golan, Chair, Committee for Closing the Gap, Pedagogical Secretariat, Ministry of Education, *Closing the Gaps in Arab Education in Israel: Data About Hebrew-Arab Education; Recommendations of the Committee for Closing the Gap; Protocol of the Meeting of the Directorship, December 13, 2000*, December 2000, p. 2 (citing data from the acting chief executive of the Northern District).

Although the above data are averages and thus allow for significant variation among individual schools, they are generally in accord with what the schools Human Rights Watch visited told us they received. For example, the principal of a primary school in Um El-Fahm with 360 children told us that the Ministry of Education gave the school 582 teaching hours per week, an average of 1.35 hours per child.[154]

Class Size and Teaching Staff

At every grade level, Arab schools' classes are, on average, larger than Jewish schools' classes.

Table 9: Average Number of Pupils Per Class 1998-1999

	Jewish schools	Arab schools
Total	26	30
Primary	25	30
Post-primary:	28	31
Intermediate	31	33
Secondary:	26	28
General secondary	28	31
Continuation classes	26	n/a
Technological/vocational	23	24
Agricultural	24	29

Source: CBS, *Statistical Abstract of Israel 2000*, no. 51, table 22.9.

In 1998-1999, the most recent year for which data were available, there were an average of twenty-six students per class in Jewish schools and thirty students per class in Arab schools. Classes for Negev Bedouin were, on average, even larger, averaging thirty-three students per class at the primary and

---

[154] Of the 582 hours, 486 were for actual teaching and the rest were for administration and "informal hours or projects." Human Rights Watch interview, Um El-Fahm, December 6, 2000.

intermediate levels, and twenty-nine students per class at the secondary level.[155]
A primary school teacher who had taught for the past four and a half years in the
Negev told us that her classes averaged forty students every year.[156]

Although the highest national average for any grade level in 1998-1999
was thirty-three students per class, many teachers we interviewed in both Jewish
and Arab schools reported having thirty to forty students in their classes. For
example, an eleven-year-old Palestinian Arab boy told us his class had forty-
three students.[157] We visited a third grade science class in an Arab school in a
mixed city with thirty-nine students and a first grade class in an unrecognized
Bedouin village in the Negev with forty-six students. "In some classes we have
thirty-nine," an eleventh-grade Palestinian Arab girl in Nazareth told us.[158] The
principal of a Jewish middle school in a development town told us that the
classes in her school were as large as forty,[159] and the principal of a Jewish
primary school told us about thirty-eight students were in her school's classes.[160]
We also saw classes with fewer than thirty-one students. Several school
principals told us that the Education Ministry capped primary classrooms at
forty students.

The Ministry of Education also allocates more total teaching staff per child
to Jewish schools than it does to Arab schools, particularly at lower grade levels.

---

[155] Center for Bedouin Studies and Development, *Statistical Yearbook of the Negev
Bedouin*, p. 75. These numbers do not include special education classes, which were
smaller.
[156] Human Rights Watch interview, village in the Galilee region, December 7, 2000.
[157] Human Rights Watch interview, village in the Triangle region, December 6, 2000.
[158] Human Rights Watch interview, Nazareth, December 9, 2000.
[159] Human Rights Watch interview with Rachel Shechori, principal of Sharet Middle
School, Nazareth Ilit, December 13, 2000.
[160] Human Rights Watch interview with Osnat Mordechai, principal, Ksulot Primary
School, Nazareth Ilit, December 13, 2000.

Table 10: Allocation of Teaching Staff: Children Per Full-Time Teacher 1999-2000[161]

	Jewish schools	Arab schools
Total	14.8	18.2
Kindergarten (official)	19.8	39.3
Primary	16.6	19.4
Intermediate	13.5	16.4
Secondary	11.0	11.3

Sources: Ministry of Education, *Proposed Budget for the Ministry of Education 2001 and Explanations as Presented to the Fifteenth Knesset*, no. 11, October 2000, p. 144; and CBS, *Statistical Abstract of Israel 2000*, no. 51, tables 22.10, 22.27.

For example, in 1999-2000 the Ministry of Education allocated the equivalent of one full-time teacher for every 16.6 children in Jewish primary schools and every 19.4 children in Arab primary schools. In kindergartens, the number of children per full-time teacher (or teacher's aide) was twice as high in Arab kindergartens (39.3 students per teacher) as in Jewish kindergartens (19.8 students per teacher). Human Rights Watch visited schools that averaged both somewhat more and somewhat fewer children per teacher.[162]

---

[161] The number of teachers is measured in work units–the number of hours per week that constitute a full teaching post. Thus, two half-time positions would be counted as one full-time position. Work hours include "teaching hours, administration hours, hours of educational guidance and other tasks at school." CBS, "Introduction to 'Education and Culture,'" *Statistical Abstract of Israel 2000*, p. (104). When actual teaching posts for primary through secondary grades, regardless of the number of hours taught, were measured, there were 109,511 posts in Jewish education, 84.1 percent of all teaching posts, and 20,772 posts in Arab education, 16.9 percent of all teaching posts. These numbers exclude teaching posts in primary schools financed by local educational authorities and parents. Ibid., p. (104) and table 22.8.

[162] For example, Human Rights Watch visited an Arab secondary school in the Triangle region with one hundred teachers for 1,200 students, an average of twelve students per teacher, slightly higher than the national average for Arab secondary schools. The students were divided into forty classes, averaging thirty students per class, again slightly higher than the national average. Human Rights Watch interview with school principal, village in the Triangle region, December 6, 2000. We visited an Arab primary school in the Triangle region with 465 students and twenty-three teachers, an average of 20.2 students per teacher, and another primary school in the region with 346 students and twenty-two teachers, an overall of 15.7 students per teacher. Human Rights Watch interviews with school principals, villages in the Triangle region, December 6, 2000. We

Class size affects the quality of education provided.[163] "It's a problem for me," a Palestinian Arab English teacher with around forty students explained. "The students should have the chance to share and talk and express themselves."[164]

Most Arab school principals whom we interviewed told us that they believed that their schools received the same budget for teaching and related expenses as Jewish schools. However, at the primary level, these funds are allocated by class,[165] and, on average, classes in Jewish schools are smaller than those in Arab schools. Thus, for all funds allocated equally by class, each Palestinian Arab child receives less on average than each Jewish child receives. Moreover, there are more teachers (of all kinds) per child in Jewish schools at every grade level. In that teachers themselves are a critical resource, Palestinian Arab students at every level receive less, on average, because their classes are larger.

Enrichment and Remedial Funding/Affirmative Action

The greatest differences in funding to Arab and Jewish schools lie in funding for enrichment and remedial programs. These programs are allocated on the basis of criteria that is weighted against Arab schools and implemented in ways that discriminate against them. Legal challenges to these practices have not been successful.

Supplementary programs–both enrichment and remedial–form an integral part of everyday education in Israeli schools. "Because we have the money, we can do what we are doing," Judith Jona, the principal of an "very good" Jewish primary school, told Human Rights Watch when she described the school's innovative programs.[166] Very little of this money comes from the municipality,

---

visited an Arab primary school in Nazareth with 630 students and thirty-five teachers, an average of eighteen students per teacher, slightly lower than the national average for Arab primary schools. Human Rights Watch interview with school principal, Nazareth, December 7, 2000.

[163] For example, the Tennessee Student Teacher Achievement Ratio ("STAR") project, a four-year longitudinal study begun in 1985, found a significant causal relationship between reducing class size and improving student achievement, especially for at-risk students. Elizabeth Word, et al., "The State of Tennessee's Student/Teacher Achievement Ratio (STAR) Project: Final Summary Report 1985-1990."

[164] Human Rights Watch interview, village in the Triangle region, December 6, 2000.

[165] Human Rights Watch interview with Dalia Sprinzak, Economics and Budgeting Administration, Ministry of Education, Jerusalem, December 19, 2000.

[166] Human Rights Watch interview with Judith Jona, Haifa, December 12, 2000. Yael Yakobi, the Chief Inspector of the District of Haifa for the Ministry of Education, categorized the school as "very good." Human Rights Watch interview with Yael

which primarily pays for maintenance and utilities, she said.   Most supplementary funding comes from the Ministry of Education. However, other government ministries fund particular programs that appear to benefit primarily Jewish education. For example, the Ministry of Housing builds kindergartens in new Jewish communities, the Ministry of Immigrant Absorption gives educational assistance to new immigrants, and the Ministry of Religious Affairs contributes to Jewish religious schools.[167] Local authorities and parents also fund programs in some schools.

The government concedes that Arab schools generally receive less government funding than Jewish schools do. In February 2001, it reported to the Committee on the Rights of the Child: "The gaps in government allocation are mainly a result of more limited allocation to enrichment and extracurricular activities such as libraries, programs for weaker students, cultural activities, and counseling and support services."[168]

Although the Ministry of Education does not release total expenditures by sector, the differences are evident in individual programs. For example, while enrichment for gifted children include both supplements to the regular curricula and special boarding schools, there are no boarding schools for gifted Palestinian Arab students. Moreover, according to the government's report to the Committee on the Rights of the Child, "associations and programs for gifted children" were only recently approved for Arab education.[169] The principal of a primary school in the Triangle region explained to Human Rights Watch how difficult it was for him to get enrichment for talented students:

> There is a boy in the school who is a genius in computers, and I asked the ministry to send him to a special school for Arabs in Israel. I waited for the reply. Every time I asked about it I was told that there wasn't any money and that he would have to wait. It was always the same. Now the boy graduated from here and is in the eighth grade in Haifa.[170]

Yakobi, Chief Inspector of the District of Haifa, Ministry of Education, December 7, 2000.

[167] Economics and Budgeting Administration, Ministry of Education, *Facts and Figures About Education and Culture in Israel*, pp. 38-39.

[168] Ministry of Justice, *Initial Periodic Report*, p. 303.

[169] Ibid., p. 280. The government reported to the Human Rights Committee that in 1996, 1,655 schoolchildren participated in a program for gifted Palestinian Arab students. U.N. Human Rights Committee, *Initial Report of States Parties Due in 1993: Israel*, para. 885(n).

[170] Human Rights Watch interview, village in the Triangle region, December 6, 2000.

Regarding remedial programs, a study by professors at Hebrew University found that Arab primary schools received 18 percent of the ministry's remedial education budget and that Arab intermediate schools received 19 percent, but that per student, Jewish students received five times the amount that Palestinian Arab students received.[171]

Variable Criteria for Allocating Resources

Although supplementary programs play an important role in all schools, the Israeli government distributes considerable resources on the basis of need and employs various indices to measure that need, such as priority area classifications and the Ministry of Education's index of educational disadvantage. This is true not only for education funding but also for many other government benefits such as transfers to local governments for development and infrastructure, which benefit schools indirectly by freeing up additional municipal monies for education.

Both the instruments purporting to measure need, as well as the implementation of need-based funding, heavily favor Jewish communities over Palestinian Arab ones. Thus, despite their greatest need, Palestinian Arabs are not receiving a share of these programs that is even proportionate to their representation in the population.

The best available measurement of general need appears to be the Central Bureau of Statistic's socio-economic scale. Sociological studies have found that a locality's socio-economic ranking clearly affects its residents' access to educational credentials in Israel.[172] The Central Bureau of Statistics ranks communities on the basis of socio-economic characteristics measured in the 1995 census and adapted in 1999 (the most recent adaptation at the time of writing).[173] The communities are then divided into ten clusters, with one being

---

[171] According to the study, the average Jewish student in need of remedial education received 0.2 hours per week of additional class time, while Palestinian Arab students received 0.04 hours per week. Kahen and Yeleneck, Hebrew University, "Discrimination Against the Non-Jewish Sector in the Allocation of Resources for Educational Development (Hebrew)."

[172] Mazawi, "Region, Locality Characteristics, High School Tracking and Equality in Access to Educational Credentials," p. 236. See Andre Elias Mazawi, "Concentrated Disadvantage and Access to Educational Credentials in Arab and Jewish Localities in Israel," *British Educational Research Journal*, vol. 25, no. 3, 1999.

[173] The socio-economic characteristics measured include: demography, standard of living, schooling and education, employment and unemployment, and receipt of public

the lowest and ten the highest.   According to the scale, Palestinian Arab communities are the poorest in Israel. In 1999, seventy-three out of the seventy-five ranked Palestinian Arab localities fell in the bottom four clusters, and no Palestinian Arab localities were ranked in the top four clusters.[174]   Jewish communal localities–kibbutzim and moshavim–and unrecognized (Arab) villages are not ranked.[175] Thus, even the best scale is not comprehensive and, indeed, excludes the poorest communities in Israel–the unrecognized villages.

In any event, the government generally uses a different criteria to allocate education-related subsidies and tax benefits.   For example, in areas the government classifies as "national priority areas," teachers receive an extra stipend for travel and living expenses, four-year tenure, and exemption from workers' compensation contributions.   The Ministry of Education also subsidizes kindergarten tuition, and residents may be eligible for loans or grants for higher education.[176] Priority areas with the highest level of classification are targets for implementation of the Long School Day Law, which funds additional informal teaching and extra-curricular activities to compensate for what wealthier parents and municipalities provide.[177] The law has never been fully implemented.[178]

---

benefits.   CBS, "Introduction (English)," *Characterization and Ranking of Local Authorities, according to the Population's Socio-Economic Level in 1999.*

[174] Ibid., table 2.

[175] Ibid.   See also Eetta Prince-Gibson "An Abundance of Despair," *Jerusalem Post,* February 16, 2001. Kibbutzim and moshavim are Jewish collective communities.

[176] See Mossawa and the Adva Center, *Status of National Priority in the Area of Education: Arab Settlements, Development Towns, and Jewish Settlements, Analysis of the Priority Area Map of the Office of the Prime Minister from 1998 and the Data of the Ministry of Education from 1997,* February 1999; David Kretzmer, *The Legal Status of the Arabs in Israel* (Boulder: Westview Press, 1990), pp. 112-113.

[177] In 1990, the first year of the Long School Day Law's implementation, only six of the 564 schools chosen for the program were Arab. Suit was brought against the Ministry of Education on the grounds that this policy was discriminatory. The High Court of Justice held that educational support to development towns meets national needs; therefore the government's policy of providing benefits only to these towns was a legitimate distinction and not discriminatory. *Agbaria v. The Minister of Education,* 45 P.D. 222 (1990). The government then renewed the program and the petitioners refiled.   The Court again dismissed the case. *Agbaria v. The Minister of Education,* 45(5) P.D. 742 (1991).

[178] Ministry of Justice, *Initial Periodic Report,* p. 259; Economics and Budgeting Administration, Ministry of Education, *Facts and Figures About Education and Culture in Israel,* pp. 15-16.

Historically, only Jewish localities were designated as priority areas. Although a few Palestinian Arab localities have since been added to the list, most are at a level that does not qualify them to receive education benefits. In May 1998, Adalah (the Legal Center for Arab Minority Rights in Israel), the Follow-Up Committee on Arab Affairs, and the Follow-Up Committee on Arab Education sued the government on the grounds that the current designation of priority areas discriminates against Palestinian Arab towns and asked that clear criteria be set for selection.[179] The case was still pending at the time of writing.

In addition to criteria used throughout the government, such as national priority areas, the Ministry of Education has developed its own "index of educational disadvantage" that it uses to allocate resources to primary and intermediate schools to improve performance and decrease dropping out.[180] The ministry applies two different standards to Arab and Jewish schools and ranks them separately. The Central Bureau of Statistics, in a 1994-1995 survey of primary and intermediate schools, explained:

> The **index of educational disadvantage** was prepared by the Ministry of Education, Culture and Sport for the purpose of differential allotment of resources to the schools, to advance weak populations. The index is determined by criteria which measure the degree of educational deprivation of each school **relative** to the other schools. Since the schools in different sectors [Jewish and Arab] differ from one another in regard to the significant causes of such deprivation, separate indices of educational disadvantage were determined for the different groups.[181]

---

[179] *Adalah, the Follow-Up Committee on Arab Affairs and the Follow-Up Committee on Arab Education v. State of Israel*, H.C. 2773/98 (filed May 1998).

[180] Ministry of Justice, *Initial Periodic Report*, p. 272.

[181] CBS, *Survey of Education and Welfare Services 1994/1995: Primary and Intermediate Schools, Hebrew and Arab Education* (Jerusalem: CBS, October 1997), p. XIX (emphasis in original). The index of educational disadvantage for Jewish education weighs the "proportion of low-income families, proportion of poorly-educated parents, proportion of large families, proportion of new immigrants, and peripheriality [sic] (distance from the three major cities)." The index for Arab education weighs the "proportion of low-income families, proportion of poorly-educated parents, proportion of large families, proportion of families living in 'unrecognized' localities, school in a mixed town (a town with both Jewish and Arab population) and a school in a small settlement." Ibid. Although the Central Bureau of Statistics justifies comparing Jewish and Arab schools separately on the grounds that certain criterion are unique to each sector, a different criteria could be developed using common measurements of need.

In other words, rather than comparing all schools against a common standard, the ministry compares Arab schools with other Arab schools and Jewish schools with other Jewish schools, but does not compare Arab schools with Jewish schools. Schools are then divided into five groups, from one–the least disadvantaged–to five–the most disadvantaged.

Table 11: Index of Educational Disadvantage–the Ministry of Education's Categorization of Primary and Intermediate Pupils and Schools 1994-1995[182]

Pupils

Degree of disadvantage	Pupils in Jewish schools (thousands)	Pupils in Arab schools (thousands)
1 (least disadvantaged)	132.2	35.0
2	142.1	33.0
3	118.0	36.9
4	107.1	30.5
5 (most disadvantaged)	76.0	34.0
Total	575.4	169.4

Schools

Degree of disadvantage	Jewish schools (absolute number)	Arab schools (absolute number)
1 (least disadvantaged)	238	69
2	249	68
3	229	70
4	233	69
5 (most disadvantaged)	235	59
Total	1,184	335

Source: CBS, *Survey of Education and Welfare Services 1994/1995: Primary and Intermediate Schools, Hebrew and Arab Education* (Jerusalem: CBS, October 1997).

As the above tables show, this index distributes both Jewish and Arab schools and Jewish and Palestinian Arab pupils into quintiles: there are roughly

---

[182] The index does not include Jewish kibbutz schools, for which a different index of educational disadvantage was applied, nor does it include either Jewish or Arab recognized but unofficial schools.

the same number of schools and pupils at every level. This distribution shows
that the need of pupils in Arab schools is being assessed in isolation from Jewish
schools. The same index of educational disadvantage was still being employed
in 2001.[183]

Given that the Arab schools by every measurement are more disadvantaged
than Jewish schools, comparing the two sectors separately is a highly misleading
indicator of the resources of Arab schools. Arab schools that rank at the top of
the index may well fall at the middle or bottom when compared with Jewish
schools. Therefore, an Arab school that would qualify for resources if compared
with Jewish schools may receive less or nothing because other Arab schools are
even worse off.[184]

Regardless of whether the ministry's index accurately measures need, Arab
schools still get fewer resources than equally ranked Jewish schools. In the
1994-1995 school year, the Central Bureau of Statistics surveyed the recognized
and official Arab and Jewish state primary and intermediate schools (with the
exception of kibbutz schools) on the provision of education and welfare
services, and found that Arab schools receive fewer services and facilities than
Jewish schools in every one of the categories assessed:

---

[183] See Ministry of Justice, *Initial Periodic Report*, pp. 271-72, 312.

[184] For example, according to Sorrell Kahen and Yakov Yeleneck at Hebrew University,

> The allocation of the [Ministry of Education's] special care [*tipuach*] basket
> is decided in two stages. In the first stage, the basket is divided into four
> sub-sectors: Arab, Druze, Jewish (official) and Jewish (non-official). In the
> second stage, the basket for each sub-sector is divided between schools (after
> a deduction of 10 percent toward a district fund).

> An examination of the special care [*tipuach*] policy shows that the allocation
> of the special care basket is decided based on educational need only within
> the sectors (except the Jewish (non-official) sector) and not between them.
> The allocation of the special care basket between the sub-sectors is arbitrary
> and ignores the differences in educational need between them.

Kahen and Yeleneck, Hebrew University, "Discrimination Against the Non-Jewish
Sector in the Allocation of Resources for Educational Development (Hebrew)"
(translation by Human Rights Watch).

Table 12: Index of Educational Disadvantage: Provision of Services 1994-1995

Index number	Schools with psychological counseling		Schools with educational counseling		Schools with counseling by a social worker	
	Jewish	Arab	Jewish	Arab	Jewish	Arab
1 (best)	95.1%	52.7%	53.9%	20.1%	47.7%	34.5%
2	91.8%	48.1%	64.2%	11.1%	61.5%	35.2%
3	87.1%	51.8%	68.4%	16.4%	69.7%	32.1%
4	91.5%	43.1%	82.8%	11.8%	69.5%	23.5%
5 (worst)	93.6%	31.1%	84.2%	8.9%	71.1%	13.3%

Index number	Schools with libraries		Mean number of educational and welfare programs	
	Jewish	Arab	Jewish	Arab
1 (best)	68.7%	61.8%	21-30	11-20
2	71.3%	44.4%	21-30	11-20
3	76.8%	52.7%	21-30	11-20
4	73.4%	51.0%	21-30	11-20
5 (worst)	71.9%	40.0%	21-30	11-20

Source: CBS, *Survey of Education and Welfare Services 1994/1995: Primary and Intermediate Schools, Hebrew and Arab Education* (Jerusalem: CBS, October 1997).

At every economic level, more Jewish schools had support services than Arab schools. For example, of schools categorized as most disadvantaged, almost all (93.6 percent) of Jewish schools offered psychological counseling to their students, while less than one-third (31.1 percent) of the Arab schools had these services. The Israeli government, in its 2001 submission to the Committee on the Rights of the Child, conceded that despite the index of disadvantage for Palestinian Arabs, which is intended to make it "easier to aptly allocate resources to schools in the Arab sector, so as to cultivate weak populations . . . the distribution of hours and budgets per schools is not equal in the two sectors, and does not take into consideration the existing gaps between the two sectors."[185]

In addition to funds allocated by the index of educational disadvantage, some funding by definition goes only to Jewish students. For example, new immigrants, who are almost entirely Jewish, receive extra educational programs.

[185] Ministry of Justice, *Initial Periodic Report*, p. 308.

The principal of a Jewish middle school told Human Rights Watch that the school received extra funding for students who immigrated less than two years ago.[186] And until 1994, children the ministry categorized as "in need of special care" (*talmid taun tipauch*) were, by definition, Jewish, and eligible for extra educational resources. In 1994, the definition was changed so that Palestinian Arabs would be eligible. However, the budget was cut at the same time, and Palestinian Arab children consequently saw little benefit.[187]

Discretion in Distribution
Considerable discretion on the part of those who administer the programs, combined with a lack of adequate Palestinian Arab representation in their administration, results in some programs never reaching Arab schools. For example, the Ministry of Education, through its Youth and Society Administration, funds what it calls "informal education": programs in both schools and public agencies such as community centers that include a weekly homeroom hour, student councils, and social programs aimed, for example, at preventing drug use, teaching leadership and decision-making skills, and instilling particular values.

Tali Yariv-Mashal, who headed a leadership program in the division from 1996 to 1999, explained how the programs worked. She supervised seven teachers, one of whom was Palestinian Arab. Some of these teachers taught in schools part-time and worked for the program part-time; others worked for more than one program. The six Jewish teachers were each assigned to a district where they supervised the teachers who actually distributed the programs in schools. "The program supervisors have discretion about where to teach. It

---

[186] Human Rights Watch interview with Rachel Shechori, principal of Sharet Middle School, Nazareth Ilit, December 13, 2000.

[187] Swirski, *Politics and Education in Israel*, pp. 179, 234.

> [T]he entire apparatus of restorative, remedial, and compensatory education was developed for Mizrahi schoolchildren, to the exclusion of Arab children. Only in 1994 did Arab pupils become eligible for "remedial hours" established in the 1960s for Mizrahim . . . . To both Mizrahim and Arabs, these allocations were construed as a sign of the privileged position of Mizrahim via-à-vis the Arabs. But the privilege carried a heavy price: the collective labeling of Mizrahim as educational failures and as the intellectual inferiors of Ashkenazim. . . . Israeli Palestinians have escaped this fate, but at the cost of exclusion from state projects and state funds.

Ibid., p. 164

depends on their relationships with the schools, and they are very free to decide," Yariv-Mashal noted.[188]

> The good teachers distribute money to everyone. Others may say, "I'm not going [to the Arab schools]. I don't understand them, and they don't understand me." They sometimes claimed that the Arab schools are the Arab teacher's responsibility–"that's what he's here for." That's where is stops. Many Arab schools don't even know about the programs that are available. The money is distributed politically, not top down but through a flat political network. You're either in or you're out.[189]

In contrast, one Palestinian Arab teacher was responsible for providing the programs to Arab schools throughout the country. Yariv-Mashal explained: "The one Arab supervisor had two days for the whole country. So the only kids that got anything were at his kids' school. . . . This is how the whole Arab system works–people are not assigned by district, versus in the Jewish system where the ministry has inspectors by districts."[190] In areas that the Palestinian Arab teacher was unable to cover, Arab schools received the programs at the discretion of Jewish teachers assigned to their district.

Yariv-Mashal also noted that the programs themselves were not adapted in any way for Palestinian Arab students. Some of the Jewish teachers who administered the programs stopped offering them to Arab schools after Palestinian Arab teachers objected to some of the content, she said.[191]

Indeed, the government reported to the Committee on the Rights of the Child in 2001 that informal education programs are implemented in the Arab sector "to a limited extent," and that "the majority of [the programs] are not as prevalent as they are in the Jewish sector."[192] For example, in 1997 only 5 percent of children in youth promotion units–a program for "youth at risk" run by the Youth and Society Administration's Youth Advancement Department–were Palestinian Arab.[193] According to the Israeli government, "it has been difficult to implement programs in Arab schools and local authorities because of

---

[188] Human Rights Watch interview with Tali Yariv-Mashal, New York, February 27, 2001.
[189] Ibid.
[190] Ibid.
[191] Ibid.
[192] Ministry of Justice, *Initial Periodic Report,* pp. 318, 321.
[193] Ibid., pp. 275-76. This was an increase from the past decade when the program served only veteran Israeli boys. Ibid.

the requirement that parents and local authorities help finance them, and because school and local staff are not always forthcoming about generating dialogue with parents. Nevertheless, some schools have succeeded in enlisting the cooperation of parents and involving them in school life."[194]

Daphna Golan, chair of the Committee for Closing the Gap in the Education Ministry's Pedagogical Secretariat, also observed that Palestinian Arabs' lack of representation in the Education Ministry keeps Arab schools from gaining access to education programs that are administered on a discretionary basis.[195]

---

[194] Ibid., p. 322.
[195] Human Rights Watch interview with Daphna Golan, Chair, Committee for Closing the Gap, Pedagogical Secretariat, Ministry of Education, Jerusalem, December 20, 2000.

The Shahar Programs

Since the 1970s, the Ministry of Education has provided a series of enrichment programs, called the "Shahar programs," to academically weak students from low socio-economic backgrounds. These programs are aimed at raising students' grades, improving their skills, and preventing them from dropping out. The Shahar programs' total budget in 1998 was approximately NIS 140 million ($35 million).[196] According to the Follow-Up Committee on Arab Education, the ministry spent on average only NIS 75 ($18.75) per Arab pupil, compared with NIS 3,628 ($907) per Jewish pupil.[197] The 1997 State Comptroller's report also criticized the unclear criteria for eligibility and the lack of monitoring of the programs' distribution, concluding that these factors led to an unjust distribution of the budget."[198]

In May 1997, Adalah, on behalf of the Follow-Up Committee on Arab Education and the Coalition of Parents' Groups in the Negev, sued to compel the Ministry of Education to provide Shahar programs equally to Arab and Jewish students. In response, the state admitted that the Education and Welfare Department had not dealt with Arab education at all until 1992, and then only in a limited scope. It subsequently promised to allocate 20 percent of the Education and Welfare Services Department budget to the Arab sector over the next five years.[199] Adalah objected to the five-year time frame and asked that the programs be immediately implemented.[200] In January 2000, the petitioners submitted evidence, which the ministry disputed, that the ministry was not complying with its promise.[201]

---

[196] Arab Association for Human Rights (HRA), *The Palestinian Arab Minority in Israel: Economic, Social and Cultural Rights*, presented to the United Nations Committee on Economic, Social, and Cultural Rights November 1998, p. 91.

[197] Press release of the Follow-Up Committee on Arab Education, 1998, cited in Arab Association for Human Rights (HRA), *The Palestinian Arab Minority in Israel: Economic, Social and Cultural Rights*, p. 91.

[198] State Comptroller, *Report*, no. 48, 1997.

[199] *Follow-Up Committee on Arab Education, et. al. v. The Ministry of Education, et. al*, ("The Shahar Case"), H.C. 2814/97 (2000), para. 1, (English translation by Adalah, http://www.adalah.org/supreme.html#2 (accessed on June 23, 2001)).

[200] Ibid., para. 3.

[201] Ibid., paras. 4-5.

In July 2000, the Israeli High Court of Justice denied the petition, finding "the matter of the present petition was thoroughly resolved and is superfluous."[202] Specifically, the Court found that "significant measures were taken to allocate funds to the Arab sector to achieve the goal of parity in educational welfare programs in accordance with the relative proportion of the Arab population in Israel."[203] Although one program, the urban renewal program, was still not being allocated equally, the Court held that this related to the Ministry of Construction and Housing's actions and was, thus, outside of the petition's scope.[204]

In its decision, the Court declined to address the state's duty to allocate educational programs equally to Palestinian Arabs:

> [T]he matter before us was not a dispute in principle over whether the state has a duty to include the Arab sector in the special programs that are part of the educational and welfare services that the Ministry of Education provides. The state admitted that the Department had not acted in the Arab sector and presented the "historic" reasons that, they contend, were inherent in the situation leading to establishment of the Department. In light of the state's position as stated in its response, it is no longer important to conduct the historical analysis, because the state does not dispute that "students from the minorities, particularly students in grave distress, are entitled to educational services that will assist them in overcoming their difficulties, just like the Jewish students receive assistance from the ministry." The state further announced that, following filing of the petition, the ministry reviewed its position on the Department's activity in the Arab sector "and decided to expand its activity such that the budget goal is that, within five years, 20 percent of the Department budget would be allocated for the minorities sector." In light of these comments, it is superfluous, of course, to discuss in principle the question of the duty of the state to ensure parity in educational allocations for the Arab sector.[205]

---

[202] Ibid., para. 7.
[203] Ibid.
[204] Ibid.
[205] Ibid., para. 3.

As of February 2001, the ministry had yet to equalize the distribution of its enrichment programs, according to Israel's submission to the Committee on the Rights of the Child.[206]

---

[206] Ministry of Justice, *Initial Periodic Report,* p. 303.

Funding from Other Sources

We give the bread. The butter and the cheese is up to the local authorities who have to get money for people. If they are impoverished, they give the children only the bread. The bread is more than 90 percent of the budget. So maybe they get bread and margarine.

–Human Rights Watch interview with Yair Levine, Deputy Director-General, Head of International Relations, Ministry of Education, Jerusalem, Israel, December 19, 2000

Households financed 6 percent of total national expenditures on primary education in 1996, and 22 percent of expenditures on post-primary education.[207] These figures exclude general administrative costs, of which local authorities financed 29 percent and the central government financed 71 percent, and "investments and capital transfers."[208] Parental funding, as well as extra monies local authorities give schools, contribute to the gap between schools in high and middle income areas and schools in low income areas.

Parental Funding

Parental funding of regular and after-school education, which in Israel is called "gray education," is much more than an after-school trumpet lesson. The State Education Law allows parent financing to increase regular school hours up to 25 percent, if 75 percent of parents in the schools request it.[209] These funds reduce class size, add hours in particular subjects, improve school infrastructure, and pay for after-school classes and activities. The nongovernmental Adva Center has documented the effect of gray education on students' performance:

---

[207] CBS, *Statistical Abstract of Israel 2000,* table 22.5. These figures include good and services but not "textbooks and stationary bought by households." Ibid.

[208] Ibid. Of financing of investments and capital transfers, which includes financing post-secondary and higher education institutions, households financed 12 percent, non-governmental nonprofit organizations financed 2 percent, government non-profit organizations financed 13 percent, local authorities financed 30 percent, and the central government financed 43 percent. Ibid.

[209] State Education Law, art. 8 (1953).

The crafters of the education budget overlook the fact that, in the absence of sufficient state funding, private money ("gray education") becomes a main player in determining the quality of education that schools provide. Schools that offer "gray education" provide a more extensive and, sometimes, a more intensive curriculum than schools in which parents can not afford to contribute. In high schools where parent co-payments in 1999 ranged from NIS 287 to NIS 2,657 [$71.75 to $664.25] per year (i.e., within the range recommended by the Education Ministry), 57 percent of students succeeded in passing their matriculation exams. In schools where co-payments ranged from NIS 1,269 to NIS 6,070 [$317.25 to $1,517.50], the proportion of matriculation-certificate eligibles was 87 percent.[210]

The Israeli government has acknowledged that gray education "increases the social inequality among population groups."[211]

Jewish households on average spend more on education than Palestinian Arab households,[212] and Arab schools, on the whole, collect less money from parents than do Jewish schools. For example, the principal of a primary school in Um El-Fahm told us that the schools asked for NIS 70 to NIS 80 ($17.50 to $20.00) per student that year.[213] This money covered security, trips, library books, insurance, and other educational activities, he explained. The school also had an active parents' committee that had raised NIS 131,000 ($32,750.00) for the year.[214] A Jewish middle school in Nazareth Ilit charged parents NIS 1,300 ($325) a year to pay for books, field trips, safety guards, a health supervisor, and extra activities.[215] A Palestinian Arab mother and English teacher told Human Rights Watch: "My daughter and son in the high school pay NIS1,500 ($375) for the psychometric exam course [a class to prepare for the exam]. If they

---

[210] Swirski, *Looking at the Budget of the State of Israel 2001* (critique of proposed 2001 Budget) (citing Yossi Gidinian, Central Bureau of Statistics, October 8, 2000). For more information about gray education, see, Swirski, *Politics and Education in Israel*, pp. 228-229.
[211] Ministry of Justice, *Initial Periodic Report*, p. 270.
[212] CBS, *Education and Educational Resources 1990-1996*, no. 99/164, July 26, 1999, cited in *Measure for Measure: An Accounting of Equality in Israel* (Hebrew), ed. Naama Yeshuvi, Association for Civil Rights in Israel (ACRI), January 2000, p. 62.
[213] Human Rights Watch interview, Um El-Fahm, December 6, 2000.
[214] Ibid.
[215] Human Rights Watch interview with Rachel Shechori, principal of Sharet Middle School, Nazareth Ilit, December 13, 2000.

don't pay, they can't take the course. My daughter told me that many good pupils can't pay. I make sacrifices so that I can pay."[216]

Funding from Local Authorities

Local authorities generally must pay for maintaining school buildings, furniture, and administrative staff.[217] For example, Human Rights Watch visited an Arab primary school in a village in the Triangle region that received NIS 6,920 ($1,730) a month (NIS 20 ($5) per child) as well as furniture from the local municipality.[218] In addition to the small amount of schools' regular budgets that they are responsible for, some local governments provide additional funding that covers many of the same kinds of things that parents sometimes pay for.

As indicated by the Central Bureau of Statistic's socio-economic scale, Palestinian Arab communities tend to be the poorest in Israel. Compared with Jewish localities, they lack an industrial tax base and depend more heavily on residential property taxes. They also receive less money generally from the central government:

> In 1999, the total regular budget for all Arab local authorities was NIS 2.2 billion [$550 million], only 8% of the regular budget for local authorities in Israel, which totaled NIS 26 billion [$6.5 billion]. Notably, Arab local authorities supply services to around 12% of the entire population. The per capita expense earmarked for residents of Arab authorities in the regular budget thus comprises only two-thirds of the per capita expense for residents of Jewish local authorities.[219]

---

[216] Human Rights Watch interview, village in the Triangle region, December 6, 2000.

[217] Human Rights Watch interview with Yael Yakobi, Chief Inspector of the District of Haifa, Ministry of Education, December 7, 2000.

[218] Human Rights Watch interview with school principal, village in the Triangle region, December 6, 2000.

[219] As'ad Ghanem, Thabet Abu-Ras, Ze'ev Rosenhek, "Local Authorities, Welfare and Community," in *After the Rift: New Directions for Government Policy towards the Arab Population in Israel*, eds. Dan Rabinowitz, As'ad Ghanem, Oren Yiftachel, November 2000, p. 27-28. See also Arab Association for Human Rights (HRA), *The Palestinian Arab Minority in Israel: Economic, Social and Cultural Rights*, p. 32-33 (stating that ordinary budgets of Arab communities are 60 percent of those of comparable Jewish communities).

Accordingly, Palestinian Arab localities must use money that other communities might spend on education for infrastructure and other development expenses.[220]

The Ministry of Education's Role

Parents are, of course, free to finance additional education for their children. However, the Ministry of Education contributes to the gaps between Arab and Jewish schools that funds from parents and local authorities create by: 1) subsidizing gray education through school infrastructure and matching funds; 2) contributing unequally to Jewish and Palestinian Arab parents' organizations; and 3) failing to distribute compensatory programs equally.

First, the ministry indirectly subsidizes parent-funded education through its infrastructure, since supplementary education takes place on school grounds and, often, during school hours. It also subsidizes supplementary education directly through matching funds. According to Israel's 2001 report to the Committee on the Rights of the Child:

> The more limited investment by local authorities and parents can be ascribed to the dire financial state of the Arab local authorities, as well as to the higher level of poverty among Arab families. It is important to note that in many cases, allocation of government funding for extracurricular activities, special programs and support services is dependent on matching funds provided by the local authority and parents. As such funds are not available in the Arab local authorities, services of this type are often not implemented in the Arab education system.[221]

Second, although parents' organizations often organize and implement gray education, the ministry funds almost no Palestinian Arab parents' organizations. Daphna Golan, chair of the Committee for Closing the Gap in the ministry's Pedagogical Secretariat, explained: "The Education Ministry gives about NIS 1.3 billion ($325 million) to nongovernmental organizations, most notably, parents' committees, each year. The nongovernmental organizations use this money for projects like after-school education, either at schools or at

---

[220] For examples of a lack of infrastructure in Palestinian Arab communities compared with Jewish communities, see Shalom (Shuli) Dichter, "The Government's Plan for Development in the Arab Localities," *Sikkuy's Report on Equality and Integration of the Arab Citizens in Israel 2000-2001*, Spring 2001.

[221] Ministry of Justice, *Initial Periodic Report,* p. 303.

local community centers. Of this amount, about 1.5 percent goes to Palestinian Arab organizations."[222]

While acknowledging the gaps that locally-funded education creates, the government argues that its supplementary programs, including the Long School Day Law, educational disadvantage index, truant officers, and support services such as counseling and other programs, counteract the gaps created by gray education. However, it also admits that these are not provided equally to Palestinian Arabs.[223]

---

[222] Human Rights Watch interview with Daphna Golan, Chair, Committee for Closing the Gap, Pedagogical Secretariat, Ministry of Education, Jerusalem, December 20, 2000.
[223] Ministry of Justice, *Initial Periodic Report*, pp. 277-78.

After-School Programs

The gaps created by supplements from the Education Ministry, parents, and local authorities are well illustrated by after-school programs held in schools.[224] Human Rights Watch visited schools with no after-school programs, schools with a few classes held after regular school hours, and schools with an extensive array of academic, athletic, and artistic programs, held on school grounds, and running from early afternoon, when the regular school day ends, well into the evening. Most of the Arab schools Human Rights Watch visited had after-school programs that were much less developed compared with the Jewish schools, and few received funding from the Education Ministry or local governments. A Palestinian Arab teacher explained:

> There is a need for clubs so students can practice other things like dance, music, sports. Money is a big problem, especially for big families. Here there is no music class–we don't have a teacher or instruments. Sometimes there is art but it is not enough–there is only one teacher. There are art teachers in the village but they don't have jobs–the ministry doesn't hire them. There are no clubs here–the children go home, watch TV, play in the street, do their homework. At the village high school where my children go there is the same problem. They finish school and go home. My youngest son always wants something to do. I bring him computer games and things. There are no clubs. When I see kids on T.V., I feel pain in my heart. We have children who can reach this level, but they don't have the chance.[225]

Human Rights Watch visited two Arab primary schools in villages in the Triangle region at which parents paid for all the after-school programs.[226] At one school, the only after-school program was a karate class. "I went to the municipality and asked the head for support," the principal explained. "They said not before 2004, and then maybe

---

[224] For information about ministry-financed after-school programs see, Economics and Budgeting Administration, Ministry of Education, *Facts and Figures About Education and Culture in Israel*, p. 19.
[225] Human Rights Watch interview, village in the Triangle region, December 6, 2000.
[226] Human Rights Watch interviews with school principals, villages in the Triangle region, December 6, 2000.

vocational programs."[227]   When we visited, the principal was sending leaflets to parents about computer, music, and art classes. "Each pupil has to pay because we bring everything in from the outside," he said. "We are a local school and these things are supposed to be given by the government."[228]

We also visited a primary school in Nazareth, and a secondary school in a recognized Bedouin town in the Negev with no after-school programs at all.   When asked about after-school programs, a Bedouin high school principal told us:

> We have plans but no budget.   We're called a "community school" but we don't have anything besides the name. We asked for the budget from the municipality. We have submitted a plan with activities, but it's only on the papers. We have no budget from the municipality–no help from the ministry or municipality. Even if I want to give after-school classes, each student has to pay–there is no additional money to plan for after-school projects. It's difficult for students to pay because of their socio-economic situation and their background: 65 to 70 percent of the total population is under the poverty line. Some students are from homes that have twenty kids in each house so the families need everything for feeding them.[229]

In contrast, students at another Arab high school in the north told us that they had many after-school programs because the Education Ministry had designated the school as an "experimental school."   These programs included a group that worked on "peace projects" and a "young investors club" that made and sold unbreakable vases.[230] We also visited an Arab vocational school where the students told us that they had after-school classes to prepare for the psychometric exam and on folkloric dancing.[231]

Jewish students at what was considered to be a very good Jewish primary school in Haifa described a wide variety of after-school programs.

---

[227] Human Rights Watch interview, village in the Triangle region, December 6, 2000.
[228] Ibid.
[229] Human Rights Watch interview, recognized Bedouin locality near Be'er Sheva, December 14, 2000.
[230] Human Rights Watch interviews with tenth-grade students, Nazareth, December 9, 2000.
[231] Human Rights Watch group interview with eleventh-grade students, Israel, December 9, 2000.

"After school we have soccer, drama, music," a fifth grade boy told us. "We got a pamphlet at the beginning of the year with about fifty activities in it [that we could sign up for after school]. You can go to as many as you want if your mom will let you." The school's principal confirmed that the school had an extensive after-school program, run by specially-paid staff, that included music classes, jazz and dance, basketball, football, soccer–"a long list."[232] Some of these classes were funded by the municipality or paid for by parents.[233]

At a Jewish intermediate school in Nazareth Ilit, a development town bordering Nazareth and a major immigrant absorption area, after-school programs are extensive and almost free for students, many of whom are recent immigrants and who come from "tough backgrounds."[234] According to the principal, the after-school programs include "lots of social and extracurricular activities that relate to values and the fact that we are in a Jewish, Zionist state. The students pay a small amount of money–a symbolic amount–we don't want to give for free because when you pay you come."[235] The after-school programs are usually taught by teachers from the school, and "sometimes the ministry will pay their salaries." The principal also applies for funding from foundations that specify a particular population, such as "Ethiopians, newcomers, learning disabled."[236] Similarly, in Be'er Sheva, where the schools are Jewish schools, the municipal government pays for after-school programs in the high schools, which are designated as community schools. Primary schools children also

---

[232] Human Rights Watch interview with Judith Jona, Haifa, December 12, 2000.
[233] Ibid.
[234] Human Rights Watch interview with Rachel Shechori, Nazareth Ilit, December 13, 2000.
[235] Ibid.
[236] Ibid.

go after schools to these high schools for programs.[237]   In contrast, we visited a Jewish primary school in Nazareth Ilit that was about to begin after-school sport, music, and computer classes for which parents would pay NIS 100 ($25) a month.[238]

[237] Human Rights Watch interview with Ruth Frankel, Head of Education, Municipality of Be'er Sheva, Be'er Sheva, December 15, 2000.
[238] Human Rights Watch interview with Osnat Mordechai, principal, Ksulot Primary School, Nazareth Ilit, December 13, 2000.

VI. SCHOOL BUILDINGS

I remember in the winter I couldn't grab the pencil because I was so cold.

> –Negev Bedouin woman, Be'er Sheva, December 15, 2000

My younger son is in the fifth grade at the public school [in Haifa]. I want to send him there because I didn't want to send him to a missionary school because I can be more involved. But there are forty-two children in the class. There is no library, labs, playgrounds, or gym class.

> –Palestinian Arab parent, Haifa, December 6, 2000

Arab schools need more classrooms, and those they have are often in poor condition, especially in the Negev. Compared with Jewish schools, Arab schools have fewer libraries, sports facilities, laboratories, and other auxiliary facilities.

School buildings are the joint responsibility of the Ministry of Education and the local governments, with the ministry funding most construction,[239] the local governments purchasing furniture, and both sharing maintenance costs. Other central government bodies, such at the Ministry of Housing, which constructs preschools in some communities, and the National Lottery, which finances auxiliary facilities, also contribute, as do parents in some instances.

Under international law, one component of the right to education is the "conditions under which it is given," and states must ensure that "in all public education institutions of the same level . . . the conditions relating to the quality of education are also equivalent."[240]

Classroom Shortage

The Follow-Up Committee for Arab Education estimated in 2001 that the Arab education system needed 2,500 additional classrooms.[241] The principal of

---

[239] At the secondary level, the Education Ministry channels the funds through local governments, which are considered to "own" the secondary schools.

[240] Convention against Discrimination in Education, arts. 1(2), 4(b)

[241] Atef Moaddi, Follow-Up Committee on Arab Education, e-mail to Human Rights Watch, July 30, 2001. The Follow-Up Committee calculated the number of classrooms needed based on the number of classes being held in rented rooms, the number of classrooms held in buildings the Education Ministry has determined are dangerous and ordered torn down (including classrooms built with asbestos), the number of classrooms

an Arab primary school in a village in the Triangle region explained: "We need more classrooms. The teachers and students complain. We are getting more and more pupils every year. We have tried for three years to get approval to widen the school grounds, and we have been refused. Even for disabled students we just don't have it."[242]

Although the Israeli government built new classrooms for the Arab system in the 1990s, the overall proportion of Arab school classrooms out of the total number of classrooms increased less than 1 percent from 1990 to 1998.

Table 13: Number of Classrooms 1990-1998

	Jewish schools	Arab schools
1990	29,448 (81.4%)	6,720 (18.6%)
1998	34,747 (80.5%)	8,423 (19.5%)
Classrooms constructed 1990-1998	5,299 (75.7%)	1703 (24.3%)

Source: State of Israel Ministry of Justice, Ministry of Foreign Affairs, *Initial Periodic Report of the State of Israel Concerning the Implementation of the Convention on the Rights of the Child (CRC)*, February 20, 2001, p. 307.

As of 1998, the proportion of Arab school classrooms–19.5 percent–still failed to reflect the proportion of students in the Arab system. Since 1998, the Ministry of Education has promised to build additional Arab school classrooms. In 2000, excluding kindergartens, 31 percent of the budget for new classrooms and continued building was designated for Arab education and 69 percent went to Jewish education.[243] In 2001, the ministry planned to build 2,000 classrooms, 585 of which (29.3 percent) were to be for Arab education.[244] The Development Administration of the Ministry of Education, which is responsible for building

---

needed for the natural annual increase in the student population, and the number of classrooms needed for kindergarten for three and four-year-old children. Ibid.; and Human Rights Watch telephone interview with Atef Moaddi, Follow-Up Committee on Arab Education, Nazareth, July 12, 2001.

[242] Human Rights Watch interview, village in the Triangle region, December 6, 2000.

[243] Ministry of Education, *Budget Instructions for 2000*, p. 50. Data on kindergartens were not available.

[244] Ministry of Education, "Classroom Construction for the Education System, 2001," www.education.gov.il/minhal_calcala/download/19.pdf (accessed June 8, 2001) (citing the Ministry of Education's Development Administration). The other classrooms planned were for Jewish education, special education, kindergartens, and Holocaust education museums. Ibid.

classrooms, did not respond to Human Rights Watch's inquiry as to how many classrooms were actually built in 2000 and 2001.

As a result of the classroom shortage, many classes in Arab schools are held in rented spaces, in some cases only a room in a private home, or in prefabricated buildings, locally called "caravans." We visited one Arab school for physically disabled children where about half of the children were deaf or hearing impaired. The school was in a rented building, which, one teacher told us, was acoustically bad for hearing impaired children because the hard stone walls, ceilings, and floors created echoes.[245] The school had placed acoustic paneling over some of the walls but could not make needed structural changes or additions. "Everything is as it is," the principal explained. "We try to improve it, but it is rented."[246]

In the unrecognized Negev Bedouin community of Al-Azazmeh, three elementary schools use forty prefabricated buildings to teach more than 1,300 students.[247] Shaqib Al-Salaam elementary school in the Negev also consists of ten prefabricated buildings.[248]

Arab school classrooms are also more crowded than those in Jewish schools. As stated above, Arab school classes have more students on average than Jewish ones. While this does not in itself mean that Arab classes are overcrowded, the Arab schools that Human Rights Watch visited, in contrast with the Jewish ones, were visibly short of space.

In 1998, the government-appointed Katz Committee found that "most" of the permanent schools in government-planned localities for Negev Bedouin were overcrowded and concluded that 146 new classrooms would be needed each year from 1998-1999 to 2002-2003.[249]

---

[245] Human Rights Watch interview, Israel, December 11, 2000.

[246] Human Rights Watch interview, Israel, December 11, 2000.

[247] Joseph Algazy, "What About the Bedouin?" *Ha'aretz Daily Newspaper (English Edition)* (Israel), May 9, 2000.

[248] Ibid.

[249] *The Investigatory Committee on the Bedouin Educational System in the Negev: A Report Requested by the Late Minister of Education, Culture and Sport, Zevulen Hammer ("Katz Committee Report")*, submitted to the Director General of the Ministry of Education, Ben Zion-Dal, March 19, 1998 (English translation downloaded from the Center for Bedouin Studies and Development website, http://www.bgu.ac.il/Bedouin /Excerpts%20from%20Katz%20report.html (accessed on September 20, 2000)), table 1.

Physical Condition/Maintenance
      More than one-third of Arab children study in flammable and dangerous structures. The situation is particularly severe in the Bedouin sector, especially in the south of the country and in the unrecognized settlements, where few classrooms have been built.

> –State of Israel Ministry of Justice, Ministry of Foreign Affairs, *Initial Periodic Report of the State of Israel Concerning the Implementation of the Convention on the Rights of the Child (CRC)*, February 20, 2001, p. 308 (citing a 1996 report by the Follow-Up Committee on Arab Education).

Human Rights Watch visited Arab schools in varying physical conditions and new schools as well as old schools. Overall, the physical differences between Jewish and Arab schools were immediately visible. A Palestinian Arab high school student noted: "Jewish schools are different. Two weeks ago I went to a sports event in a Jewish town. I saw courts and buildings–there was a special building for the eighth grade. It was the same as other Jewish schools in Akka [Acre]. There was a big building for only 700 students."[250]

We visited an Arab primary school in a village in the Triangle region made of concrete block and with a stench of urine in the halls. One hallway was blocked off at the end and filled with trash. In another school in the region that we visited, the parents' committee had just built a new addition with five new classrooms. "If we waited for the municipality to support it, it could have taken years," the principal explained. "I didn't sit and wait."[251]

School buildings are worse in the Negev, especially in the unrecognized villages, although Human Rights Watch saw also schools in poor condition in recognized Bedouin towns. Israel reported to the Committee on the Rights of the Child in 2001 that:

> Schools attended by the Bedouin children are located in both permanent settlements (where they were established by the State),

---

[250] Human Rights Watch interview, Acre, December 10, 2000.
[251] Human Rights Watch interview with primary school principal, village in the Triangle region, December 6, 2000.

and in unplanned, unrecognized encampments and settlements. The latter are well below par: Their budgets are low, they lack appropriate buildings or even electricity and water, in some cases, and they lack appropriate supplies and equipment. Schools in permanent settlements are better equipped and in better physical condition, but they lack equipment such as laboratories, and the level of crowding in them is very high. [252]

Similarly, the Katz Committee in 1998 found that in Negev Bedouin schools:

> Facilities and equipment are insufficient, and in some cases, altogether lacking. This is especially true for the schools in spontaneous tribal settlements which the government considers temporary. Currently there are eleven temporary and eighteen permanent Bedouin primary schools in the Negev. These temporary schools in unplanned settlements are poorly equipped, have low budgets, inadequate facilities, poor buildings and furnishings, and few teaching materials. They often suffer from a complete lack of facilities and materials such as audiovisual, computers, laboratory and sports equipment, etc. They are mostly housed in tin, wooden, or concrete buildings with insufficient classroom and office space. In general, they are not supplied with running water and electricity, although some are found next to water pipes or electric lines. As a rule, these schools are not expanded and are poorly maintained. In contrast to temporary schools, permanent schools are located in government planned settlements or on the sites of future developments, and are better equipped. Most of them are housed in modern buildings, and have electricity and running water. But even they do not have sufficient laboratories, libraries or other teaching materials.[253]

In April 1998, the Israeli High Court of Justice ruled that the government must provide electricity to all government schools in unrecognized villages.[254] Since then, the government has provided generators to at least some of these schools.

---

[252] Ministry of Justice, *Initial Periodic Report*, pp. 312-13.

[253] *Katz Committee Report.*

[254] *Abu-Frech et al. v. The Education Authority for the Bedouins in the Negev et al.*, H.C. 4671/98 (1998).

Although the magnitude of the problem is difficult to quantify, it is generally recognized that a school's physical condition affects its students' academic performance.[255]

---

[255] For example, a New York state court, finding that the conditions of New York City schools negatively affected students' performance, relied on testimony from the former Commissioner of State Education Department Thomas Sobol:

> If you ask the children to attend school in conditions where plaster is crumbling, the roof is leaking and classes are being held in unlikely places because of overcrowded conditions, that says something to the child about how you diminish the value of the activity and of the child's participation in it and perhaps of the child himself. If, on the other hand, you send a child to a school in well-appointed or [adequate facilities] that sends the opposite message. That says this counts. You count. Do well.

Campaign for Fiscal Equality, et al., v. New York, 719 N.Y.S.2d 475 (N.Y. Sup. Ct. 2001).

Primary Schools for Negev Bedouin

On a wet day in December with the temperature in the 50s Fahrenheit (around 10 degrees Celsius), Human Rights Watch visited two primary schools in a recognized Bedouin locality in the Negev near Be'er Sheva. The buildings were run-down and surrounded by mud and standing water. In the schoolyard were a few pieces of playground equipment, including a plastic horse mounted on a spring with its head half broken, and its base submerged in mud. Most of the buildings were made of concrete block, and each classroom door opened directly to the outside. One building, with a sign reading "Center for Young Children and Families," was made of corrugated metal that was rusted more than halfway up the sides. According to a parent of a five-year-old child at the school, the building was still being used.[256]

Despite desert temperature extremes of hot and cold, the school had no central heat or air conditioning.[257] Indeed, until a few years ago, the school had no electricity at all. When we visited, some classrooms had a small space heater and a small fan mounted on the wall; others had nothing. A second grade teacher showed us the small space heater at the front of the classroom that was intended to provide heat for her thirty-nine students. But her class, like all of the classes we visited, was as cold as the outside air, and the children wore winter coats while seated at their desks. The teacher told us that "the bathrooms are far away and it's cold, so the kids don't want to go out. Some children just wet themselves."[258]

Human Rights Watch then visited another primary school, constructed in 1992, in the same area. This building was obviously newer–the corridors were enclosed, the paint was not flaking, and the pavement was intact. Nevertheless, it did not have heating or air conditioning, and the building was very cold inside. According to the vice-principal, the school had almost 900 pupils and already needed more classrooms.[259]

---

[256] Human Rights Watch interview, recognized Bedouin locality near Be'er Sheva, December 14, 2000.

[257] It should be noted that not all Jewish schools in the Negev have air conditioning. For example, as of September 2000, schools in Ofakim, Dimona, Sderot, Yeroham, and Eilat lacked air conditioners. See Gil Hoffman, "Eleventh-hour Talks to Avert Teachers' Strike," *Jerusalem Post*, September 1, 2000.

[258] Human Rights Watch interview, recognized Bedouin locality near Be'er Sheva, December 14, 2000.

[259] Human Rights Watch interview, recognized Bedouin locality near Be'er Sheva, December 14, 2000.

Several days later we visited a school bordering an unrecognized Bedouin community outside Be'er Sheva. An electrical plant was visible nearby and electric wires ran overhead; however, neither the community nor the school was connected to a central power supply. Two years ago, following the Israeli High Court's 1998 ruling that the state was obligated to provide electricity to all government schools in unrecognized villages, the Ministry of Education provided the school with a generator.[260] When we visited, the generator was operating but was noisy and disruptive inside the classrooms. According to a representative of the parents' committee, it is weak and often shuts down.[261] Like all Bedouin schools in the Negev that we visited, the building had no central heat or air conditioning. The principal described the extreme desert temperatures–both heat and cold– and showed us a small space heater and a small fan mounted on the wall. "That's it," he told us.[262]

Most of the buildings at this school were concrete block, although two were new prefabricated buildings. To one side of the school were eight toilets, housed in a separate concrete structure. These served all fifty-two teachers and 1,330 children, except for the kindergarteners who had a single toilet in their classroom. Next to the toilets and about twelve feet from a classroom was an open, foul-smelling garbage pile, taller than a kindergarten child. We were told that the school is supposed to burn the pile every few days, but it had not done so recently because the fumes blow into the school and the nearby houses.[263] There are cyanide and bromine factories in a nearby industrial zone, and a first grade teacher complained to us that a bad smell, which she attributed to the factories, often fills her classroom.[264]

[260] Eitan Michaeli, Coordinator, Negev Coalitions, Shatil (The New Israel Fund's Empowerment and Training Center for Social Change Organizations in Israel), e-mail to Human Rights Watch, April 12, 2000.
[261] Human Rights Watch interview, unrecognized village near Be'er Sheva, December 17, 2000.
[262] Human Rights Watch interview, unrecognized village near Be'er Sheva, December 17, 2000.
[263] Human Rights Watch interview with Eitan Michaeli, Shatil, Be'er Sheva, December 17, 2000.
[264] Human Rights Watch interviews, unrecognized village near Be'er Sheva, December 17, 2000.

Travel Distances

Many unrecognized Bedouin villages lack a school of any kind, and according to some reports, more than 6,000 Bedouin children must travel dozens of kilometers to school every day.[265] In October 1999, a journalist reported:

> Every morning, 8-year-old Yasser and 9-year-old Saalem, of the Azazma tribe, wake up at 5:00 a.m. and hike two kilometers from their corrugated tin shack to the main road. There, a bus picks them up for the 100-kilometer ride to their school in Segev Shalom. At the end of the day, they make the return trip. The two travel over 200 kilometers every day. "It's hardest in winter, because Mom wakes us up in the dark," Saalem says, "it's really cold and raining and we run very fast to catch the bus. But if we're a little late, the bus doesn't wait."[266]

Similarly, Human Rights Watch visited a school near an unrecognized village in the Negev where the children came from as far as fifty kilometers away.[267] A first grade teacher told us that some of her students travel more than an hour to reach the school.[268] A municipal official in the recognized Bedouin town of Kseife, told Human Rights Watch that 42 percent of children attending school there come from outside the town.[269] Students also travel as far as fifty kilometers to reach elementary schools in Al-Azazmeh, another unrecognized village.[270] Saud al-Haroumi, a teacher at a school in the recognized Bedouin community Shaqib Al-Salaam/Segev Shalom noted: "What do you expect a student to learn, when he has to get up early in the morning and travel for an hour or more by bus," asks.[271]

In response to this situation, Moshe Shohat, the government head of the Bedouin educational system in the Negev, told a journalist that it is not possible to build a school "on every hill and under every luxuriant tree where the

[265] Aliza Arbeli, "Distance Learning: Thousands of Bedouin Children Travel Dozens of Kilometers Daily to Reach Their Schools," *Ha'aretz Daily Newspaper (English Edition)* (Israel), October 20, 1999.
[266] Ibid.
[267] Human Rights Watch interviews with school principal and head of the parents' committee, unrecognized village near Be'er Sheva, December 17, 2000.
[268] Human Rights Watch interview, unrecognized village near Be'er Sheva, December 17, 2000.
[269] Human Rights Watch interview, Kseife, December 14, 2000.
[270] Algazy, "What About the Bedouin?"
[271] Ibid.

Bedouin are dispersed. We have 14 schools located in centers of temporary residences and they're spread out all over the Negev."[272]

In July 2000, Adalah and the Association for Civil Rights in Israel (ACRI) filed a petition on behalf of the Regional Council for the Unrecognized Villages, Parents' Committees, and residents of Be'er Hadaj against the Minister of Education and the Ramat HaNegev regional council demanding they establish schools in the unrecognized community of Be'er Hadaj.[273] Local children were traveling thirty-two to forty kilometers each way to reach their schools, and 33.9 percent of children (215 out of 635 children) between the ages of three and eighteen did not attend school. In 1998, only two of thirteen eighth graders were girls. Although the Ministry of Education provided transportation, only one out of seven buses entered the village. To reach the other six buses, children walked four kilometers to unmarked bus stops along the highway.[274] The Israeli High Court granted an *order nisi* in July 2000 ordering the government to respond and then accepted the government's promise to build a temporary school closer to the community than the old school. However, the new school would not be located in the community, but rather in an area where the government planned to resettle the community but where no town yet existed.[275]

The situation in Be'er Hadaj and the low numbers of girls who made it to the eighth grade demonstrate the disparate impact that long travel distances have on girls' education: parents are often more reluctant to send their daughters on long bus rides and so keep them at home. We visited a primary school in an unrecognized Bedouin village that continued through the ninth grade. The head of the local parents' committee told us that for many of the girls, this would be their last year of school because they would not travel the longer distance to the nearest high school.[276] Similarly, a Bedouin teacher told us that his eighteen-year-old sister had dropped out of school after the eighth grade. "The long distance between home and school makes it difficult for a girl to walk alone in the desert," he explained.[277]

[272] Arbeli, "Distance learning."
[273] *Dahlala Abu Ghardud, et. al. v. Ramat HaNegev Regional Council, et. al.,* H.C. 5221/00 (*order nisi* granted July 2000).
[274] *Adalah,* "Adalah and ACRI Submit a Petition to Supreme Court Calling for the Establishment of Arab Schools in the Area of the Ramat HaNegev Regional Council," July 20, 2000. http://www.adalah.org/news32000.html#9 (accessed on May 31, 2001).
[275] Marwan Dalal, attorney for Adalah, e-mail to Human Rights Watch, July 20, 2001.
[276] Human Rights Watch interview, unrecognized village outside Be'er Sheva, December 17, 2000.
[277] Human Rights Watch interview, Be'er Sheva, December 16, 2000.

International law requires that schools be physically accessible for the right to education to be fulfilled. The United Nations Committee on Economic, Social, and Cultural Rights has stated that to be physically accessible, schools must be "within safe physical reach, either by attendance at some reasonably convenient geographic location (e.g. a neighbourhood school) or via modern technology (e.g. access to a 'distance learning' programme)."[278] In addition, the Convention on the Elimination of All Forms of Discrimination against Women, to which Israel is a party, obligates states to "eliminate discrimination against women in order to ensure them equal rights with men in the field of education and in particular to ensure, on the basis of equality of men and women . . . [t]he same conditions . . . for access to studies."[279]

Auxiliary Facilities

The lack of auxiliary facilities in Arab schools–libraries, laboratories, gymnasiums, and art rooms–compared with those we saw in Jewish schools was especially striking. For example, we went from an Arab school where children played on the roof for lack of even an empty parking lot, to a Jewish school with a separate gymnasium with tiered stadium seating; from an Arab school where the special education classroom contained only desks and chairs, some of which were missing their plastic backs leaving bare metal rods, to a Jewish school with an art therapy room. While not all Jewish schools have art therapy rooms, national data from the Israeli government documents the shortage of auxiliary facilities in Arab schools compared with Jewish schools.

The problem is compounded by the fact that many Palestinian Arab communities lack services such as local libraries and recreational facilities that might compensate for shortages in schools. This is especially true in Negev Bedouin localities, both recognized and unrecognized. But a parent in Haifa and a representative of a parents' committee in Acre both complained about the lack of Arabic libraries with children's literature in their cities as well.[280]

Libraries

There is no library, no room with books in it that the students can use. And a laboratory. Students need a way to do research for themselves and collect material–it is necessary for university. We can't train them to do research because we don't have a library.

---

[278] *General Comment 13, The Right to Education*, Committee on Economic, Social and Cultural Rights, para. 6.

[279] CEDAW, art. 10.

[280] Human Rights Watch interview, Haifa, December 6, 2000; and Human Rights Watch interview with Sami Hawary, Acre, December 10, 2000.

There was one in the village but it is closed now, so most pupils only
have the ministry's book, and they don't get any more information
than that.

–Palestinian Arab teacher, village in
the Triangle region, Israel, December
6, 2000.

More Jewish schools than Arab schools have libraries. According to
Israel's Central Bureau of Statistics, 64.4 percent of Arab schools, compared
with 80.7 percent of Jewish schools, had libraries.

Table 14: Schools with Libraries 1994-1996

	Jewish schools	Arab schools
Primary schools (1994-1995)	73.0% (836 of 1,145)	55.0% (179 of 326)
Intermediate schools (1994-1995)	91.1% (293 of 322)	72.6% (57 of 78)
Secondary schools (1995-1996)	91.6% (453 of 494)	90.8% (83 of 91)
Total schools with libraries	80.7% (1,582 of 1,961)	64.4% (319 of 495)

Sources: CBS, *Survey of Education and Welfare Services 1994/1995: Primary and
Intermediate Schools, Hebrew and Arab Education* (Jerusalem: CBS, October 1997);
and CBS, *Survey of Education and Welfare Services 1995/1996: Secondary Schools,
Hebrew and Arab Education* (Jerusalem: CBS, May 1999).

No data was available on the quality of libraries in schools that had them.
We visited an Arab primary school in the Triangle region where the "library"
consisted of a single shelf on which about ten books were propped flat against
the wall, held in place by a length of string. We visited a secondary school with
over seven hundred students in a recognized Bedouin town in the Negev. The
building was new and had a small room designated as a library. Although over a
third of the shelves were empty, the principal told us proudly that the students
had raised NIS 50,000 ($12,500) that had paid for the books. "The ministry
brings the workers and the tools and just builds the building," he explained.
"The school must bring the books and the furniture."[281]   We also visited a

[281] Human Rights Watch interview, recognized Bedouin locality near Be'er Sheva,
December 14, 2000.

primary school in an unrecognized Bedouin village and an Arab primary school in a village in the Triangle region that had no libraries. In contrast, we visited the English language library in a Jewish primary school in Haifa which had a large closet with shelves of books in English.

According to its annual budget, the Ministry of Education provides funding for library services, including librarians.[282]

Sports Facilities

> One week a month we can use the gym because of the rotation. Girls and boys are separated for sports, and often we give up our time to the girls. The building itself is good, but there is not much equipment for sports. There are two balls and two baskets–basic equipment. It is hard to arrange games.
>
> —Palestinian Arab high school student, Acre, December 10, 2000.

The Arab schools Human Rights Watch visited often lacked sports facilities. For example, a Palestinian Arab first grade teacher of thirty-one children told us that while she did teach a sports class, she usually taught it inside.[283] When we went to see her school in a small village in northern Israel, we understood why. The class was taught in a single-room prefabricated building at the edge of a rocky dirt road. Next door was another prefabricated building. In between were several pieces of playground equipment in a yard smaller than the classroom itself. The entire area was on a steep hill and thickly carpeted with spiny bushes. The only place where a child could run was in the road.

The principal of a primary school in Nazareth told us that his students received two hours of sports instruction a week. The school did have balls, but no other sports equipment.[284] A physical education teacher at a primary school in a village in the Triangle region told us: "We need a gym for every school. In the kibbutz I see a gym. We don't need one like the N.B.A., just a little one, suitable for the needs of the school."[285]

Human Rights Watch visited another primary school in the region where the physical education teacher came two days a week, which was not, he said,

---

[282] Ministry of Education, *Proposed Budget for the Ministry of Education 2001*, pp. 173-75.
[283] Human Rights Watch interview, Israel, December 7, 2000.
[284] Human Rights Watch interview, Nazareth, December 7, 2000.
[285] Human Rights Watch interview, village in the Triangle region, December 6, 2000. N.B.A. stands for the U.S. National Basketball Association.

enough time to teach every class.[286] The school did not have a gymnasium. The only recreation space was a concrete parking lot with soccer nets at each end. The building was built on the side of a hill. Except for the parking lot, the surrounding area was steep, full of trash, and fenced off.

We visited a Jewish intermediate and high school that shared a large new gymnasium built with money from the national lottery (*Mifal Hapayis*).[287] In another building was a dance studio with mirrored walls, a ballet *barre*, and lighting.[288]

The Israeli government in its initial submission to the Committee on the Rights of the Child acknowledges that there is "a lack of sports and games facilities for [Palestinian Arab] elementary school children, for whom the streets are a favored playing field. . . . Arab youth tend to explain their lack of involvement in informal activities as being due to a lack of services, not a lack of interest."[289]

Laboratories

Human Rights Watch visited Arab schools with full computer labs, and schools with no computers at all. At a primary school in Um El-Fahm, the Education Ministry had just provided NIS 50,000 ($12,500) for computers and a science lab.[290] Previously, the school had three computers that only the staff used. We also visited a primary school in a village in the Triangle region that had enough computers for one class of students to each use a computer, and secondary school for Negev Bedouin with thirty-four computers for over 700 students.

In contrast, a teacher at another primary school in the Triangle region told us, "[m]ost of all we need computers—the children don't even know what they are."[291] A second grade teacher at a school in a recognized Bedouin community

---

[286] Human Rights Watch interview, village in the Triangle region, December 6, 2000.

[287] The national lottery (*Mifal Hapayis*) was frequently cited as a source of funding for auxiliary buildings. According to the principal of an Arab primary school in the Triangle region that received funding from the lottery for computer programs, the national lottery administers funding on a discretionary basis and "only gives to schools that are recommended by counselors and social workers." Human Rights Watch interview, village in the Triangle region, December 6, 2000.

[288] Human Rights Watch interview with Israel Vargist, principal, Alon High School, Nazareth Ilit, December 13, 2000.

[289] Ministry of Justice, *Initial Periodic Report*, pp. 322-23.

[290] Human Rights Watch interview with primary school principal, Um El-Fahm, December 6, 2000.

[291] Human Rights Watch interview, village in the Triangle region, December 6, 2000.

in the Negev showed us the computer supplied to her class. It didn't work. "We should just throw it away," she said.[292] Another school in northern Israel that we visited had eight computers for one hundred students.

Many Palestinian Arab principals, teachers, and students told us that their schools' computers were old or that there were not enough computers for students to spend much time on them. "In our school we don't have time to use the computers," an eleventh-grade girl explained.[293] A high school teacher told us:

> There is no internet. The textbooks assume a familiarity with it, but hardly any students know about it. I had to copy websites on a disk and put them on the computer. It couldn't show pictures, but I tried to give them an idea of what the internet is. Two students out of twenty-two knew what "www" and "e-mail" stood for.[294]

Human Rights Watch visited a Jewish primary school in Haifa with a large computer lab with a color printer. "Computers are fun. We can play on the computer at recess," a fifth grade boy commented.[295] We visited another Jewish primary school in Nazareth Ilit with thirty-five computers for 300 students.[296]

Human Rights Watch also toured the science laboratory of a secondary school in a recognized Bedouin locality. The lab had a storage annex for equipment; however, the shelves were empty. When we asked why, the science teacher told us that there was nothing to put on them.[297]

The Israeli government reported to the United Nations Human Rights Committee in 1998 that the Ministry of Education had built laboratories in forty Arab primary schools, thirty-five Arab intermediate schools, and forty-seven high schools and had sent science and technology instructional kits to fifteen Palestinian Arab localities.[298]

---

[292] Human Rights Watch interview, recognized Bedouin locality near Be'er Sheva, December 14, 2000.

[293] Human Rights Watch interview, Nazareth, December 9, 2000.

[294] Human Rights Watch interview, mixed city, December 10, 2000.

[295] Human Rights Watch interview, Haifa, December 12, 2000.

[296] Human Rights Watch interview with Osnat Mordechai, principal, Ksulot Primary School, Nazareth Ilit, December 13, 2000.

[297] Human Rights Watch interview, recognized Bedouin locality near Be'er Sheva, December 14, 2000.

[298] U.N. Human Rights Committee, *Initial Report of States Parties Due in 1993: Israel*, para. 843.

Communications Facilities at Jewish Schools

Human Rights Watch visited Jewish schools with communications facilities far beyond what we saw at any Arab school. For example, we visited a primary school in Haifa with a school radio station that the students used to broadcast inside the school. In Nazareth Ilit, a development town with a large immigrant population, we visited a primary and secondary school, each with television studios, complete with editing equipment, and dark rooms for developing photographs.[299] The principal of secondary school showed us several rooms he called the "communications studio" that students used for filming and computerized editing. The studio cost NIS one million ($250 thousand)–"very expensive"–which came from the municipality and the Ministry of Education, he said.[300] In addition, we visited two Jewish primary schools with school newspapers and one with a separate drama room, with racks of costumes, several mannequins, and lighted mirrors.

None of the Arab schools that Human Rights Watch visited had similar facilities.

---

[299] Ibid.

[300] Human Rights Watch interview with Israel Vargist, principal, Alon High School, Nazareth Ilit, December 13, 2000.

VII. IN-SCHOOL SUPPORT SERVICES

Despite the increase in the number of positions available for support staff (truant officers, social workers, educational psychologists, speech therapists), support services in the Arab sector are still very inadequate, and are still not commensurate with the percentage of Arab children and youth in the population.

> —State of Israel Ministry of Justice, Ministry of Foreign Affairs, *Initial Periodic Report of the State of Israel Concerning the Implementation of the Convention on the Rights of the Child (CRC)*, February 20, 2001, p. 309.

Psychologists, counselors, social workers, and truant officers play an important role in schools, and one that is complementary to that of classroom teachers. They identify and address problems that affect students' academic performance, help identify students needing special education, provide services that keep some disabled children in regular classrooms, and prevent students from dropping out. Despite higher rates, on average, of dropping out and lower academic performance among Palestinian Arabs, far fewer Arab schools than Jewish schools offer these services.

Educational and Psychological Counseling

Fewer Arab schools than Jewish schools have counselors of any sort, and those schools that do offer some counseling provide fewer services. The shortage is an issue for both regular and special education Arab schools.

Table 15: Counseling in Schools 1994-1996

	Educational Counseling		Psychological Counseling		Counseling by a Social Worker	
	Jewish	Arab	Jewish	Arab	Jewish	Arab
Primary (1994/95)	67.4% (772 of 1,145)	18.7% (61 of 326)	91.3% (1,045 of 1,145)	44.4% (145 of 326)	63.4% (726 of 1,145)	51.1% (167 of 326)
Intermediate (1994/95)	95.7% (308 of 322)	64.4% (50 of 78)	81.0% (261 of 322)	27.4% (21 of 78)	72.8% (234 of 322)	64.4% (50 of 78)
Secondary (1995/96)	94.0% (464 of 494)	74.4% (68 of 91)	65.8% (325 of 494)	34.8% (32 of 91)	61.1% (302 of 494)	53.5% (49 of 91)
All schools	78.7% (1,544 of 1,961)	36.2% (179 of 495)	83.2% (1,631 of 1,961)	40.0% (198 of 495)	64.4% (1,262 of 1,961)	53.7% (266 of 495)

Source: CBS, *Survey of Education and Welfare Services 1995/1996: Secondary Schools, Hebrew and Arab Education* (Jerusalem: CBS, May 1999).

For example, 36.2 percent of Arab schools, compared with 78.7 percent of Jewish schools, offered educational counseling, and 40 percent of Arab schools, compared with 83.2 percent of Jewish schools, offered psychological counseling.

Part of the problem is in implementing stated policy. The 1997 State Comptroller's Report criticized the government for the large gap between the number of counseling hours to which Arab schools are legally entitled and the number that they actually receive. According to the report, Arab schools received only 35 percent of the counseling hours to which they were entitled.[301]

"We ask the ministry for special counselors for special cases, but we just don't get them," a history teacher at an Arab primary school in the Triangle region told Human Rights Watch.[302] The school's English teacher confirmed that the school had no counselors, although she said she could think of at least ten children who needed some form of psychological help. The parents would

---

[301] State Comptroller, *Report*, 1997, p. 317.
[302] Human Rights Watch interview, village in the Triangle region, December 6, 2000.

not agree to send them to private psychologists, she explained, because of the stigma and the cost.[303]

We visited an Arab primary school in a mixed city with 1,370 pupils that was supposed to have two psychologists or counselors, the vice-principal told us. However, neither one was working when we visited because one was on maternity leave and the other was on strike.[304] Human Rights Watch also visited an Arab school for physically disabled children that had no psychologist or counselor when we were there. Usually a psychologist came one day a week, but she was on maternity leave.[305] The special education teacher at a regular Arab school in the Triangle region told Human Rights Watch, "[f]or three years we have tried to get help from the ministry for a girl in the class who has many psychological problems, but we cannot get anything."[306] The school had no counselors or psychologists.[307]

Those counselors who do work in Arab schools often have caseloads that are too large for them to provide adequate individualized care. Orna Cohen, an attorney for Adalah, wrote in March 2000 to the Education Ministry-appointed committee (called the "Margalit Committee") that was examining the implementation of the Special Education Law: "The number of psychologists and educational consultants allocated for Arab schools is much lower than for schools for the Jewish population. . . . The great shortage compels psychologists in the schools and local authorities that have slots for psychologists to spend most of their time in locating and diagnosing children and almost no time for treating them."[308] Human Rights Watch interviewed a social worker in Nazareth who told us that she went to a different Arab school every day and was responsible for four schools and five kindergartens. "I don't have enough time," she said.[309] A Palestinian Arab psychologist employed by a local municipality to work at several schools told us that his case load was double that of Jewish

---

[303] Human Rights Watch interview, village in the Triangle region, December 6, 2000.

[304] Human Rights Watch interview with vice-principal, mixed city, December 10, 2000.

[305] Human Rights Watch interview with school principal, Israel, December 11, 2000.

[306] Human Rights Watch interview, village in the Triangle region, December 6, 2000.

[307] Human Rights Watch interviews with English teacher and special education teacher, village in the Triangle region, December 6, 2000.

[308] Orna Cohen, attorney for Adalah, letter to Professor Malka Margalit, Chairperson, Public Commission to Examine Implementation of the Special Education Law, March 22, 2000, on file at Human Rights Watch, paras. 18, 20. Tel Aviv University professor Malka Margalit headed the committee, which reported its findings to the Ministry of Education in July 2000.

[309] Human Rights Watch interview, Nazareth, December 11, 2000.

psychologists who work in schools.[310]   When we interviewed him, he was working at a school where he had one day and a half a week for one hundred children with various mental disabilities.   The principal of an Arab primary school in Haifa told us that there was one psychologist responsible for all Arab schools in Haifa and Ibtin. In the past month, he said, the psychologist had come once. "When we need him, we call him. But we need someone full-time for this school," he explained.[311]

Truant Officers

Despite drop-out rates among Palestinian Arab students that are triple those of Jewish students, there are fewer truant officers in Arab schools than in Jewish schools.   Truant officers play an important role in reducing drop-out rates in Israel, according to the Israeli government's report to the Committee on the Rights of the Child in 2001: "Truant officers play a key role in addressing the problem of irregular attendance. . . .   Their job is to reduce dropping out by identifying and reporting visible and hidden dropping out, by returning students who have dropped out to school, and by involving educational and therapeutic agents in preventing students from dropping out."[312]   Despite this recognition, the government provides proportionately fewer truant officers for Palestinian Arab students.

In 1994-1996, 53.7 percent of Arab schools, compared with 65.1 percent of Jewish schools, had a truant officer, according to the Central Bureau of Statistics. In contrast, the State Comptroller reported in 1997 that truant officers were available in only 29.8 percent of Arab schools.[313]

---

[310] Human Rights Watch interview, Israel, December 11, 2000.

[311] Human Rights Watch interview, Haifa, December 4, 2000.

[312] Ministry of Justice, *Initial Periodic Report*, p. 273.

[313] State Comptroller, *Report*, 1997, p. 318.

Table 16: Truant Officers 1994-1996

	Jewish schools	Arab schools
Primary schools (1994-1995)	64.7% (741 of 1,145)	51.1% (167 of 326)
Intermediate schools (1994-1995)	72.8% (234 of 322)	64.4% (50 of 78)
Secondary schools (1995-1996)	61.1% (302 of 494)	53.5% (49 of 91)
All schools with truant officers	65.1% (1,277 of 1,961)	53.7% (266 of 495)

Sources: CBS, *Survey of Education and Welfare Services 1994/1995: Primary and Intermediate Schools, Hebrew and Arab Education* (Jerusalem: CBS, October 1997); and CBS, *Survey of Education and Welfare Services 1995/1996: Secondary Schools, Hebrew and Arab Education* (Jerusalem: CBS, May 1999).

Again, part of the problem is implementation of policy, as agreed staffing levels are simply not met. According to a 2001 report by the State Comptroller, "while funds sufficient for the employment of 346 such officials in the Arab sector should be available, during the year 2000 Education Ministry funding for just 53 posts reached the schools, via local councils. Established standards in Rahat [a recognized Negev Bedouin town] call for at least 14 truancy officer positions, but money has been allocated for just one such official."[314] When we asked the principal of an Arab primary school in the Triangle region if the school had a truant officer, he replied that a truant officer came "once in a blue moon." However, he noted, dropping out was more a problem at the high school level than at his school.[315]

Negev Bedouin

Bedouin schools, in particular, lack social services. The principal of a secondary school in a recognized Negev Bedouin town told Human Rights Watch that the school had no counselors for over 700 students, although there was a regular psychologist in the town. "We get forms from the ministry for counselors and evaluations," he said. "I have to fill them out myself."[316]

---

[314] Algazy, "What About the Bedouin?"

[315] Human Rights Watch interview, village in the Triangle region, December 6, 2000.

[316] Human Rights Watch interview, recognized Bedouin locality near Be'er Sheva, December 14, 2000.

Another primary school that we visited in an unrecognized area in the Negev
had 1,330 students and no counselor.[317]

A 1993-1994 survey of seventeen of the thirty-seven Bedouin schools that
existed at the time in the Negev found that only five were visited by
psychologists, four by a truant officer, two by social workers, and that only four
had school guidance counselors. None were regularly visited by a doctor or
nurse.[318] According to the Katz Committee:

> there is a lack of Bedouin school counselors, which contributes to the
> large gap in this area between the Bedouin and Jewish sector. At the
> elementary school level, there are 69 counselors in the Jewish
> schools of the Southern District, and none in the Bedouin schools.
> At the intermediate school level, there are 48 counselors in the
> Jewish schools and 3 in the Bedouin schools.[319]

---

[317] Human Rights Watch interviews with head of the parents' committee and school
principal, unrecognized village near Be'er Sheva, December 17, 2000.
[318] Abu-Rabiyya, "Survey of Bedouin Schools in the Negev," pp. 20-21. The schools
surveyed included eleven primary schools, two intermediate schools, and four high
schools.
[319] *Katz Committee Report* (citing Ministry of Education, *Personnel Data in Education
for 1995-96* (in Hebrew), (Jerusalem: Israel, 1995)).

VIII. VOCATIONAL AND TECHNICAL EDUCATION

Vocational education is less available to Palestinian Arab students than to Jewish students, and a smaller proportion follow vocational tracks. Those who do follow vocational tracks receive education of a lower quality in more limited areas and perform less well on the matriculation examinations.

Vocational education is an important part of the right to education, and the prohibition on discrimination in education includes discrimination in vocational education. The International Covenant on Economic, Social and Cultural Rights specifies in article 13(2) that "[s]econdary education in its different forms, including technical and vocational secondary education, shall be made generally available and accessible to all by every appropriate means."[320] The Convention on the Rights of the Child contains a similar provision.[321]

Vocational education in Israel (also called technological education) includes both schools devoted only to vocational subjects as well as "comprehensive schools" offering both academic and vocational subjects, or "tracks." Students who elect a vocational track may take matriculation examinations with either a vocational or an academic emphasis.

Approximately eighty vocational schools (also called industrial or technological schools) provide work-oriented education for secondary students and are recognized by the government as an important tool in retaining students who might otherwise drop out.[322] Israel's vocational schools were originally designed to absorb low-achieving Jewish students, primarily *Mizrahim.* Nongovernmental organizations, which run most vocational schools, did not begin running vocational schools in Palestinian Arab villages until the 1980s.[323]

To provide vocational education, the government contracts with other bodies, namely ORT, `Amal, and Amit. ORT is a vocational and technological training organization founded in Russia in 1880 for needy Jewish communities and currently operating around the world.[324] `Amal is a school network run by

---

[320] ICESCR, art. 13(2). See Universal Declaration of Human Rights (UDHR), art. 26(1), *adopted* December 10, 1948, G.A. Res. 217A(III), U.N. Doc. A/810; *General Comment 13, The Right to Education,* Committee on Economic, Social and Cultural Rights, para. 15-16.

[321] Convention on the Rights of the Child, art. 28(1).

[322] Ministry of Justice, *Initial Periodic Report,* p. 279.

[323] Human Rights Watch interview with Yair Levin, Deputy Director-General, Head of International Relations of the Ministry of Education, Jerusalem, December 19, 2000; Swirski, *Politics and Education in Israel,* pp. 180-182.

[324] "ORT" is a Russian acronym for "*Obshestwo Propostranienia Truda*," meaning "The Society for Handicrafts and Agricultural Work"; however, the organization now calls itself the "Organisation for Rehabilitation and Training." World ORT, "The World ORT Union," http://www.ort.org/ort/wou/wou.htm (accessed on May 28, 2001).

the Ministry of Labor and Social Affairs, established in 1928. Amit is a Jewish women's organization that runs religious schools. The Ministry of Education gives the money it would otherwise give to local authorities for secondary education directly to these organizations[325]; in 1997 this constituted 20.8 percent of its funds allocated for secondary schools' budgets. According to the ministry, it allocates more per pupil in technological/vocational education than general education because technological/vocational education costs more to provide.[326]

Participation in Vocational Education

For many Palestinian Arab students, vocational education is not the buffer against dropping out that it is for Jewish students. By any measurement, a smaller proportion of Palestinian Arab students than Jewish students participate in vocational education. Of all students enrolled in vocational schools in 1999-2000, 12.6 percent were enrolled in Arab schools and 87.4 percent were enrolled in Jewish schools.[327] (In contrast, 18.9 percent of all students in general secondary schools were Palestinian Arab.)[328] By sector, 30.0 percent of students in Arab secondary schools were enrolled in vocational schools, compared with 38.9 percent of students in Jewish secondary schools.[329]

By age seventeen, most Jewish students who have left the academic track have gone to vocational or agricultural schools. In contrast, most Palestinian Arab students who have left the academic track have dropped out. Roughly half of both Jewish and Palestinian Arab seventeen-year-olds students were still in a general secondary school in 1998-1999—48.9 percent of Palestinian Arab seventeen-year-olds and 56.1 percent of Jewish seventeen-year-olds.[330] Moreover, the number of Jewish students attending a general secondary school included students in continuation classes in kibbutzim, an option not available for Palestinian Arab students. If these students were not included in the total, presumably the difference in Jewish and Palestinian Arab students attending

---

[325] Sherrie Gazit, Director, Foreign Relations Section, Department of Marketing, Public Relations, and Foreign Affairs, ORT/Israel, e-mail to Human Rights Watch, March 1, 2001; and Human Rights Watch interview with Director, ORT Technological High School, Israel, December 9, 2000.
[326] Economics and Budgeting Administration, Ministry of Education, *Facts and Figures About Education and Culture in Israel*, p. 50.
[327] CBS, *Statistical Abstract of Israel 2000*, table 22.10.
[328] Ibid.
[329] Ibid. Altogether, 14,472 students were enrolled in Arab technological/vocational schools and 100,657 students were enrolled in Jewish technological/vocational schools. Ibid.
[330] Ibid., table 22.12.

general secondary school would be even smaller. Of those seventeen-year-olds not in general secondary schools, 33.5 percent of Jews attended vocational and agricultural schools and 10.4 percent had dropped out, compared with 19.4 percent of Palestinian Arab seventeen-year-olds who attended vocational schools and 31.7 percent who had dropped out.[331] Thus, while more Jewish students stayed in other kinds of education, more Palestinian Arab students dropped out all together.

One reason for this difference appears to be that there are simply fewer Arab vocational schools. When we asked the Ministry of Education for data about vocational schools, we were referred to ORT.[332] When we asked how many of its schools were for Palestinian Arabs, ORT/Israel's spokesperson responded that ORT did not maintain these statistics.[333] However, the director of an ORT school attended only by Palestinian Arabs, who requested that his name be withheld, told Human Rights Watch that there were three ORT schools for Palestinian Arabs: one each in Haifa, Nazareth, and Na'ura.[334] "This is the only [Arab] vocational school in the whole area, I'm sure," he said. "Students come by bus. Some travel a long way. Students break the fast [during the month of Ramadan] here because of the distance."[335] According to ORT/Israel's website, it operates ninety-three high schools, industrial high schools, and junior high schools in the country.[336]

Quality of Vocational Education

At issue is not only the availability of vocational education but also the quality of what is offered. The Israeli government concedes that the level of vocational education varies significantly among schools. It reported to the Committee on the Rights of the Child in 2001: "The level of education offered to students in technological/vocational tracks varies widely from school to school. Some technological tracks are on a very high level and prepare students to take matriculation examinations . . . while others provide only low-level

---

[331] Ibid.

[332] Human Rights Watch interview with Yair Levin, Deputy Director-General, Head of International Relations of the Ministry of Education, Jerusalem, December 19, 2000.

[333] Sherrie Gazit, Director, Foreign Relations Section, Department of Marketing, Public Relations, and Foreign Affairs, ORT/Israel, e-mails to Human Rights Watch, March 1 and March 18, 2001.

[334] Human Rights Watch interview, Israel, December 9, 2000.

[335] Human Rights Watch interview with Director, ORT Technological High School, Israel, December 9, 2000.

[336] ORT Israel, "Schools Site: Result," http://www3.ort.org.il/archive/schools/ (accessed on May 15, 2001).

vocational training, and prepare students for matriculation examinations only in part, if at all."[337]

The distinction between vocational and technological education is critical. Sherrie Gazit, ORT/Israel's spokesperson, wrote to Human Rights Watch:

> ORT's principle is to equip a student with the tools to enable him to provide a living for himself—once this related to vocations such as carpentry, joinery, mechanics. Nowadays this is not vocational as the skills which are in demand nowadays (in Israel at least) are related to hi-tech professions. Consequently we emphasize advanced science and technology subjects in our schools.[338]

However, according to Zafer Shurbaji, of the Fund for the Development of Technological Education in the Arab Sector in Israel:

> Vocational education is doing by hand; technological education is doing by mind, like programming the computer. We can see technological education in the Jewish sector. They say it is there in the Arab sector but it is not. It is called the same thing but inside, it is different, the program is different. . . . In the Arab sector there are not the same books and not the same projects as the Jewish sector. . . . ORT and 'Amal are teaching both vocational and high-tech education, called "technological education." They prepare Jewish students for the army. They don't teach the same things in the Arab and Jewish sectors because the level is different. We see the consequences in the university—there are fewer Arab students in technology.[339]

Palestinian Arab students have fewer vocational subjects to choose from than Jewish students do. According to a 1996 study, nineteen vocational subjects were offered in Arab schools in Israel, compared with more than ninety offered in Jewish schools.[340] ORT/Israel's website lists fifty-six possible

---

[337] Ministry of Justice, *Initial Periodic Report*, p. 264.
[338] Sherrie Gazit, Director, Foreign Relations Sections, Department of Marketing, Public Relations and Foreign Affairs, ORT/Israel, e-mail to Human Rights Watch, March 1, 2001.
[339] Human Rights Watch interview with Zafer Shurbaji, The Fund for the Development of Technological Education in the Arab Sector in Israel, Haifa, Israel, December 7, 2000.
[340] The Fund for Promoting Technological Education in the Arab Community in Israel (Arabic), unpublished paper presented to the "Equality Conference," Nazareth, December

subjects of study but indicates that in 1999 ORT Nazareth Technological (Arab) High School offered: "Electronics and Electrotechnics" (128 students), "Mechanics" (331 students), and "Secretarial Studies" (116 students).[341] Similarly, Human Rights Watch visited an Arab ORT vocational school that offered only five vocational subjects: "electronics, automobile mechanics, machinery, accounting, and computers."[342] According to the school's director, the best students studied computers, which included a biotechnology component.[343]

A physics teacher at the school, when asked if there were differences between his school and Jewish vocational schools, told Human Rights Watch that, "they have more activities, types of vocations, and after-school programs."[344] When we asked the director to compare tracks that were offered in Jewish vocational schools with those at his school, he responded: "This is the main difference between us and the Jewish schools. They [Jewish students] can find work in [these areas]."[345] Similarly, a Bedouin graduate of an `Amal comprehensive secondary school in the Negev, with both academic and vocational tracks, when asked how many vocational subjects were taught at his school, responded: "There are few vocational programs–it's not enough. It's difficult to be an expert after you graduate from school in technology or computers. And even if you have a specialty in one subject, it's hard to get a job afterwards. Even for students with great artistic skills, they lack courses in schools in arts and dance."[346]

An eleventh-grade girl in Nazareth at a comprehensive Arab secondary school explained how her school was different from an ORT high school: "We have physics and math and they don't," she said. "They have other lessons–

1996, on file with the Follow-Up Committee for Arab Education, cited in Adalah and the Arab Association for Human Rights (HRA), *Equal Rights and Minority Rights for the Palestinian Arab Minority in Israel: A Report to the UN Human Rights Committee on Israel's Implementation of Articles 26 and 27 of the International Covenant on Civil and Political Rights*, July 1998, p. 56.

[341] ORT Israel, "Schools Site: Info," http://www3.ort.org.il/archive/schools/ (accessed on March 8 and May 15, 2001). According to an ORT Israel representative, this database was updated until 1999. Sherrie Gazit, Director, Foreign Relations Section, Department of Marketing, Public Relations, and Foreign Affairs, ORT/Israel, e-mail to Human Rights Watch, March 18, 2001.

[342] Human Rights Watch interview, Israel, December 9, 2000.

[343] Ibid.

[344] Human Rights Watch interview, Israel, December 9, 2000.

[345] Human Rights Watch interview, Israel, December 9, 2000.

[346] Human Rights Watch interview, Be'er Sheva, December 16, 2000.

mechanics, electronics."[347]   Human Rights Watch also visited an Arab comprehensive high school in the Triangle region that offered vocational classes, which the principal categorized as either "low" or "high," as well as academic classes.   The vocational subjects were: electronics, mechanics, fashion, engineering of buildings, communications, tourism, sports, ecology and environmental studies, computers and information technology, and biotechnology.[348]   The "higher" technological subjects were introduced about three years ago, he said.

Palestinian Arab students in vocational education fare worse than Jewish students on the matriculation examinations. In 1999, 35.7 percent of Palestinian Arab students who took vocational matriculation examinations passed, compared with 52.2 percent of Jewish students.[349]   In total, Palestinian Arab students made up only 9.7 percent of all students passing technological matriculation examinations in 1999.[350]

---

[347] Human Rights Watch interview, Nazareth, December 9, 2000.

[348] Human Rights watch interview, village in the Triangle region, December 6, 2000.

[349] CBS, *Statistical Abstract of Israel 2000,* table 22.22.

[350] Ibid.

IX. TEACHER QUALIFICATIONS

While there are many qualified and dedicated teachers in the Arab school system, teachers in Jewish schools have, on average, a higher level of education and more years of teaching experience. This is attributable in part to the fact that Palestinian Arab teachers have had fewer opportunities to obtain academic credentials: a self-perpetuating cycle, discrimination against one generation produces less well-trained teachers in the next. Moreover, Arab teacher training colleges were accredited to provide academic degrees only in the last five years, and the Education Ministry provides more in-service training to Jewish than to Palestinian Arab teachers. International law specifically prohibits discrimination in "training for the teaching profession."[351]

Teachers' wages are determined both by their teaching experience and their level of education.[352] Because teachers in Jewish schools have, on average, a higher level of education and more years of experience, they are, on average, paid more than teachers in Arab schools.[353] Thus less money in the form of teacher salaries flows to Arab schools.

Education

Individuals may become certified teachers either by attending a university or a teachers' training college, or by being certified as "qualified" without a formal degree by Education Ministry officials. Not all teachers, however, are certified, and there is a separate salary grade for uncertified teachers.[354]

Teacher training colleges award certifications and, in some cases, academic degrees. In 1990-2000, there were forty Jewish teacher training colleges and three Arab teacher training colleges, with only two Arab teacher training colleges accredited to award an academic degree (B.Ed.).[355] Some Jewish teacher training colleges reportedly exclude Palestinian Arab students. For example, the Ohalo College of Education and Sports in Katsrin only allows non-

---

[351] Convention against Discrimination in Education, art. 4(b), (d).

[352] See Ministry of Education, "Criteria for Assigning Salary and Seniority," www.education.gov.il/sherut/download/1_29_1_2.rtf (accessed on June 8, 2001).

[353] According to Israel's Central Bureau of Statistics, "the grade according to which the teachers' wages are calculated is generally determined by the teacher's educational attainment and pedagogical qualification." CBS, *Statistical Abstract of Israel 2000*, p. (104).

[354] Ministry of Education, "Criteria for Assigning Salary and Seniority."

[355] The accredited Arab teachers' training colleges are Haifa Arab Teachers' College (accredited in 1996) and a program for Palestinian Arab teachers at Beit Berl Teachers' College (accredited 1998). A few Jewish teacher training colleges offer programs tailored for Palestinian Arabs. For example, Kaye College in Be'er Sheva offers a special class to train Bedouin teachers.

Jews to study physical education, excluding them from studying kindergarten or primary education. "The Arab College in Haifa does not offer a course in physical education and therefore we are obliged to accept the non-Jewish students for this path of studies," Hagit Harel, the head of student administration, told a journalist. Although Harel stated that the policy was based on a directive from the Ministry of Education, the ministry denied that it had issued such an order.[356]

There is evidence that the quality of education at Jewish teacher training colleges is higher than at Arab ones. On average, the Jewish colleges were smaller and had the equivalent of more full-time teachers per student than the Arab colleges.[357] In addition, some Palestinian Arab instructors complained that the level of teaching in programs for Palestinian Arabs is lower. "Jewish programs are more like university, and we are more like high school," an instructor at Haifa Arab Teachers' College told us.[358] "The problem begins with teacher training," said a former instructor at a program for Bedouin at a Jewish teachers' college. "They treat students like they are in secondary school. Notes were sent to the women's parents about dress and modesty."[359]

In 1997-1998, a lower proportion of teachers in Arab schools than in Jewish schools had academic degrees, a higher proportion were rated only as "qualified," and a higher proportion were rated "not qualified."

---

[356] David Ratner, "College Bars Non-Jews from Education Studies," *Ha'aretz Daily Newspaper (English Edition)* (Israel), July 16, 2001. Harel subsequently affirmed that the Ministry of Education had issued the order and elaborated: "The directive of the Education Ministry is not new and stipulates that Arabs should study education at the Arab College because of the language and the fact they go back to teach in their own places and do not need to learn about Passover and Hanukkah with us. They learn about their heritage and things." Ibid.

[357] There were 4,338 full-time equivalent teaching posts and 28,442 students at Jewish teacher training colleges in 1999-2000. In the Arab colleges there were 288 full-time equivalent posts and 2,621 students. CBS, *Statistical Abstract of Israel 2000*, table 22.31.

[358] Human Rights Watch interview with Hala Espanioly, Haifa, December 4, 2000.

[359] Human Rights Watch interview, Haifa, December 6, 2000.

Table 17: Teacher Qualifications: Primary, Intermediate, and Secondary Schools 1997-1998

	Jewish schools	Arab schools
Teachers with an academic degree (B.A., M.A., or Ph.D.)	59.5%	39.7%
Teachers rated "qualified"	36.4%	52.3%
Teachers rated "not qualified"	4.1%	7.9%

Source: CBS, *Statistical Abstract of Israel 2000*, no. 51, table 22.28.

Thus, 59.5 percent of teachers in Jewish primary and secondary schools had a degree of B.A., M.A. or Ph.D., compared with 39.7 percent in Arab schools. In Jewish schools, 4.1 percent of teachers were on the "not qualified" salary grade, compared with 7.9 percent in Arab schools. The discrepancy was worst at the lower grade levels. The majority of "not qualified" teachers were primary teachers: 6.3 percent of primary teachers in Jewish schools fell into this category, compared with 10.7 percent of teachers in the Arab system.[360] In a 1993 survey of 121 Arab preschool programs in ten localities, the nongovernmental organization Shatil found that "40.1% of the teachers had no structured and defined training. Some studied in courses organized by the program operator or by a local institution. Some had no training at all. . . . Only 3.4% of the teachers employed in pre-school programs which were surveyed were graduates of accredited institutions."[361] Also, the lack of preschool teacher training programs in the Arab sector acts as a barrier to preschools obtaining a license.

Human Rights Watch visited an Arab primary school in Um El-Fahm with twenty-six teachers, including six half-time teachers and the principal, who also taught. Of these, four had university degrees, three were still studying at the university, and the rest had attended a teachers' training college.[362] In Haifa, we interviewed a kindergarten teacher who told us she was "certified through experience."[363]

---

[360] Ibid.

[361] Ghada Abu Jaber, *A Survey of Early Childhood Education in the Arab Sector of Israel*, ed. Hamutal De-Lima (Israel: Shatil, January 1994), pp. 21, 45.

[362] Human Rights Watch interview with primary school principal, Um El-Fahm, December 6, 2000.

[363] Human Rights Watch interview, Haifa, December 4, 2000.

In-Service Training

The Ministry of Education provides less in-service training to teachers in Arab schools than to teachers in Jewish schools. In a survey of 404 Arab primary and intermediate schools and 1,467 Jewish primary and intermediate schools, Israel's Central Bureau of Statistics found that the following "programs to improve teaching" were offered in schools at the following rates:

Table 18: Programs to Improve Teaching: Primary and Intermediate Schools 1994-1995[364]

	Jewish Schools	Arab Schools
Voluntary school-based training	87.9%	60.1%
Preparing and administering tests to measure achievement	35.9%	43.3%
Other programs to improve teaching	26.9%	24.0%
Offered no programs at all	6.4%	21.5%

Source: CBS, *Survey of Education and Welfare Services 1994/1995: Primary and Intermediate Schools, Hebrew and Arab Education* (Jerusalem: CBS, October 1997).

Thus, Jewish schools had much higher rates of school-based in-service training, while Arab schools had somewhat higher rates of programs on preparing and administering achievement tests. Of Arab schools, 21.5 percent offered no programs at all to improve teaching, while 6.4 percent of Jewish schools had no such programs.

One reason for this difference may be that in-school programs are frequently administered at ministry officials' discretion and that their curricula are not always appropriate for Palestinian Arabs. As explained above, this results in fewer programs reaching Arab schools. Another reason is where some classes are held. Shlomo Swirski, coordinator of the Adva Center's Budget Analysis Project, explained: "in principle [the classes] are open to everyone, but fewer of the special programs get to Arab villages . . . One could argue it's not

---

[364] It should be noted that a small number of teacher training programs–between 0 and 6.3 percent of programs, depending on the type and grade level–in both Jewish and Arab schools were primarily funded by parents. CBS, *Survey of Education and Welfare Services 1994/1995*, pp. 80-81, 100-01, 110-11, 118-19, 154-55, 166-67, 190-91, 196-97.

discrimination, it's geography, since most courses are in Tel Aviv and most Arab settlements are in the north or south. Outlying Jewish villages suffer from the same."[365]

A Palestinian Arab high school English teacher in a mixed city told us that she participated in in-service training both for Palestinian Arab teachers and for Jewish teachers. She concluded: "They have more serious lectures. The Jewish training is provided on a much higher level. Things are taken more seriously."[366] Human Rights Watch also interviewed the principal of an Arab primary school in Nazareth who said that as part of an experimental program, the school had received a special budget for teacher training for the past five years that would end in 2001.[367]

In-service training of teachers tends to improve students' performance, according to a study published in 2001, which found that in secular primary schools in Jerusalem, an in-service training program "raised children's achievement in reading and mathematics."[368]

Experience

Teachers in Jewish schools had a median of 14.8 recognized years of teaching in 1997-1998, with 17.8 being the median in secondary schools. Teachers in Arab schools had a median of 10.8 recognized years, with 11.0 years being the median in secondary schools.[369]

Special Education

Special education teachers had the highest rate of uncertified teachers in Arab education–19 percent in 1995-1996.[370] In that year, 64 percent were certified and 17 percent held academic degrees.[371] A greater proportion of teachers in the Negev were uncertified. The nongovernmental organization Shatil reported in 2000 that:

---

[365] Human Rights Watch interview with Shlomo Swirski, coordinator of the Adva Center's Budget Analysis Project, Tel Aviv, November 30, 2000.

[366] Human Rights Watch interview, Israel, December 10, 2000.

[367] Human Rights Watch interview, Nazareth, December 7, 2000.

[368] Joshua D. Angrist and Victor Lavy, "Does Teacher Training Affect Pupil Learning? Evidence from Matched Comparisons in Jerusalem Public Schools," *Journal of Labor Economics*, vol. 19, no. 2, April 2001.

[369] CBS, *Statistical Abstract of Israel 2000*, table 22.28.

[370] Yosef Khory, Economic Advisor, Mossawa Center, *Information Book: The Education System in the Arab Sector*, April 1998, p. 15 (citing CBS).

[371] Ibid.

> Of ninety special education teachers in special education schools in Southern Arab areas, 40 or 44 percent are not certified. In the school in Kseife, eleven of twenty-eight teachers are not certified. In the school in Rahat, only three teachers gained certification. . . . Of six paramedical workers in physiotherapy or speech therapy in the Southern Arab areas, five work without certification from the Health Department. . . . Two of the speech therapists do not speak Arabic.[372]

The government acknowledged this gap to the Committee on the Rights of the Child in 2001: "Many special education teachers [for Palestinian Arab students] lack appropriate training, although their number is diminishing due to the opening of suitable frameworks of study."[373]

In-service training for experienced special education teachers is also lacking. Human Rights Watch visited a school for physically disabled children that conducts its own in-service training because its teachers get no additional training from the state. A teacher of blind and low-vision students explained: "If teachers specialize in special education at the university and then come here, they need more courses, for example Braille, so we do special courses here and sometimes other places for newcomers. When we hire new teachers, it stops there–the ministry doesn't give additional training–we have to train our new teachers."[374] A municipal employee in the town where the school was located confirmed that there was "no budget for additional training."[375] According to the principal, "it's not enough–we can't teach everyone here. This year we gave a general course about language. The teachers teach each other–there's no money to bring teachers from outside. They do it on their breaks, teach Braille for example. At the end of the day it is hard for them to stay."[376]

Israel's Special Education Law explicitly requires special education teachers to be qualified and to have special education training or a temporary

---

[372] Parents' Committee for Special Education for Arabs in the Negev, Shatil, *Arab Special Education in the Negev: Discrimination in Affirmative Action* (Hebrew), 2000, p. 7 (translation by Human Rights Watch).

[373] Ministry of Justice, *Initial Periodic Report*, p. 311. The government also stated that the Ministry of Education's Department of Manpower in Education had allocated NIS 10 million ($2.5 million) annually from 2001 to 2006 to train teachers and staff working in Arab special education. Ibid., p. 312. Like other allocations to Arab education, it remains to be seen whether these funds will actually be allocated in annual budgets.

[374] Human Rights Watch interview, Israel, December 11, 2000.

[375] Human Rights Watch interview, Israel, December 11, 2000.

[376] Human Rights Watch interview, Israel, December 11, 2000.

permit from the Ministry of Education.[377] Likewise, psychologists, paramedical professionals, and other non-teachers employed in special education must be qualified or licensed according to the standards of their profession.[378]

Negev Bedouin

While there is a surplus of Palestinian Arab teachers in northern Israel, there is a shortage of local Bedouin teachers in the southern part of the country. The Ministry of Education has addressed this problem by bringing teachers from outside the region to Bedouin schools. In 1995, only about 60 percent of teachers in Bedouin schools were Bedouin.[379] Human Rights Watch visited a secondary school in a recognized Bedouin locality where half of the forty-four teachers were from outside of the Negev.[380] As teachers gain more experience, they frequently return to their own communities. Accordingly, teachers in the Negev are generally more inexperienced, and the turnover rate is very high.

The ministry recruits teachers for the south both by requiring Palestinian Arab graduates of teacher training institutions to work in Bedouin schools in the Negev for several years following graduation and by offering teachers various financial incentives. However, a recent comparative study found that "bonuses given to Jewish teachers who work in national priority development areas are almost twice as lucrative as those which go to educators who teach in Bedouin communities in the Negev."[381]

---

[377] Special Education Law, sec. D(16) (1988) (English translation downloaded from the website of the Special Education Department, State of Israel Ministry of Education, http://www.education.gov.il/special/english2.htm (accessed on April 6, 2001)).
[378] Ibid., sec. D(18).
[379] *Katz Committee Report* (citing a 1995 study).
[380] Human Rights Watch interview, recognized Bedouin locality near Be'er Sheva, December 14, 2000.
[381] Algazy, "What About the Bedouin?" According to news reports, the study found that: The Jewish teachers have their seniority status accelerated by three or four years (meaning that their wages are higher), and the worker's share of payments in "retraining and further study" funds (keren hishtalmut) are subsidized for these teachers. Nothing like that is provided to teachers who head south to teach Bedouin pupils in Negev schools. Teachers who work in Jewish schools in priority development areas receive rent subsidies worth NIS 12,000 ($3,000) a year; and they can receive an additional NIS 8,000 ($2,000) for travel expenses, and higher education tuition fees. Teachers who go south to work in the Negev Bedouin schools are eligible for annual rent and travel expense incentives worth just NIS 10,000 ($2,500) total. Ibid.

A high proportion of teachers in Negev Bedouin schools are uncertified: 23 percent in 1994.[382] A 1993-1994 study also found that the proportion of uncertified teachers was twice as high in unrecognized as recognized localities and the proportion of teachers with academic degrees much lower.[383] According to the 1998 Katz Committee Report, the number of teaching positions in the Negev is expanding at a rate faster than Bedouin teachers are being trained. The committee called for "serious intervention, and all efforts . . . starting with high school students, to identify and support potential local candidates for teacher's education."[384]

---

[382] Ministry of Justice, *Initial Periodic Report*, p. 313. See also, *Katz Committee Report* (citing 1994 Ministry of Education records).
[383] Abu-Rabiyya, "Survey of Bedouin Schools in the Negev," pp. 25-27 (using 1993-1994 data).
[384] *Katz Committee Report.*

X. KINDERGARTENS

Kindergarten in Israel begins at age two and continues through age five or six, when children begin the first grade. In addition to government kindergartens, local governments and private and religious organizations also run schools, the latter two usually charging a monthly fee ranging from a few hundred to several thousand shekels. This chapter addresses discrimination from age three, when Israeli law obligates the state to provide free and compulsory kindergarten. At the time of writing, attendance rates for three and four year-old Palestinian Arabs were less than half that of Jewish children, and many of the most impoverished Palestinian Arab communities had no kindergartens at all for three and four-year-olds (often called "preschools"). Of the Arab kindergartens that do exist, many suffer from the same problems as the rest of the Arab school system: poor physical plants, less-developed curricula, and fewer university-trained teachers.

Preschool from ages three and four appears to have long-term academic and social benefits, including reducing drop-out rates.[385] Education is cumulative, and, therefore, most Palestinian Arab children start out two years behind Jewish children.

Attendance Rates

In the 1999-2000 school year, 359,000 children ages two to six attended kindergarten in Israel, 49,000 (13.6 percent) of whom were Palestinian Arab.[386] In 1998-1999, the most recent year for which data were available, Jewish three-year-olds attended preschool at four times the rate of their Palestinian Arab counterparts; Jewish four-year-olds at three times the rate.

---

[385] In a fifteen-year study of low income children in Chicago public schools who attended preschool from age three or four, compared with children who began kindergarten at age five, researchers found that children who participated in preschool had a higher rate of school completion; more years of completed education; and lower rates of juvenile arrests, violent arrests, school dropout, grade retention (being "held back"), and use of special education services. The researchers concluded that the better educational and social outcomes from preschool were evident for up to age twenty. Arthur J. Reynolds, Judy A. Temple, Dylan L. Robertson, and Emily A. Mann. "Long-Term Effects of an Early Childhood Intervention on Educational Achievement and Juvenile Arrest: A Fifteen-Year Follow-Up of Low-Income Children in Public Schools," *Journal of the American Medical Association*, vol. 285, no. 18, May 9, 2001.

[386] CBS, *Statistical Abstract of Israel 2000*, table 22.10. Data exclude East Jerusalem. Ibid., p. (103).

Table 19: Attendance Rates: Private, Municipal, and State Kindergartens 1998-1999[387]

Age	Jewish students	Palestinian Arab students
3	89.3%	22.5%
4	92.9%	33.5%
5	94.0%	80.7%

Source: CBS, *Statistical Abstract of Israel 2000*, no. 51, table 22.11.

Some have argued that attendance rates are lower among Palestinian Arab children because of parental choice–that Palestinian Arab parents do not recognize the value of preschool education. However, among Jewish parents, the government has campaigned to raise awareness among Jewish parents about the values of preschool. Nabila Espanioly, director of the Al-Tufula Pedagogical Center, commented:

> They say Arab parents won't send their kids to kindergarten, but when we open kindergartens, children do come. . . . They don't ask whether Jewish immigrants want to send their kids to kindergarten. They know it is important so they don't ask–they build kindergartens and the need is created. When it exists and is easy to access, then people use it. If I don't know about it, it doesn't mean that I don't want it.[388]

A father of three and four-year-old children from a village outside of Haifa told Human Rights Watch:

> I pay for private preschool because the law doesn't extend to my village. I can because I work and my wife works. But most in my village cannot. If the law extended to [was being implemented in]

---

[387] Data exclude East Jerusalem. Ibid. In contrast, Dalia Limor, director of the Education Ministry's preschool department, stated that in February 1998, only 68 percent of Jewish three-year-olds (54,000) and only 5 percent of Arab children that age (4,000) attended kindergarten. By age four the rates rose to 90 percent in the Jewish population but still only 8 percent in the Arab population. Relly Sa'ar, "Bill on Free Schooling for Toddlers Advances," *Ha'aretz Daily Newspaper (English Edition)* (Israel), December 15, 1998, p. 3. See also "Free, Compulsory Nursery School," *Ha'aretz Daily Newspaper (English Edition)* (Israel), January 12, 1999.

[388] Human Rights Watch interview with Nabila Espanioly, Director, Al-Tufula Pedagogical Centre, Nazareth, December 8, 2000.

my village, preschool would be free. Parents know about the law and ask. There are two Arab villages near the sea that got preschools, and they are sending their kids."[389]

State Funding

In the 1999-2000 school year, only 11.5 percent of teaching hours for government-run ("official") kindergartens went to Arab kindergartens.[390]

Kindergarten attendance from age three has been compulsory by law since 1984, when the age was lowered from five to three years old. However, no serious steps were taken to implement the law until 1999, when the Knesset passed a bill calling on the state to subsidize education fees for three and four-year-olds.[391] The law is to be gradually implemented over a ten-year period, during which the Education Minister has the authority to decide which towns will receive funding. After ten years, all three and four-year-olds are to be exempted from preschool fees.

Although the government was not effectively obligated by law to provide kindergarten for children ages three and four until 1999, the government has long subsidized preschools for many Jewish children, especially for Mizrahi children. According to Israel's 2001 submission to the Committee on the Rights of the Child:

> These data [on kindergarten attendance rates] indicated that although free education from age three is not implemented due to budgetary limitations, the State of Israel has attained nearly universal participation in pre-compulsory education (ages two to four) in the Jewish sector. The high level of participation in early education in this sector is a result of investment of resources in the construction of preschools and day care centers and the training of teachers and aides, which was accelerated in the 1970s in recognition that beginning education at the earliest possible opportunity promotes equality and equal opportunity. This recognition is also reflected in

---

[389] Human Rights Watch interview with Basem Kanane, Haifa, December 3, 2000.

[390] Ministry of Education, *Proposed Budget for the Ministry of Education 2001*, p. 144.

[391] "Free, Compulsory Nursery School"; and Relly Sa'ar, "Free Education Law Won't Cover More Preschoolers Next Year," *Ha'aretz Daily Newspaper (English Edition)* (Israel), February 16, 2000.

the efforts made to enable families with little means to send their children to such frameworks.[392]

Palestinian Arab children have not enjoyed the same support from national and local governments. The government's submission to the Committee on the Rights of the Child continues:

> There are a number of reasons for the differences in preschool attendance rates of Jews and Arabs. The availability of preschools in the Arab sector is relatively limited, and there is a lack of preschool teachers and teacher training programs. In addition, there is no structured preschool program. This is the result of the relatively small government investment in this sector, as well as of the fact that Arab local authorities have to finance the construction of preschools and cover 25% of the tuition for municipal preschools for children ages three-four. As noted, Arab local authorities have financial difficulties and a negative financial balance, and cannot allocate the financial resources necessary to construct preschools.[393]

Despite a greater deficit among Palestinian Arab children, to date, the 1999 law to subsidize preschool education has primarily benefited Jewish communities. After the bill was passed, the Minister of Education at the time, Yitzhak Levy, decided that the law would be implemented by the "priority areas" ranking system. As explained above, the rankings, which are based in part on geographic location and need, are weighted towards Jewish settlements in the West Bank and Gaza and towns with many new immigrants, and include few Palestinian Arab communities in Israel. Towns with an "A" ranking would be the first to receive preschool funding. When the Ministry of Education released the list of initial recipients, there were 195 Jewish localities on the list. Almost all were settlements in the West Bank and Gaza; only three Palestinian Arab localities were on the list. Moreover, many of these communities were already receiving free preschool.[394] In July 1999, the next Education Minister, Yosi Sarid, added to the list towns from the two lowest levels of the Central

---

[392] Ministry of Justice, *Initial Periodic Report*, p. 262. As is the case here, many government publications still do not refer to kindergarten for three and four-year-olds as compulsory, although it is now compulsory by law.
[393] Ibid., p. 304. See also Adva Center, "Early Education in Israel," *Israel Equality Monitor*, no. 3, May 1993, pp. 2-3.
[394] Human Rights Watch interview with Dalia Sprinzak, Economics and Budgeting Administration, Ministry of Education, Jerusalem, December 19, 2000.

Bureau of Statistic's socio-economic scale because, he said, the list "included hardly any Arab communities."[395] Accordingly, twenty-three Palestinian Arab communities were added.[396] Nevertheless, in the 1999-2000 school year, most of the children who received exemptions from fees under the law were reportedly Jewish children already exempt for other reasons, for example, as residents of "frontline settlements," communities with national priority status, and neighborhood renewal areas.[397] In 2000, the ministry announced that it would not add any children to the program because it lacked funding,[398] meaning that the imbalances created in 1999 were not corrected in 2000. Thus the Education Ministry, in implementing the 1999 law, has neglected Palestinian Arab children, who have fewer preschool opportunities, who rank the lowest on the socio-economic scale, and who currently attend preschools at much lower rates than Jewish children.

Classroom Conditions

Palestinian Arab children who do attend kindergarten face classes that are nearly twice as large as those that Jewish children attend. And while the number of children per staff decreased slightly in Jewish education from 1998-1999 to 1999-2000, the number increased slightly in Arab education.

Table 20: Pupils Per Teaching Staff: Government Kindergartens 1999-2000

	Jewish schools	Arab schools
1998-1999	20.1	37.9
1999-2000	19.8	39.3

Source: Ministry of Education, *Proposed Budget for the Ministry of Education 2001 and Explanations as Presented to the Fifteenth Knesset*, no. 11, October 2000, p. 144.

A major barrier to opening preschools in Palestinian Arab communities is the lack of a building, as funding for construction or rent is not included in the 1999 Knesset law. For example, at a school in an unrecognized village outside of Be'er Sheva that Human Rights Watch visited, two prefabricated classrooms

[395] Aryeh Dean Cohen, "More Arab Communities Made Eligible for Free Preschool," *Jerusalem Post*, July 29, 1999, p. 3.
[396] Relly Sa'ar, "Free Kindergarten List Expanded," *Ha'aretz Daily Newspaper (English Edition)* (Israel), July 29, 1999; and Cohen, "More Arab Communities Made Eligible for Free Preschool" (stating that thirty-three Palestinian Arab communities were added).
[397] Sa'ar, "Free Education Law Won't Cover More Preschoolers Next Year."
[398] Ibid.

had been brought in at the start of the school year, intended to be used for kindergartens for three and four-year-olds. However, because other classes at the school were so large, two additional first and second grade classes were created instead. A kindergarten class for five-year-olds with one teacher, an assistant, and thirty-six students were housed in one of the buildings. As of December 2000, the area still had no classes for three and four-year-olds.

The nongovernmental organization Shatil, in a 1993 study, found that: "50% of [Arab] pre-school programs are located in rented facilities, most of which were not designed to serve this purpose. The lack of appropriate facilities was cited by operators of early childhood programs as one of the key obstacles in providing pre-school education. In the absence of financial support, establishing and equipping programs according to the directives of the ministry is not feasible."[399]

Although the 1999 law does not address kindergarten construction, the state has paid for kindergarten construction through other mechanisms, primarily in Jewish communities. For example, the Ministry of Housing constructs kindergartens in newly-built towns with more than 5,000 residents and in new neighborhoods with at least 1,000 apartments. No Palestinian Arab town or neighborhood of this size has been built since 1948.[400] Jewish agencies have also financed kindergarten construction in Jewish communities. The government states in its 2001 submission to the Committee on the Rights of the Child that the Ministry of Education financed the construction of one hundred Arab kindergarten classes from 1995 to 1996.[401]

Teacher Qualifications

As discussed above, the largest gaps between Jewish and Arab schools in teacher training and experience occur at the kindergarten level. Although the government claims that in 1995 it expanded training for Palestinian Arab kindergarten teachers, six years later the gaps were still great.[402]

Negev Bedouin

They talk around the issues but don't change anything. I have a daughter five years old. I thought last year with [former Education

---

[399] Abu Jaber, *A Survey of Early Childhood Education in the Arab Sector of Israel*, p. 45.
[400] Follow-Up Committee on Arab Education, *A Report on the Education of the Arabs in Israel* (1995) cited in Adalah, *Legal Violations of Arab Minority Rights in Israel: A Report on Israel's Implementation of the International Convention on the Elimination of all Forms of Racial Discrimination* (Israel: Adalah, March 1998), p. 79, note 116.
[401] Ministry of Justice, *Initial Periodic Report*, p. 305.
[402] Ibid.

Minister] Yosi Sarid's promise she would go to [a government] preschool, but there were none there. There are private preschools but their content is weak. My daughter started going last year to a private preschool, but she told us, "I have more books, toys, papers, and colors at my house than at school." So we didn't make her go.

–parent, Laqiya (recognized Bedouin locality), Israel, December 14, 2000

Kindergarten attendance is lowest among Negev Bedouin. Out of approximately 14,500 non-Jewish children ages three to five in the Be'er Sheva sub-district in 1998-1999, only 5,084 Bedouin children were registered in kindergartens and preschools.[403] A study by the Center for Bedouin Studies and Development and the Negev Center for Regional Development at Ben Gurion University attributes the low enrollment rates to three factors:

a) lack of kindergartens in both recognized and unrecognized localities

b) inability of parents to pay tuition in kindergartens for children aged 3-4 (nursery school)

c) parents' lack of awareness about the importance of formal education before primary school. The fact that most women do not work contributes to the keeping of small children at home.[404]

The lack of kindergartens is attributable to the Ministry of Education, and in smaller part to local governments. Although the Ministry of Education operated kindergartens for five-year-olds in every recognized Bedouin locality and twelve unrecognized localities in 1998-1999, it did not provide classes for most three and four-year-old Bedouin children.[405] At the time of writing, the Ministry of Education operated kindergartens for three and four-year-olds in only two localities, Shaqib Al-Salaam/Segev Shalom and Tal Al-Saba/Tel Sheva, and one "mixed" class for three to five-year-olds in Kseife, Rahat, and Tal Al-Saba/Tel Sheva.[406] Local authorities ran kindergartens for three and

---

[403] Center for Bedouin Studies and Development, *Statistical Yearbook of the Negev Bedouin*, p. (31).

[404] Ibid., pp. (31)-(32).

[405] Ibid., p. 74.

[406] Ismael Abu-Saad, e-mail to Human Rights Watch, March 23, 2001. In the 1998-1999 school year, the preschool in Shaqib Al-Salaam/Segev Shalom served fifteen children, the preschool in Tal Al-Saba/Tel Sheva served 316, and mixed facilities in Kseife, Rahat, and Tal Al-Saba/Tel Sheva served twenty-four, thirty-five children, and thirty-five

four-year-olds in three recognized localities, and nonprofit associations and the Islamic movement ran kindergartens in ten localities, both recognized and unrecognized.[407] In unrecognized villages in 1998-1999, 167 three and four-year-old children attended kindergarten, all of which were run by private organizations, as there were no government preschools.[408] "There is a severe shortage of compulsory kindergartens or preschools" for Bedouin children in unrecognized villages, the Israeli government reported to the Committee on the Rights of the Child in 2001.[409]

Children's failure to attend kindergarten because their parents are unable to pay tuition fees should be wholly the government's responsibility, now that kindergarten is to be free by law.

---

children, respectively.   Center for Bedouin Studies and Development, *Statistical Yearbook of the Negev Bedouin*, p. 74.
[407] Center for Bedouin Studies and Development, *Statistical Yearbook of the Negev Bedouin*, p. 74.
[408] Ibid.
[409] Ministry of Justice, *Initial Periodic Report*, pp. 312-13.

Shaqib Al-Salaam/Segev Shalom
   The Minister of Education in July 1999 added the recognized locality of Shaqib Al-Salaam/Segev Shalom to the list of towns slated for free preschool. In October 1999, the municipality opened four classes–each a single room–for about two hundred children, about half of those eligible. The local government closed the schools on November 3, 1999, on the grounds that they were unsafe. The schools lacked fencing, playground facilities, and games, and some lacked basic furnishings such as tables and chairs. [410] The classes, averaging fifty students each, were also severely overcrowded. When the local government failed to repair and reopen the facilities, Adalah, on behalf of the local parents' committee, petitioned the Israeli High Court of Justice to compel the local government and the Minister of Education to establish kindergartens for all four hundred Bedouin children in the locality. Following the issuance of an *order nisi* by the Court, which required the government to respond to the petition, the respondents re-opened kindergartens for two hundred children.[411] It should be noted that at the time, the local government of Shaqib Al-Salaam/Segev Shalom was not elected; rather the national government had appointed non-Bedouins from outside of the community to a governing council.

---

[410] Aliza Arbeli, "Bedouin Parents Protest Preschool Closure," *Ha'aretz Daily Newspaper (English Edition)* (Israel), November 4, 1999.
[411] *Parents Committee in Segev Shalom, et. al. v. The Government-Appointed Council in Segev Shalom, et. al.,* H.C. 8534/99 (2000). See also, Arbeli, "Bedouin Parents Protest Preschool Closure"; and Moshe Reinfeld, "High Court Petition Claims 400 Bedouin

XI. SPECIAL EDUCATION

One of the largest gaps is in the area of special education, where, compared with Jewish children, Palestinian Arab children with mental, sensory, and physical disabilities receive less funding and fewer in-school services, have fewer special schools, and lack appropriate curricula. This is true despite higher rates of disability among Palestinian Arab children.

Under Israel's Special Education Law, the state must provide free special education to "special needs children" from ages three to twenty-one.[412] A special needs child is one with a "physical, mental, emotional, or behavioral developmental impairment" that limits the child's "ability to adjust behaviors."[413] A placement committee appointed by the Ministry of Education decides whether a child is eligible for special education and, if so, what kind:[414] integration in a regular classroom (mainstreaming); placement in a special education classroom within a regular school; or placement in a separate special education school. Placement in regular schools is the preferred option under the law. The Minister of Education has the discretion to regulate class size and the provision of psychological and medical services, extend the regular school day or school year for certain schools, and determine what ancillary services to provide during these extra class hours.[415]

Palestinian Arab children are discriminated against in each of these three options. It is less likely that a Palestinian Arab child will be accommodated in a local school because the Ministry of Education allocates fewer resources per Palestinian Arab child for integration and fewer special education services to help Palestinian Arab children stay in regular schools. The special education classes are also larger in Arab schools than in Jewish schools. The separate Arab special education schools are inferior to the Jewish ones, and only a handful exist. Thus, many Palestinian Arab children face an unsatisfactory choice: to attend regular classes that do not meet their needs, to travel very long distances to attend an Arab special education school, or, if one is available, to attend a Jewish special education school. Faced with these choices, some parents just keep their children at home.

---

[412] Special Education Law, secs. A(1)(a), A(3) (1988). Although the law was passed in 1988, the sections concerning children ages three and four, and over eighteen, and the provision of ancillary services were intended to be implemented gradually, with full implementation by the start of the 1999 school year. Ibid., sec. E(22)(a).

[413] Ibid., sec. A(1)(a).

[414] Ibid., sec. C.

[415] Special Education Law, secs. D(14), (15), (17), (18) (1988).

International law explicitly guarantees the right to education without discrimination for disabled children.[416]

"Special Needs" Children

In the 1999-2000 school year, 35,998 children attended special education classes in separate and regular schools.[417] In addition, about 80,000 children in regular classes received special education services.[418] The Israeli government, in its 2001 submission to the Committee on the Rights of the Child, stated that 18 percent of these children were Palestinian Arab.[419] However, the Committee for Closing the Gap, in the Education Ministry's Pedagogical Secretariat, reported to the ministry's leadership in December 2000 that 30 percent of children *needing* special education were Palestinian Arab.[420]

Palestinian Arab children are diagnosed with "special needs" at a slightly higher rate than Jewish children, 8.5 percent of all children versus 7.6 percent.[421] They also have higher rates of severe disabilities, 5.4 percent of all children versus 3.3 percent.[422] About 7 percent of Negev Bedouin are hearing impaired, compared with 3 percent of the general Israeli population.[423] But these numbers still underestimate the rate of disability among Palestinian Arab children,

---

[416] Convention on the Rights of the Child, arts. 2, 23(3); Declaration on the Rights of Disabled Persons, paras. 2, 6, 10, G.A. Res. 3447 (XXX), 30 U.N. GAOR Supp. (No. 34) at 88, U.N. Doc. A/10034 (December 9, 1975).

[417] Ministry of Education, *Proposed Budget for the Ministry of Education 2001*, p. 158. This number includes students at special education preschools, special education classes within regular schools, and special education schools.

[418] Ministry of Justice, *Initial Periodic Report*, p. 205.

[419] Ibid., p. 311.

[420] Golan, *Closing the Gaps in Arab Education in Israel*, p. 3.

[421] D. Naon, et. al., *Children with Special Needs Stage I and Stage II: An Assessment of Needs and Coverage by Services* (Hebrew), (Jerusalem: JDC-Brookdale Institute, 2000) cited in JDC-Brookdale Institute Disabilities Research Unit, *People With Disabilities in Israel: Facts and Figures*, September 2000, downloaded from the institute's website, http://www.jdc.org.il/brookdale/disability/index.htm (accessed on March 15, 2001). The children with special needs identified in the report "suffer from disabilities or chronic conditions such as deafness, paralysis, retardation, learning disabilities, severe behavioral problems, cancer, or renal failure and need medical or para-medical care on a regular basis." Ibid. It should be noted that the study uses a more detailed definition of special needs than the Special Education Law.

[422] Ministry of Justice, *Initial Periodic Report*, p. 311 (citing Naon, *Children with Special Needs Stage I and Stage II*).

[423] Parents' Committee for Special Education for Arabs in the Negev, Shatil, *Arab Special Education in the Negev* (Hebrew), p. 8.

according to a 2000 study by the JDC-Brookdale Institute, a nonprofit organization that operates as a partnership between the American Jewish Joint Distribution Committee (AJJDC) and the government of Israel:

> The proportion of children with special needs is higher in Arab towns than in Jewish ones–8.3% versus 7.6%. It should be noted that this is an underestimate; it may be assumed that the actual gap is greater. The underestimate is a consequence of the lack of an appropriate system of identification and diagnosis of children with learning disabilities in the Arab sector.[424]

The Israeli government, which cites the JDC-Brookdale study in its 2001 submission to the Committee on the Rights of the Child, blames the under-diagnosis of learning, behavior, and speech disabilities on a lack of awareness among Palestinian Arabs of "the need to identify and diagnose disability" and "a severe lack of diagnostic services in the Arab sector."[425]   By failing to adequately diagnosis disabled Palestinian Arab children, the Ministry of Education denies them appropriate treatment.   In addition, the difference in disability rates among Palestinian Arab and Jewish children increases the proportion of special education resources Palestinian Arab children should receive.

Unequal Distribution of Resources
     Despite higher rates of disability, Palestinian Arab children receive proportionately fewer special education resources than Jewish children. According to official data from the Education Ministry, it allocated only 10.8 percent of the total special education hours to Palestinian Arabs in 1996.[426] By 1999-2000 it had increased their share, but only to 14.1 percent, with 2 percent of the total to Bedouin.[427]

---

[424] Naon, *Children with Special Needs Stage I and Stage II.*
[425] Ministry of Justice, *Initial Periodic Report,* p. 193.
[426] Ministry of Education, *Proposed Budget for the Ministry of Education 2001,* p. 158.
[427] Ibid.

Table 21: Distribution of Teaching Hours for Special Education

	Jewish schools	Arab schools
Weekly special education hours for primary and secondary levels 1999-2000	85.9% (288,662)	14.1% (47,342)
Weekly hours for integration 1998-1999	91.6% (75,819)	8.4% (6,992)

Sources: Ministry of Education, *Proposed Budget for the Ministry of Education 2001 and Explanations as Presented to the Fifteenth Knesset*, no. 11, October 2000, p. 158; and Daphna Golan, Chair, Committee for Closing the Gap, Pedagogical Secretariat, Ministry of Education, *Closing the Gaps in Arab Education in Israel: Data About Hebrew-Arab Education; Recommendations of the Committee for Closing the Gap; Protocol of the Meeting of the Directorship, December 13, 2000*, December 2000, p. 3.

In addition, the Margalit Committee, appointed by the Ministry of Education to review the Special Education Law, concluded in 2000 that not enough funds had been allocated "for developing the grounds and physical structures to respond to [Palestinian Arab] students' needs."[428]

Funding for Integration (Mainstreaming)

Resources for integrating special education students into regular classes–the preferred option under the Special Education Law–are particularly inequitable: only 8.4 percent (6,992 hours) of integration hours in 1998-1999 went to Arab schools.[429] Although there were sixty-one Jewish integration kindergartens, there were none for Palestinian Arab children. [430] The ministry

---

[428] *Report of the Committee to Examine the Implementation of the Special Education Law (1988)* (Hebrew), July 20, 2000, p. 29-30 (translation by Human Rights Watch).

[429] Golan, *Closing the Gaps in Arab Education in Israel*, p. 3. The Ministry of Education's integration services in regular schools include special education teaching; paramedical and therapeutic services; special aids and services for blind, visually impaired, deaf, and hearing impaired students; remedial education; and creative and expressive therapies. See Special Education Department, Ministry of Education, *Points Emphasized in the Introduction to the Director General's Circular 59(c) 1999*, http://www.education.gov.il/special/english6.htm (accessed on April 6, 2001); and Ministry of Justice, *Initial Periodic Report*, p. 205.

[430] Ibid. A kindergarten is considered integrated when eight to ten children with sensory, linguistic, or developmental impairments are placed in the kindergarten by a special education placement committee. Special education teachers work with regular teachers in integrated kindergartens. Preschool Education Division, Pedagogical Administration, Ministry of Education, "Special Needs Populations in the Preschool Education System,"

distributes integration hours to local authorities based on a criteria that takes into account the school's "development index."[431] As explained above, this index discriminates against Arab schools.

Palestinian Arab parents and school officials told Human Rights Watch of trying to get assistance for special needs students in regular classes without success. The mother of an eleven-year-old disabled boy in a regular class told us: "There are forty-three kids in his class. There is no open space. Because of my son's condition he needs calm surroundings, but with forty-three kids he cannot concentrate. Every day because of the lack of help and assistance I come to sit with my son."[432] An English teacher in an Arab high school said that in her school, "the special education students are integrated into the classrooms, and they are illiterate. We lack the money and tools to deal with the problem."[433]

In some cases, integration takes the form of a special teacher who works with students who are integrated into regular classes. Human Rights Watch visited two Jewish primary schools with such special education teachers.[434] None of the Arab schools we visited had this kind of service.

Psychologists and counselors also help children integrate. According to Adalah, "[t]he shortage of psychologists and educational consultants in regular Arab schools also affects the ability of those schools to integrate suitable children with special needs. This problem exists despite the strong current trend to prefer integration over placement in separate special education frameworks."[435]

---

http://www.education.gov.il/preschool/English/special_needs.htm (accessed on April 23, 2001).

[431] "Each local authority is allocated a quota of teaching hours [for services for children with disabilities who attend regular schools] based on the number of students in its jurisdiction, the school's 'development index', and the percentage of students with slight disabilities who are referred to placement committee in an effort to encourage their mainstreaming." Ministry of Justice, *Initial Periodic Report,* p. 206.

[432] Human Rights Watch interview, village in the Triangle region, December 6, 2000.

[433] Human Rights Watch interview, mixed city, December 10, 2000.

[434] The No Fim Primary School had one special education teacher. Human Rights Watch interview with special education teacher, Haifa, December 12, 2000. The Ksulot primary school had two special education teachers. Human Rights Watch interview with Osnat Mordechai, principal, Ksulot Primary School, Nazareth Ilit, December 13, 2000.

[435] Cohen, attorney for Adalah, letter to Professor Malka Margalit, Chair, Public Commission to Examine Implementation of the Special Education Law (1988), paras. 20-21.

The discriminatory allocation of integration hours was the subject of a lawsuit in August 2000, which caused the Ministry of Education to promise to equalize the hours over a four to five year period.[436]

In-School Services

Part of the state's legal obligation to provide special education includes a duty to provide "physiotherapy, speech therapy, occupational therapy, and other areas of professional treatment, as well as ancillary services, as required in order to meet the child's special needs."[437] Palestinian Arab children receive fewer of these services, according to both the JDC-Brookdale Institute[438] and the Israeli government, which reported to the Committee on the Rights of the Child in 2001: "A significant proportion of disabled Arab children do not receive the pedagogical, psychological, and paramedical services, or the hours of instruction, for which they are eligible."[439] The Margalit Committee, appointed by the Ministry of Education to review the implementation of the Special Education Law, also concluded in 2000 that, "the Arab education system is discriminated against in an insufficiency of professional personnel and outdated equipment."[440]

The Israeli government blames the gap in services in part on a lack of awareness among Palestinian Arabs "of the importance of education for the disabled child."[441] However, parents, teachers, and principals reported to Human Rights Watch that their requests to the ministry for special education services were often unheeded.

We interviewed the parents and teachers of Ali M., a Palestinian Arab boy suffering from *xeroderma pigmentosum*, a rare genetic defect in DNA repair

---

[436] Human Rights Watch telephone interview with Yousef Taiseer Jabareen, former attorney for the petitioners, Washington, D.C., July 17, 2001.

[437] Special Education Law, sec. A(1)(a) (1988). Ancillary services include "transportation, meals, auxiliary aides, medical, paramedical, psychological, and social services, and any other services ordered by the Minister." Ibid.

[438] "Services in many areas are lacking in the Arab sector, including diagnosis of learning disabilities in Arabic, educational counseling, para-medical services, and psycho-social services, etc." JDC-Brookdale Institute Disabilities Research Unit, *People With Disabilities in Israel* (citing Naon, *Children with Special Needs Stage I and Stage II*; and M. Margalit, *Report of the Commission to Maximize the Ability of Students with Learning Disabilities, Presented to the Minister of Education and Culture and the Minister of Science* (Hebrew) (1997)).

[439] Ministry of Justice, *Initial Periodic Report*, p. 311.

[440] *Report of the Committee to Examine the Implementation of the Special Education Law (1988)* (Hebrew), p. 29-30 (translation by Human Rights Watch).

[441] Ministry of Justice, *Initial Periodic Report*, p. 310.

causing severe sensitivity to ultraviolet radiation, especially to sunlight. Patients are highly susceptible to skin and eye cancer, and must therefore avoid any exposure to the sun. Ali M. was small and covered with dense freckles. The whites of his eyes were red, and his skin was scaly and flaking. His father told us:

> My son is not allowed to be in the sun. He needs constant care and has to stay inside. He needs special services. In his classes there are no curtains, and the sun comes in and hits him. The government doesn't supply the needed tools. We have been asking for special support for many years. Usually we go to the Ministry of Education, and they tell us to go to the local municipality, and we go and are denied.[442]

The boy attends a regular school but does receive special transportation, albeit somewhat erratic, because he cannot walk in the sun. The school principal told us that he had been asking the Ministry of Education for "special tools and care" without success for the past three years.[443]

According to the school's special education teacher, it is difficult for her to get extra help for any of her students who need it. About Sami G., another physically disabled child, she stated, "[f]or four years we have been asking for someone to attend to him–to help him go to the toilet, to go outside–and we can't get anyone to help."

In particular, Arab special education schools lack speech therapists. The nongovernmental Arab Association for Human Rights (HRA) reported in 2000 that of 1,185 speech therapists in Israel, only twenty-one were Palestinian Arab.[444] This shortage results in some Palestinian Arab children being treated by speech therapists who do not speak Arabic. For example, it was reported in July 2000 that at the Niv school for the deaf in Be'er Sheva, where more than half of the children are Bedouin, speech therapy was conducted in Hebrew by a therapist who did not speak Arabic.[445]

---

[442] Human Rights Watch interview, village in the Triangle region. December 6, 2000.

[443] Human Rights Watch interview, village in the Triangle region. December 6, 2000.

[444] Arab Association of Human Rights (HRA). "The Dynamics of Arab Special Education in Israel." *Discrimination Diary*. August 28. 2000. http://www.arabhra.org /dd2808.html (accessed on September 6, 2000). See also Tamar Rotem, "Special Education for Arab Children is Only Available in Hebrew," *Ha'aretz Daily Newspaper (English Edition)* (Israel), July 16, 2000 (describing a lack of Palestinian Arab speech therapists).

[445] Rotem, "Special Education for Arab Children is Only Available in Hebrew."

The shortage also causes Arabic-speaking therapists to be responsible for more children than they can reasonably treat. Human Rights Watch visited an Arab special education school with approximately seventy children who were deaf or hearing impaired. The school had two part-time speech therapists who, between the two of them, worked five days a week. This was not enough time to provide speech therapy for every child, one speech therapist told us. "Other kids need it and you feel bad," she said.[446] A municipal employee explained that it was difficult to find speech therapists because only one school in Israel teaches speech therapy, only a few Palestinian Arabs attend each year, and graduates could earn more money in private clinics than working for the school system.[447]

In addition, speech therapists may not be appropriately trained to treat Arabic-speaking students. In a March 22, 2000 letter to the Margalit Committee, an attorney for Adalah wrote:

> the few Arab students who study in these fields [paramedical fields including communication therapy, occupational therapy, physiotherapy, and art therapy] at the universities are not trained to handle the special needs of Arab children. For example, the curricula in the study of communication disorders do not relate to treating disorders of pronunciation of consonants that do not exist in Hebrew.[448]

Human Rights Watch interviewed a Palestinian Arab speech therapist with a B.A. in Arabic and special education, and a master's degree in reading disabilities from Israeli universities. All of her university training, except for her reading disabilities exam, was in Hebrew. Applying her training for Arabic-speakers has been difficult for this reason, she told us.[449]

In addition to needing more trained professionals, some schools lack proper equipment. "We need audiological rooms and audiological meters for the deaf children, and we don't have them," a speech therapist told us.[450] A teacher for blind and low vision children elaborated: "Jewish schools are modern and have good equipment. We suffer from a lack of equipment. When we compare ourselves with Jewish schools, we find a drastic lack of equipment.

---

[446] Human Rights Watch interview, Israel, December 11, 2000.

[447] Human Rights Watch interview, Israel, December 11, 2000.

[448] Cohen, attorney for Adalah, letter to Professor Malka Margalit, Chair, Public Commission to Examine Implementation of the Special Education Law, para. 17.

[449] Human Rights Watch interview, Israel, December 11, 2000.

[450] Human Rights Watch interview, Israel, December 11, 2000.

All we have is a machine for printing Braille. Computers for the blind are very expensive. But we can't make a lot of progress today without computers."[451] A special education teacher at a regular Arab primary school told us she lacked sufficient instruments and tools, and that she had received nothing new from the Education Ministry for two years. "The government says there is money but we haven't seen anything yet."[452]

Palestinian Arab children with special needs also receive proportionately fewer services from government bodies outside of the Ministry of Education.[453] According to the JDC-Brookdale Institute: "In the case of most [in-kind] services, the percentage of children with special needs receiving services in Jewish areas is much higher (in most cases double or even triple) than the percentage of children living in Arab areas."[454] A lack of services outside of school makes the work of special education schools even more difficult. A principal at an Arab special education school noted, "[w]e know that it is not enough in school. Not many children have funds for therapy."[455]

Fewer Schools/Larger Classes

Proportionately, there are fewer special education schools for Palestinian Arab children than for Jewish children. In 1998-1999, only 8.5 percent of special education kindergartens and only 16.5 percent of other special education schools were Arab schools.

---

[451] Human Rights Watch interview, Israel, December 11, 2000.

[452] Human Rights Watch interview, village in the Triangle region, December 6, 2000.

[453] Ministry of Justice, *Initial Periodic Report*, pp. 194-96, 199. However, a higher proportion of Palestinian children than Jewish children received National Insurance Institute disability benefits in accordance with the greater rate of severe disabilities among Palestinian children. Ibid.

[454] JDC-Brookdale Institute, *First Results of Study on Children with Special Needs in Israel: 160,000 Children and Youth Suffer from Functional Problems or Chronic Disease Requiring Ongoing Medical Care*, December 23, 1999 (citing Naon, *Children with Special Needs Stage I and Stage II*), http://www.jdc.org.il/brookdale/special.htm, (accessed on November 8, 2000)).

[455] Human Rights Watch interviews, Israel, December 11, 2000.

Table 22: Special Education Institutions 1998-1999

	Jewish schools	Arab schools
Special education kindergartens	484 (91.5%)	45 (8.5%)
Integrated kindergartens	61 (100%)	0 (0%)
Special education schools (excluding kindergartens)	222 (83.5%)	44 (16.5%)
Students in primary schools for "handicapped children" 1999-2000	13,165 (85.4%)	2,253 (14.6%)

Sources: Daphna Golan, Chair, Committee for Closing the Gap, Pedagogical Secretariat, Ministry of Education, *Closing the Gaps in Arab Education in Israel: Data About Hebrew-Arab Education; Recommendations of the Committee for Closing the Gap; Protocol of the Meeting of the Directorship, December 13, 2000*, December 2000, p. 3; and CBS, *Statistical Abstract of Israel 2000*, no. 51, table 22.10.

On February 26, 2001, the Israeli High Court of Justice issued a order giving the government two months to reply to charges that there is a severe shortage of special education classes in the Arab sector.[456] The case, which was pending at the time of writing, was the most recent of several cases filed at the beginning of a school year when there have not been enough classes for disabled Palestinian Arab children. For example, in response to a previous petition and resulting court order, the Education Ministry had stated that it would provide funds to open fifty additional classrooms for Palestinian Arab children with emotional or learning disabilities.[457] However, the ministry has not changed its procedures to ensure that each year there are enough Arab special education classes.[458]

---

[456] Dan Isenberg, "Government Ordered to Explain Lack of Special Ed Classes in Arab Sector," *Jerusalem Post*, February 26, 2001, p. 5. The petition was submitted on behalf of six Palestinian Arab children aged nine to fourteen whom the Education Ministry's placement committees found to be eligible for special education under the Special Education Law. Some of the children were placed in regular classes and others in special education frameworks that did not meet their needs.   According to news reports, "[b]efore the petition was submitted, the Education Ministry claimed it didn't have a budget for the special classes in the Arab sector. In response to the petition, however, it argued that it did not have trained manpower to teach the disadvantaged children." Ibid.

[457] Moshe Reinfeld, "Education Ministry to Budget NIS 50 Million for Arab Special-Ed," *Ha'aretz Daily Newspaper (English Edition)* (Israel), November 9, 1999.

[458] Human Rights Watch telephone interview with Yousef Taiseer Jabareen, formerly an attorney for the Association for Civil Rights in Israel (ACRI), Washington, D.C., July 17, 2001.

Because there are so few classes or special schools in the Arab system, students often must travel long distances to reach an appropriate school. At one Arab school for physically handicapped children that we visited, students came from approximately forty villages, some as far as seventy kilometers away, traveling an hour and a half each way. With the school day lasting from 8:00 a.m. to 3:00 p.m., some children were away from home for as long as eleven hours a day, the principal explained.[459] Under the Special Education Law, a special needs child is entitled to education at "a special education school near his home," or, if there is no school nearby, then "as near to his home as possible."[460] State and local authorities bear joint responsibility for maintaining special schools, and the Ministry of Education has the power to order local authorities to open such schools.[461]

In addition, Arab special education classes are, on average, larger than Jewish ones,[462] and children with a wide range of abilities are often placed in the same class. Human Rights Watch interviewed a special education teacher in a regular Arab school who, with the help of an assistant, taught twelve primary students whose disabilities included "hearing, seeing, mental problems, hyperactivity, serious disabilities, and dyslexia." She told us that:

> The fact that each one has a different level makes it hard to teach, so everyone has to go at the same pace. There are a few students that are just slow, but because they are with the disabled children they have to go even slower and they cannot develop. If we had another class and more space, we could separate them into six and six.

However, she said, there is simply no more space in the school for another class.[463] Human Rights Watch interviewed another Palestinian Arab special education teacher who taught one class of twelve students in four different grades, ranging from kindergarten to the sixth grade. She is supported by a psychologist who comes one day a week; there is no school social worker or counselor.[464] We also visited an Arab school for mentally disabled children

---

[459] Human Rights Watch interview, Israel, December 11, 2000.

[460] Special Education Law, sec. A(3) (1988).

[461] Ibid.

[462] "Despite the increase in Arab children attending special education frameworks and the increase in special education classrooms, special education classes are still more crowded in the Arab than in the Jewish sector." Ministry of Justice, *Initial Periodic Report*, p. 311.

[463] Human Rights Watch interview, village in the Triangle region, December 6, 2000.

[464] Human Rights Watch interview, Um El-Fahm, December 6, 2000.

where the average class had fourteen students,[465] and an Arab elementary school in Haifa with two rooms for forty disabled children.[466] The Ministry of Education's regulations cap special education classrooms in regular schools at eight to fourteen students, depending on students' disabilities.[467]

The government's 2001 submission to the Committee on the Rights of the Child confirms that, "many special education schools in the Arab sector do not meet the minimum level or conditions required of an educational institution. Consequently, special education is 'uniform', and children with differing needs are placed in the same class and receive the same care."[468] The Special Education Law requires that each special needs student have an individualized education plan based on the child's particular needs.[469]

Moreover, some disabled Palestinian Arab children simply receive no special education at all. For example, a speech therapist and the principal of an Arab school for physically disabled children told us that there are no high schools for Palestinian Arab deaf students who are unable to integrate into regular classrooms.[470] Israel reported to the Committee on the Rights of the Child in 2001 that, "the lack of special education institutions in the Arab sector often means that placement committees' decisions cannot be implemented. Children who have been diagnosed as needing special education do not necessarily receive it."[471] Tel Aviv University senior lecturer Andre Elias Mazawi, who was a member of the Margalit Committee appointed by the Education Ministry in 1998 to review the Special Education Law's implementation, told Human Rights Watch that during its investigations the committee found a placement committee that had stopped screening children for special education because there was no place to send them. The children were being stigmatized by the placement committee's label of "disabled," but they were getting no benefit.[472] Similarly, a report on special education in the Negev by the nongovernmental organization Shatil found:

---

[465] Human Rights Watch interview with school principal, Israel, December 11, 2000.
[466] Human Rights Watch interview with school director, Haifa, December 4, 2000.
[467] Special Education Department, Ministry of Education, *Regulations on the Composition of Special Education Classes,* http://www.education.gov.il/special/types_of.htm (accessed on April 6, 2001), para. 2.
[468] Ministry of Justice, *Initial Periodic Report,* p. 311.
[469] Special Education Law, sec. D(19) (1988).
[470] Human Rights Watch interviews, Israel, December 11, 2000.
[471] Ministry of Justice, *Initial Periodic Report,* p. 311.
[472] Human Rights Watch interview with Andre Elias Mazawi, senior lecturer and head of the Sociology of Education Program, School of Education, Tel Aviv University, Tel Aviv, November 30, 2000.

at the beginning of the year 2000, approximately 250 students were referred to preliminary classes. And yet, no existing classrooms could receive them. The school system was advised to open new classrooms in a short span of time and was hard-pressed to provide proper teaching hours and transportation . . . . This year, twenty Negev students were diagnosed with hearing disabilities, but a proper arrangement could not be made, and in the end they were either sent for integration into normal schools or left at home with a lack of proper arrangements. [473]

Palestinian Arab teachers and administrators confirmed that children are being turned away from special education for lack of space. The special education teacher at an Arab primary school, who with an assistant teaches twelve children, told us: "We cannot accept more than twelve because we lack the instruments, the tools. Many children need to be in the class, but I cannot have more than twelve. Each kid needs special and private help, and it's just me alone. I cannot help all these kids." [474]

At one Arab school for mentally disabled children, the principal told Human Rights Watch that although enrollment was officially restricted to eighty students, one hundred students were enrolled, and she had another forty-five to fifty students on her waiting list. "Every day I get phone calls from parents, especially parents in the villages, wanting to get their children in," she said. "I have to turn them away." [475] Also, the school cannot accept any children with physical disabilities that prevent them from navigating the steep stairways leading to the classrooms and the toilets. [476] Indeed, the school appeared cramped when Human Rights Watch visited. The one hundred students were divided among ten long, narrow classrooms that seemed to have once been five full-size rooms. Half of the classrooms were windowless. One class of about ten children had arranged their chairs in a tight circle–the room was so narrow that the circle spanned the width of the room. Teachers provided individual therapy in whatever leftover space they could find. When Human Rights Watch visited, every room, including the teachers' room, the kitchen, and the principal's office, was being used for teaching. The teachers' room was too small to seat all twenty-four teachers for a faculty meeting; when they met, some

---

[473] Parents' Committee for Special Education for Arabs in the Negev, Shatil, *Arab Special Education in the Negev* (Hebrew), pp. 6, 8 (translation by Human Rights Watch).
[474] Human Rights Watch interview, village in the Triangle region, December 6, 2000.
[475] Human Rights Watch interview, Israel, December 11, 2000.
[476] Ibid.

had to stand.[477] Other than the roof, there was no recreational space, not even a parking lot as we saw being used at other schools. The roof was surrounded by a high fence and partially shaded by a long sheet of corrugated metal. When it was raining or too hot for the children to play on the roof, the principal told us, the children play in the school's single hallway, which was about two meters wide.

Similarly, when Human Rights Watch visited an Arab school for physically disabled children, the principal told us that the school was at maximum capacity. Usually students could be worked in, she said, although they often had to wait a year. The school had no room for a library; two days a week a social worker used the principal's office because there was no other space.[478]

In contrast, Human Rights Watch visited a regular Jewish middle school in Nazareth Ilit, a development town near Nazareth, that had a special room for art therapy. The room was sunny, well-stocked with paints, paper, and other supplies, and larger than the classrooms at the school for mentally disabled Palestinian Arab children.

Negev Bedouin

The shortage of classes is particularly acute for Bedouin in the Negev. In 1998-1999, only 446 (1.4 percent) of the 32,501 Bedouin students in grades one through twelve in the Negev were in special education classes,[479] compared with national averages in 1997 of 3 percent of Jewish children and 2 percent of Palestinian Arabs.[480]

There are two schools in the Negev for Bedouin with disabilities such as mental retardation, autism, and emotional or behavioral disorders: one in Kseife and one in Rahat. The nongovernmental organization Shatil, in a 2000 study, concluded that both of these schools were inadequate.[481] Shatil first found that that the physical buildings did not comply with the Ministry of Education's regulations:

> Each school's classrooms are housed in old buildings, many of them built in the 1970s. Today these structures do not meet their

---

[477] Human Rights Watch interview with teacher, Israel, December 11, 2000.

[478] Human Rights Watch interview with principal, Israel, December 11, 2000.

[479] Center for Bedouin Studies and Development, *Statistical Yearbook of the Negev Bedouin*, p. 75.

[480] Ministry of Justice, *Initial Periodic Report*, p. 206.

[481] Parents' Committee for Special Education for Arabs in the Negev, Shatil, *Arab Special Education in the Negev* (Hebrew), p. 9.

objectives, and their physical status is worse yet. At the Kseife school, structures are built with asbestos, a carcinogenic material whose use is prohibited for security reasons by the Director-General under recommendation from the Ministry of Health. . . . At both schools there are no specified rooms for private treatment like physiotherapy, although many of the students need such therapy. . . . There is no climate control in most of the classrooms in these schools (except a few classrooms at the Kseife school). . . . In some of the classrooms, the number of students exceeds regulations.[482]

Second, Shatil found that the social services provided in school failed to fulfill the students' needs:

Lack of individual treatment: . . . For example, last year at the Kseife school there was no physiotherapist for two months. In several of the other months, only one worker served in this position although two are needed. . . . Lack of complete education: . . . Playgrounds, or an area fit for recreation, which are important means for developing the social abilities of the students. . . . Disparities in service: Some of the children cannot enjoy a long day of education and depend on being transported outside the village, and therefore leave school at 2:30 p.m.; as is the case with children from the unrecognized villages."[483]

Jewish Special Education Schools
Where Arab special education schools do not exist or are of poor quality, some Palestinian Arab parents send their children to Jewish special education schools, if there is one nearby. However, these schools are designed for Jewish children, from the curricula and holiday schedule to the language of instruction, Hebrew. Orna Cohen, an attorney for Adalah, explained to a journalist: "The problem is especially serious for children whose ability to acquire language is limited. This situation, where children are not taught in Arabic, prevents them from deriving full benefit from the education given to them and undermines their ability to acquire language and integrate into their own society."[484]

---

[482] Ibid. (English translation by Human Rights Watch).
[483] Ibid.
[484] Quoted in Rotem, "Special Education for Arab Children is Only Available in Hebrew."

Ofakim School, Haifa[485]

The Ofakim school in Haifa is considered one of the best schools in Israel for children with cerebral palsy and muscular dystrophy. About 40 percent of the students are Palestinian Arab. Despite this, teaching is conducted in Hebrew; Palestinian Arab children study Arabic only one hour a week, and as of December 2000, there was only one Palestinian Arab teacher.[486] Palestinian Arab holidays and customs are not observed. Although Haifa's population is about 8.4 percent Palestinian Arab,[487] there is no Arab special education school, apart from one day-care center for learning disabled toddlers.

The mother of a student at the school, a sixteen-year-old boy with cerebral palsy, told us that her son "has to go to Jewish school because there is no Arab school." Her son has faced a significant language barrier there:

> For many years the school dealt with him as if he was suffering from deep mental retardation, but we saw him communicate and progress at home. He has to deal with two languages. No one talked to him there, so the family had to pay someone to go with him and translate. We send someone every day with him and we pay [the person] NIS 2,500 ($625). This person doesn't go on Sunday, so he stays at home that day. He doesn't like to go alone. What happens if he wants to go to the bathroom?[488]

---

[485] Except where otherwise indicated, information about the school is from: Rotem, "Special Education for Arab Children is Only Available in Hebrew"; and Human Rights Watch interview with a parent, Haifa, December 6, 2000.

[486] According to the parent of a student at the school, the principal agreed to have a second Palestinian teacher come several times a week for three hours but this had not yet begun. Human Rights Watch interview, Haifa, December 6, 2000.

[487] Strategic Planning Research Unit, Haifa Municipality, *Haifa's Population by Religion and Age Gge [sic] Groups—1999—percent,* http://www.Haifa.gov.il/Muni/spr/PressRpro/dataEng/36.shtml (accessed on June 1, 2001).

[488] Human Rights Watch interview, Haifa, December 6, 2000.

Niv School for the Deaf, Be'er Sheva

Most of the students at the Niv school for the deaf in Be'er Sheva are Bedouin.[489]   However, according to news reports, instruction, including speech therapy, is in Hebrew.[490] Sa'id Nassara, a parent with three children at the school, testified before the Knesset Education Committee:

> None of the children know Arabic; they don't know anything about the Muslim holidays. The most astonishing thing is that the school cannot accept the fact that the children do not eat during Ramadan or that the parents want them let out early because of a holiday. I cannot accept that my children do not learn about their own customs, yet they know what Sukkot is. I talk to them about 'Id al-Adha and all they know about is Hanukkah. In Be'er Sheva there are a lot of Bedouin and we have our own customs. They cannot simply ignore us.[491]

According to a report by Shatil, the school also lacks an electrical system sufficient to install air conditioning and heating, and adequate equipment for hearing impairments (including "linoleum floor tiling, acoustic ceiling, and hearing equipment"). In addition, the furniture is "old and not maintained. Moreover, the school lacked games, and only through pressure from the Negev Parents Committee for Special Education were proper games purchased for the children." The report also states that some classes are larger than Ministry of Education regulations permit.[492]

---

[489] Shatil reports that 110 out of 118 students are Bedouin. Parents' Committee for Special Education for Arabs in the Negev, Shatil, *Arab Special Education in the Negev* (Hebrew), p. 8. Other reports state that 60 percent of the students are Bedouin. Rotem, "Special Education for Arab Children is Only Available in Hebrew."

[490] Rotem, "Special Education for Arab Children is Only Available in Hebrew."

[491] Quoted in Rotem, "Special Education for Arab Children is Only Available in Hebrew."

[492] Parents' Committee for Special Education for Arabs in the Negev, Shatil, *Arab Special Education in the Negev* (Hebrew), p. 8 (English translation by Human Rights Watch).

Curricula

Israel, in its 2001 submission to the Committee on the Rights of the Child, states that under the Special Education Law "[i]t is assumed that [special needs children] have special educational needs; that meeting these needs requires special teaching materials and methods; and that without these, the children will not enjoy equal developmental opportunities."[493] However, as documented below in the chapter on curricula, Human Rights Watch found that Arab special education schools lacked special curricula and teaching materials from the Ministry of Education. Khawla Saadi, Director of Curriculum for Arab Israeli Schools, told us that her department had just developed primary level special education books in Arabic in 2000.[494] These had not been distributed to any of the special education schools Human Rights Watch visited.

"In the Education Ministry, they think about the Jewish child," the principal of an Arab school for disabled children told us:

Lots of things are not suitable for our children. Some things are not even suitable for all Jewish children, only for the very strong sector. Sometimes the rules don't fit. For example, hours. The Long Day is O.K., but our pupils have to travel, which makes for a *very* long day, but it's the law. Many don't get home until 5:00 p.m. And the main subjects in school–last year Zionism was to be the main theme for school. They forget that even if I wanted to teach it, for our kids it is very hard.[495]

---

[493] Ministry of Justice, *Initial Periodic Report,* pp. 201-02.

[494] Human Rights Watch interview with Khawla Saadi, Director of Curriculum for Israeli Arab Schools, Ministry of Education, Jerusalem, December 20, 2000.

[495] Human Rights Watch interview, Israel, December 11, 2000.

XII. CURRICULA

Israeli and International Law

The aim of the state educational system, according to Israel's State Education Law is:

> to base elementary education in the state on the values of Jewish culture and the achievements of science, on love of the homeland and loyalty to the state and the Jewish people, on practice in agricultural work and handicraft, and *chalutzik* [pioneer] training, and on striving for a society built on freedom, equality, tolerance, mutual assistance and love of mankind.[496]

The State Education Law also provides that "in non-Jewish educational institutions, the curriculum shall be adopted to the special conditions thereof."[497]

The Arab education system, however, has been widely criticized by Palestinian Arabs as failing to adequately consider the Palestinian identity of Arabs in Israel. Although some changes have been made recently in the curriculum, the overarching aims of education remain based on the transmission of Jewish values and culture, and Zionist thought. This type of education may be appropriate for Jewish children, but it is inappropriate for children belonging to the Palestinian Arab minority within Israel, who comprise over 20 percent of children in Israeli schools. Article 29(1) of the Convention on the Rights of the Child focuses on the aims of children's education:

> (a) the development of the child's personality, talents and mental and physical abilities to their fullest potential;

> (b) the development of respect for human rights and fundamental freedoms, and for the principles enshrined in the Charter of the United Nations;

> (c) the development of respect for the child's parents, his or her own cultural identity, language and values, for the national values of the country in which the child is living, the country from which he or she may originate, and for civilizations different from his or her own;

---

[496] State Education Law, art. 2 (1953).
[497] Ibid., art. 4.

143

(d) the preparation of the child for responsible life in a free
society, in the spirit of understanding, peace, tolerance, equality of
the sexes, and friendship among all peoples, ethnic national and
religious groups and persons of indigenous origin; and

(e) the development of respect for the natural environment.[498]

The convention does not attempt to prescribe the specific content of
education but makes clear that the development of respect for the child's cultural
identity shall be one of the purposes of education. While the diverse aims of
article 29 at times may appear to be in conflict with one another, the U.N.
Committee on the Rights of the Child has stated that "the importance of this
provision lies precisely in its recognition of the need for a balanced approach to
education and one which succeeds in reconciling diverse values through
dialogue and respect for difference."[499] Thus while instruction on the state's
national values shall be a part of education, state authorities should make special
effort to harmonize this with lessons on the child's own cultural identity,
language, and values, even where perceived to be in conflict. Pursuit of one aim
shall not trump another, but rather all aims must be considered together in the
best interests of the child.

The Committee on the Rights of the Child has commented that article
29(1) emphasizes the child's "individual and subjective right to a specific quality
of education" that is "child-centered," and where "the curriculum must be of
direct relevance to the child's social, cultural, environmental, and economic
context. . . ."[500] The U.N. Committee on Economic, Social and Cultural Rights
has similarly stated that "the form and substance of education, including
curricula and teaching methods, have to be acceptable (e.g. relevant, culturally

---

[498] Article 29(1) builds upon the aims of education as articulated in Article 13(1) of the
International Covenant of Economic, Social and Cultural Rights:

[States parties] agree that education shall be directed to the full development
of the human personality and the sense of its dignity, and shall strengthen the
respect for human rights and fundamental freedoms. They further agree that
education shall enable all persons to participate effectively in a free society,
promote understanding, tolerance and friendship among all nations and all
racial, ethnic or religious groups, and further the activities of the United
Nations for the maintenance of peace.

[499] *General Comment 1, The Aims of Education (Article 29(1))*. Committee on the Rights
of the Child. U.N. Doc. CRC/GC/2001/1 (April 17, 2001), para. 4.

[500] Ibid., para. 9.

appropriate and of good quality) to students . . . ."[501]   Curricula must be culturally relevant for children in order for them to receive the full benefits of education.

Children belonging to ethnic, religious, or linguistic minorities, or of indigenous origin, are entitled to further special consideration and protection, taking into account their unique group identities. The Committee on Economic, Social and Cultural Rights, interpreting article 13 of the ICESCR on the right to education, has declared that states must "fulfil (facilitate) the acceptability of education by taking positive measures to ensure that education is culturally appropriate for minorities and indigenous peoples. . . ."[502]   Article 30 of the Convention on the Rights of the Child provides further general protection to children belonging to ethnic, religious, or linguistic minorities, or who are indigenous; such a child "shall not be denied the right, in community with other members of his or her group, to enjoy his or her own culture, to profess and practice his or her own religion, or to use his or her own language."[503]

Finally, regarding the content of education, religious instruction is singled out for special consideration in international law. Interpreting article 13(3) of the ICESCR, on the right of parents to ensure the religious and moral education of their children, the Committee on Economic, Social and Cultural Rights has stated that the ICESCR

> permits public school instruction in subjects such as the general history of religions and ethics if it is given in an unbiased and objective way, respectful of the freedoms of opinion, conscience and expression. . . . [P]ublic education that includes instruction in a particular religion or belief is inconsistent with article 13(3) unless

---

[501] *General Comment 13, The Right to Education*, Committee on Economic, Social and Cultural Rights, para. 6(c).

[502] Ibid., para. 50.

[503] Convention on the Rights of the Child, art. 30. In addition, the U.N. Declaration on the Rights of Persons Belonging to National or Ethnic, Religious or Linguistic Minorities, which is not binding but which provides authoritative guidance to states, declares that: "States should, where appropriate, take measures in the field of education, in order to encourage knowledge of the history, traditions, language and culture of the minorities existing within their territory." Declaration on the Rights of Persons Belonging to National or Ethnic, Religious or Linguistic Minorities, art. 4(4), *adopted* December 18, 1992, G.A. Res. 47/135.

provision is made for non-discriminatory exemptions or alternatives that would accommodate the wishes of parents and guardians.[504]

Similarly, under the Convention against Discrimination in Education, "no person or group of persons should be compelled to receive religious instruction inconsistent with his or their conviction."[505]

Curricula in Arab Schools
Curriculum Development and Palestinian Arab Participation
Subjects in Arab schools can be divided into three categories: 1) subjects such as math and science that are the same for students in Arab and Jewish schools, where the curriculum is translated from Hebrew into Arabic; 2) subjects such as civics that are taken from those developed for Jewish schools and adapted for use in Arab schools; and 3) subjects unique to Arab education such as Hebrew as a second language and Arabic as mother tongue that are developed solely for use in Arab schools. For each subject a "curriculum" or syllabus is developed and published by the Ministry of Education as a guide for teachers in all schools throughout the country.

Curricula for the various subjects are developed by the Curriculum Department within the Pedagogical Administration of the Ministry of Education. Khawla Saadi currently holds the position of Director of Curriculum for Arab Israeli Schools, within the Curriculum Department. According to Saadi, she works with a team of twenty people who fill the equivalent of five full-time positions (within a department with sixty full-time positions) to oversee and develop the curricula for all subjects from kindergarten through grade twelve in Arab schools.[506] In practice, committees of educators and experts are formed to develop the curricula for a particular subject for particular grade levels. For subjects unique to Arab schools and subjects that must be adapted for use in Arab schools, Palestinian Arab educators and experts, along with Jewish educators, develop the curricula. However, Palestinian Arabs' opportunity to participate in the committees that develop the common subjects is limited, further fueling students' feelings of alienation from their education's content.

Senior lecturer Andre Elias Mazawi, head of the Sociology of Education Program at Tel Aviv University, commented on the importance of considering Palestinian Arab identity in all subjects, not only the special subjects: "There

---

[504] *General Comment 13, The Right to Education,* Committee on Economic, Social and Cultural Rights, para. 28.
[505] Convention against Discrimination in Education, art. 5(1)(b).
[506] Human Rights Watch interview with Khawla Saadi, Director of Curriculum for Israeli Arab Schools, Ministry of Education, Jerusalem, December 20, 2000.

are questions of culture in all subjects. All subjects need to take into account the background of the students. Most curricula are just translated into Arabic and not specially adapted. Even in less value-laden subjects, there is bias."[507] This bias is reflected, for example, in the use of Hebrew names and Jewish references as examples in textbooks, in which Arabs appear to be nonexistent or are portrayed in stereotype. "Books still present us as working in the fields," remarked a high school Hebrew teacher in Nazareth.[508] Nabila Espanioly, director of the Al-Tufula Pedagogical Center in Nazareth, showed Human Rights Watch an example given in a kindergarten textbook of "traditional work": four photographs depicting a Jewish scribe writing, an Arab cutting stone, an Arab making ceramics, and an Arab cleaning shoes.[509]

Some Palestinian Arab teachers attempt to adapt the published curricula to make them more sensitive to their cultural identity, values and needs, and bring in outside teaching materials and lessons that they develop on their own to address issues of Palestinian identity. For example a sixth grade geography teacher explained how he independently adapts the curricula for his students: "There are many paragraphs related to the geography of the Jewish people and Israel, and I add that Palestine has a relation."[510] However, teachers do this at a price, as they are still responsible for covering the material in the syllabus and may risk censure and punishment if found out: "I tried to introduce other texts but I didn't try to ask for permission. I took the risk that I would get fired. It makes more work for the kids because we have to do the basic texts anyway," said one Hebrew language teacher in an Arab high school.[511] Another teacher in a primary school in an unrecognized village similarly stated, "[I]t makes it difficult to teach because [the curriculum] is not adapted to the Arab students, only the Jewish student's way of life, thinking. If we try to adapt the curriculum to the Arab students, we'll have bad results [on exams]."[512]

---

[507] Human Rights Watch interview with Andre Elias Mazawi, senior lecturer and head of the Sociology of Education Program, School of Education, Tel Aviv University, Tel Aviv, November 30, 2000.
[508] Human Rights Watch interview with high school Hebrew teacher, Nazareth, December 8, 2000.
[509] Human Rights Watch interview with Nabila Espanioly, Director, Al-Tufula Pedagogical Center, Nazareth, December 8, 2000.
[510] Human Rights Watch interview with primary school teacher, village in the Triangle region, December 6, 2000.
[511] Human Rights Watch interview with high school Hebrew teacher, Nazareth, December 8, 2000.
[512] Human Rights Watch interview with fifth and sixth-grade teacher, unrecognized village near Be'er Sheva, December 16, 2000.

Consideration of Palestinian Arab identity requires greater participation of Palestinian Arab educators in curriculum development. "Right now there are not Arabs in all departments dealing with them in education. We asked the ministry to make a clear statement on representation in all the departments for Arab education–this is basic," Saadi remarked. The area where positive changes have taken place are, not surprisingly, in subjects that are unique or adapted for Arab education where Palestinian Arab educators have participated in curriculum development and have pushed for reform. The most notable changes have recently taken place in the subjects of high school history, geography for grades five to nine, and civics. These changes will be discussed in greater detail below.

Delays in Translation and Development of Curricula

On the whole, children in Arab schools receive a Jewish education, using curricula and teaching materials first developed by Jewish educators for use in Jewish schools and later translated into Arabic.[513] "The ministry's curriculum is translated from the Hebrew which is a different culture. It's a bad translation and it's old curriculum," the vice-principal of an Arab primary school told Human Rights Watch.[514] Delays in translation result in Arab schools lagging behind Jewish schools, relying on outdated curricula or, in some cases, no curricula at all. "We can't even dream about closing the gap between us and Jewish schools. We started ten years later with a low budget and few people. We can't close the gap ever–maybe narrow it, but never close it," stated Khawla Saadi, Director of Curriculum for Arab Israeli Schools.[515] She explained that "[s]ome syllabi are not translated because teachers can read Hebrew."

With few resources dedicated to Arabic curriculum development, Palestinian Arab educators working on curriculum development are overextended, and advances are slow. A school counselor at an Arab high school in Nazareth explained:

---

[513] Problems in translation relate not only to delays in translation, but also to the quality of translation, which several interviewees noted was mixed. Translation problems extend to other areas of education as well. Several interviewees complained about the quality of the Arabic translation of the psychometric exam (a standardized exam required for all students seeking admission to university), resulting in poorer exam results for Arab students.
[514] Human Rights Watch interview, mixed city, December 10, 2000.
[515] Human Rights Watch interview with Khawla Saadi, Director of Curriculum for Israeli Arab Schools, Ministry of Education, Jerusalem, December 20, 2000.

It's not just the material, the main problem is that when the ministry does an educational program, they never do it in Arabic. Many things aren't even translated. We have to translate them and fit them to our needs. For example, the life skills program–it doesn't fit our needs and our specialties in Arab society, and we have to get funds to translate. We always ask them to do in Arabic, to put an Arab person on the committee. We have to work double time.[516]

A review of the published curricula for Arab schools shows curricula in some subjects that is ten, and in a few cases, over twenty years old. Deneis A., a parent who sent her daughter to a Jewish school and later to an Arab school, commented on the disparity between the two systems. In the Jewish school, she explained "[e]very two years there were new books, and teachers have lots of books to choose from." In contrast, in the Arab school "[t]he Arab children have to wait two or three years until the Hebrew curriculum is translated, so they are always behind."[517]

Special Education

Human Rights Watch found no special education curricula adapted for Arab students in the special education schools and classes we visited. "We just get the normal curriculum," explained a speech therapist working in an Arab school for physically disabled children.[518] The principal of the school confirmed: "We just get the normal curriculum, nothing special. We look for special material and we create some. If we need a work book, we make it here."[519] Another speech therapist in an Arab school for mentally disabled children commented on the absence of curricula: "we don't have programs for special education. "We have to make everything–exams, papers–everything." When asked how she created her own curriculum, she replied "I take it from regular Arabic books and prepare some questions. We adapt curriculum for regular schools and try to make it easier."[520]

Khawla Saadi told Human Rights Watch that four or five Arabic special education books for the primary level were published in 2000, and that she had

---

[516] Human Rights Watch interview, Nazareth, December 8, 2000.
[517] Human Rights Watch interview, Haifa, December 6, 2000.
[518] Human Rights Watch interview, Israel, December 11, 2000.
[519] Human Rights Watch interview, Israel, December 11, 2000.
[520] Human Rights Watch interview, Israel, December 11, 2000.

given most of her budget that year to their development.[521]   The materials had
not yet been distributed in any of the schools Human Rights Watch visited.

Finally, although published curricula do exist for most subjects in Arab
schools, there is still a dearth of teaching materials and textbooks available in
Arabic. Thus even with a sound curriculum in place, implementation is difficult
without the appropriate Arabic textbooks. The result is that children in Arab
schools perceive their education as second hand and second rate compared to
their counterparts in Jewish schools.

Teaching Material and Textbooks

A critical dimension of Palestinian Arabs' education lies with the
availability of materials used to teach the required curricula, and the lack
thereof. "There is an enormous difference in the quantity of material. Material
for Arab schools must be translated from Hebrew," commented Daphna Golan,
the chair of the Committee for Closing the Gap within the Pedagogical
Secretariat of the Ministry of Education.[522] "We have all the syllabi but not all
syllabi have materials.   This is the gap," stated Khawla Saadi.[523]   Thick
catalogues of teaching materials for Jewish schools stand in stark contrast to the
thin catalogues of materials available for Arab schools.

For example, a kindergarten teacher may turn to a guidebook of in-class
programs and find that although there may be many suggested lessons, there are
few materials to support him or her in the classroom. "If I am a good teacher, I
go to the catalogue and pick an environmental program. The Arab teacher
doesn't have any material to support her work on the environment, so she invents
it or goes without," explained Nabila Espanioly, director of Al-Tufula
Pedagogical Center, commenting on a guidebook of programs for kindergarten
teachers.[524]   This criticism was echoed by many teachers and educators
interviewed by Human Rights Watch.   Zafer Shurbaji, of the Fund for the
Development of Technological Education in the Arab Sector, stated that there
are no computer programs in Arabic: "Maybe you have the computers, but not
the programs in Arabic. It's starting to change, but not enough. I think we are

---

[521] Human Rights Watch interview with Khawla Saadi, Director of Curriculum for Israeli
Arab Schools, Ministry of Education, Jerusalem, December 20, 2000.
[522] Human Rights Watch interview with Daphna Golan, Chair, Committee for Closing the
Gap, Pedagogical Secretariat, Ministry of Education, Jerusalem, December 20, 2000.
[523] Human Rights Watch interview with Khawla Saadi, Director of Curriculum for Israeli
Arab Schools, Ministry of Education, Jerusalem, December 20, 2000.
[524] Human Rights Watch interview with Nabila Espanioly, Director, Al-Tufula
Pedagogical Center, Nazareth, December 8, 2000.

twenty years behind the Jewish sector."[525]   Khawla Saadi confirmed that there
are no Arabic computer books for Arab schools.[526]

The scarcity of teaching materials for Arab schools is attributable in large
part to the absence of government resources devoted to the development of such
materials.   "The Jewish system of education is very dynamic and always
evolving. The Arab system is fixed, stagnant. Until now we don't have a center
to do research on education, to develop teaching texts for the Arab community,"
commented Professor George Kanazi', a former adviser to the Ministry of
Education.[527]   Professor Butrus Abu-Manneh, an expert on Arab history
curriculum at Haifa University, explained: "In Hebrew schools, each curriculum
department would have a committee that would approve textbooks and develop
materials for many different subjects.   Arabs don't have a committee for
preparing books and so forth. It's left to be done in the form of unofficial
publications."[528]

Without the financial commitment and support of the Israeli government,
development of Arabic teaching materials will continue to lag behind.
According to Khawla Saadi:

The biggest difference between the two systems is the material.
There is a big lack of specialists in the Arab system who can write
books according to the curriculum. It is also hard to get published
because the market is so small that it is not profitable for private
companies to publish them. So if the government doesn't publish
them, no one will.[529]

In recent years the Ministry of Education has moved towards decentralizing the
development and publication of textbooks, giving responsibility of drafting

[525] Human Rights Watch interview with Zafer Shurbaji, Fund for the Development of
Technological Education in the Arab Sector, Haifa, December 7, 2000.
[526] Human Rights Watch interview with Khawla Saadi, Director of Curriculum for Israeli
Arab Schools, Ministry of Education, Jerusalem, December 20, 2000.
[527] Human Rights Watch interview with Professor George Kanazi', Professor of Arabic,
Haifa University, former adviser to Ministry of Education in 1992-95, former member of
committee to prepare curriculum for Arabic language and literature, and a former
member of committee to evaluate achievement of Arabic mother tongue instruction for
grades four through eight, Haifa, December 8, 2000.
[528] Human Rights Watch interview with Professor Butrus Abu-Manneh, Haifa University,
member of committee charged with revising history curriculum for Arab high schools,
Haifa, December 5, 2000.
[529] Human Rights Watch interview with Khawla Saadi, Director of Curriculum for Israeli
Arab Schools, Ministry of Education, Jerusalem, December 20, 2000.

textbooks to private institutions.[530]   The move towards privatization is viewed by Palestinian Arab educators as likely to further hinder the development of Arabic teaching materials.

Hebrew as a Second Language and Religious Instruction

Regarding specific subjects, Palestinian Arab parents, students and teachers alike complain of compulsory instruction in Tanach (Jewish bible) and Judaism through the teaching of Hebrew language and literature in Arab high schools. Students in Arab schools begin learning Hebrew in the third grade and continue the subject through high school.[531] Although both Hebrew and Arabic are recognized as official languages, in practice, Hebrew is the principal language of the state of Israel, and fluency in the language is a necessary tool for all children to participate fully in society. Aside from the goals of advancing communication between Palestinian Arabs and Jews and enabling Palestinian Arab students' participation in the life of the state, other official goals of Hebrew instruction in Arab schools are: for children in grades three through six, to "strengthen loyalty to the state of Israel," and to advance "familiarity with the Hebrew cultural and literary inheritance of the Jewish people and their descendants and the values of that inheritance;"[532] and for children in grades seven through nine, "to increase familiarity of students with part of the cultural

---

[530] Human Rights Watch interview with Said Barghouti, Inspector of History for Arab Schools, Ministry of Education, Nazareth, December 9, 2000.

[531] Instruction in Arabic as a second language for Jewish students is not a compulsory subject in all Jewish schools, despite the fact that Arabic is recognized as an official language of Israel. Human Rights Watch received different reports from principals of Jewish schools on whether Arabic was a required subject in their schools. Two ninth-grade students from a Jewish intermediate school who did study Arabic told us that some students in their school took French instead. Human Rights Watch group interview, Nazareth Ilit, December 13, 2000. We also talked with three seventh-grade students, two girls who studied French and one boy who studied Arabic. In their school, they said, the third language was determined by their English grades. High scorers took French; low scorers took Arabic. Human Rights Watch group interview, Haifa, December 12, 2000. An expert on Arabic language and literature explained, "the Ministry of Education decided it should be compulsory in Jewish schools some years ago, but it has not been implemented yet." Human Rights Watch interview with Professor George Kanazi', Professor of Arabic, Haifa University, Haifa, December 8, 2000. What is certain is that Arabic is not a compulsory subject in the matriculation exams for Jewish students. Hebrew has long been a required subject on the matriculation exams for Palestinian Arab students.

[532] Ministry of Education, Hebrew Curriculum for Arab Students (1978), Grades 3-6, section on goals.

and literary heritage of the Jewish people and with the value of Hebrew culture."[533]

In the lower grades, children in Arab schools learn basic reading and writing in Hebrew, and study the Jewish religious holidays and their significance. The curriculum for grades seven through nine allocates 10 to 15 percent of the studied literature to biblical sources and an additional 10 percent to literature of the sages, which include Jewish Talmudic scholars.

There is no written curriculum for Hebrew instruction for grades ten to twelve,[534] but the matriculation exam (*bagrut*), which all students graduating from high school must take, contains a mandatory unit on Tanach. While the Ministry of Education states that Palestinian Arab students may take the bible portion of the matriculation exams on Christianity, Islam or the Druze religion, Palestinian Arab students and teachers stated that their Hebrew language exam covers Jewish religious texts. Also, the Central Bureau of Statistics has written that compulsory subjects in Arab education include "Hebrew (incl. Bible and literature)."[535] All students in Arab high schools thus must study Tanach in Hebrew language class, without exception. A Hebrew language teacher in an Arab high school in Nazareth described her pupils' reaction to the subject: "Some children see it as imposed on them. It makes it hard for the teacher to motivate students to study. It doesn't relate to Arab children as whole. . . but because of the *bagrut* we have to cover the material."[536]

Instilling in children an appreciation for different cultures and values is a vital part of education. However, when one considers the relatively minimal instruction available to Palestinian Arab children on their own cultural identity and religion, compared to their counterparts in Jewish schools, the state's educational emphasis on instilling Jewish religion in Palestinian Arab children is problematic. For example, according to the Ministry of Education, seven hours per pupil are scheduled for "Arab culture or Islam or Christianity or Druze

---

[533] Ministry of Education, *Hebrew Curriculum for Arab Students (1988), Grades 7-9,* section on goals. For comparison, the goals of Arabic literature in Arab schools include: "Developing the students pride in the Arabic language with respect to the fact that it is the national language and a main component of his character," and "Students' absorbing high ethics and human values from both Arabic and global heritage and culture." Ministry of Education, *Arabic Literature Curriculum for the Secondary Level, Grades 10-12,* p. 6; and Ministry of Education, *Arabic Literature Curriculum for Grades 7 - 9 in Arabic Schools,* p. 5 (English translation by Human Rights Watch).

[534] Human Rights Watch interview with Khawla Saadi, Jerusalem, December 20, 2000.

[535] CBS, *Pupils Who Took Matriculation and Final Exams and Are Entitled to Certificates 1995/1996,* no. 1129, (Jerusalem: CBS, July 2000), p. XXIII.

[536] Human Rights Watch interview, Nazareth, December 8, 2000.

heritage" for grades seven through nine in Arab schools.[537] By contrast, for grades seven through nine in Jewish schools[538] double that amount (fourteen hours) are scheduled for "Bible and Judaic Studies."[539] The imbalance is greater in grades ten through twelve; in Arab schools three to four hours per pupil are scheduled for "Arab culture or Islam or Christianity or Druze Heritage" compared to nine hours per pupil in Jewish schools for "Bible and Judaic Studies."[540] When one considers the broader framework of Arab education, with its overriding emphasis on instilling Jewish values and culture as whole, the imbalance is even more stark.

Another criticism of Hebrew language instruction is of the infrequent use of Arab writers in Hebrew. Although the official curriculum for Hebrew in Arab schools for grades seven through nine provides for the inclusion of Arab writers of the Hebrew language,[541] few examples are found in practice. "I teach literature of the Jews, poems of Jewish writers, religion of the Jews. There are Arabs who write in Hebrew, poems in Hebrew, but they are not taught," noted a Hebrew language teacher at an Arab technical high school in Haifa.[542]

On a similar note, in Arabic language and literature classes in Arab schools, students and educators expressed a desire to study the works of more Palestinian writers, on issues related to identity. It was widely commented that the works of well known Palestinian writers were used only when lyric in nature or to describe scenes of natural beauty, and that essays and poems addressing Palestinian identity were omitted from the curriculum. "The great Palestinian writers, such as Mahmoud Darwish, Emil Habibi, Jabra Ibrahim Jabra, Tawfiq Ziyad, Samih al-Qasim are not studied," stated Ameer Makhoul, director of Ittijah, a network of nongovernmental organizations working on Palestinian youth issues.[543]

---

[537] Economics and Budgeting Administration, Ministry of Education, *Facts and Figures About Education and Culture in Israel*, p. 73.
[538] Children in Jewish state religious schools receive twenty-four to twenty-six hours in Bible and Judaic Studies. Ibid., p. 72.
[539] Ibid.
[540] Ibid., pp. 74-75. Children in grades ten to twelve in Jewish state religious schools receive twenty to twenty-six hours per pupil on "Bible and Judaic Studies." Ibid.
[541] Ministry of Education, *Hebrew Curriculum for Arab Students (1987), Grades 7-9*, section on assumptions.
[542] Human Rights Watch interview, Haifa, December 4, 2000.
[543] Human Rights Watch interview with Ameer Makhoul, Director of Ittijah, Haifa, December 5, 2000.
[544] Human Rights Watch interview with fifth and sixth grade history teacher, primary school in Um El-Fahm, December 6, 2000.

Palestinian History and Recent Reforms

The teaching of Palestinian history is important in establishing children's respect and appreciation for their own cultural identity. Palestinian Arab students, parents, and teachers interviewed by Human Rights Watch uniformly criticized existing curricula for their failure to educate children on this subject:

> When we learn about the Greek or Roman period we learn so much about it, but it is not connected to us. Why don't we learn a little of our own history? Yes, they teach us a little of Arab history, but only from a small period, like Mohammed and the Caliphs. In Jewish schools, they learn lots about Jewish history and about all the Jews. Sometimes the [Palestinian Arab] students would learn Palestinian history at an event, where the teachers would themselves talk to children about it. But it's not part of the syllabus.[544]

> They taught us nothing on Palestinian history in elementary or junior high school. Yes, they taught us world history, and old Arab history, but not Palestinian history. I would like to learn more. I learn Palestinian history in a special program outside the school.[545]

> I would like to learn, not for us but for any age, about what happened from 1948 because the new generation, people our age, don't know about this—we lack information about our past. When the intifada happened last October we learned out[side] of the curriculum what happened. . . . We realized it didn't just happen like that. We connected what happened now with the past. . . . It happened because of history.[546]

Other interviewees echoed the sentiment that the Israeli education system as it exists today is designed to separate Palestinian children from their past and from the Palestinian people. "It's taking us out of our culture and history. . . . They try to separate us from the Palestinian people–they say, 'You are not Palestinian,'" said Amal Elsana-Alhooj, a Bedouin woman who works with the nongovernmental organization Shatil.[547]

In response to such criticism, the Ministry of Education published a new history curriculum in 1999 for use in Arab high schools. For the first time, one

---

[545] Human Rights Watch interview with eleventh-grade girl, Mar Elias College, I'blin, December 5, 2000.

[546] Human Rights Watch interview with tenth-grade girl, Nazareth, December 9, 2000.

[547] Human Rights Watch interview, Be'er Sheva, December 15, 2000.

of the stated goals of teaching history in Arab high schools is "to develop the pupils' feelings towards his Arab Palestinian nation and the Arab world and culture from one side, and the state of Israel and its citizens from the other," commented Said Barghouti, inspector of history for Arab schools, who participated in reviewing the new curricula for history, geography, and civics.[548] Professor Butrus Abu-Manneh, who participated in the drafting of the new curricula, remarked:

> For the first time ever, we did it. We did it from the period of Arab conquest of Palestine up until 1948. We wanted to teach pupils the history of their own people. We thought the kids had emptiness about their own life. We wanted them to feel his roots and feel proud of his people and history.[549]

The new curriculum contains five units, including a specific unit on Palestinian history, heretofore an untouched subject in Arab schools.[550] This marks a significant step forward in the Arab education system, and for the Israeli education system as whole. "It may be difficult to implement these goals into textbooks and actual teaching, but at least it is now being recognized on paper," added Barghouti.[551]

The implementation of any new curriculum, however, is difficult without the appropriate teaching materials. The new curriculum has not yet been fully implemented in Arab schools as textbooks are lacking. "Still more textbooks are needed for the new curriculum to be implemented–a patchwork approach is being used now . . . [t]rying to find materials to make do," said Barghouti.[552] Jony Mansour, Dean of Mar Elias College, explained that only one textbook exists for the new curriculum, "The Middle East in the Modern Period," which was published in two volumes by the Ministry of Education in 1995 and 1998. He noted that the new textbook, which is used to teach the first of the five units

[548] Human Rights Watch interview with Said Barghouti, Inspector of History for Arab Schools, Ministry of Education, Nazareth, December 9, 2000.
[549] Human Rights Watch interview with Professor Butrus Abu-Manneh, Haifa University, member of committee charged with revising history curriculum for Arab high schools, Haifa, December 5, 2000.
[550] Human Rights Watch interview with Said Barghouti, Inspector of History for Arab Schools, Ministry of Education, Nazareth, December 9, 2000.
[551] Ibid.
[552] According to Barghouti, two new textbooks were developed for history in Arab high schools, but only one had been published at the time of writing, on "the Middle East from the nineteenth century to 1948."

of the history curriculum, was published *before* the new curriculum was published in 1999. "In the Jewish sector, they publish the curriculum first, then the books, and lots of them. For us the Arabs, for each subject we have only one choice, no choice," said Mansour.[553] Again, as discussed above, the problem lies with the absence of government funds devoted to research and development of teaching materials in Arabic.

Other positive reforms have taken place in the subjects of geography and civics, which are subjects that are adapted for use in Arab schools. Related to history, a new geography curriculum for grades five to nine was published in 1998 for both Jewish and Arab schools. Thanks to the efforts of Palestinian Arab educators in the curriculum development process, which took over ten years, students will not be taught that Palestinian Arab and Druze communities were one of the "problems" or obstacles that Jewish settlers faced; rather there will be separate sections on Palestinian Arab communities and on Jewish settlements.[554] And in new geography textbooks in Arab schools, "we're trying to put Hebrew and Arabic names [for places] side by side," said Barghouti, whereas in the past Arabic names were largely omitted from texts.[555] Still, the primary emphasis in the curriculum in Arab schools is on the significance of places within Israel to Judaism, with some attention paid to Christianity and Islam, and there are no references to Palestine or Palestinian territory.

A "rationale," or guideline, for a new civics curriculum was presented in 1996, entitled "To be Citizens During the 21st Century: Education for Citizenship for all Students of Israel." Based on this, a new civics curriculum was developed and published for use in Jewish and Arab schools (the Arabic curriculum is adapted), which addresses, in part, issues of majority and minority rights in a state that defines itself as Jewish and democratic.[556] According to Barghouti, the new curriculum was implemented in Jewish schools last year, but was introduced as experimental in only fifteen Arab schools. Again, delays in implementation are attributed to lack of textbooks: "the textbook writers for Jewish schools began their work a year earlier," he explained.[557]

---

[553] Human Rights Watch interview with Jony Mansour, Dean of Mar Elias College, I'blin, December 5, 2000.
[554] Human Rights Watch interview with Said Barghouti, Inspector of History for Arab Schools, Ministry of Education, Nazareth, December 9, 2000.
[555] Ibid.
[556] Civics is taught in high school and is a compulsory subject on the matriculation exam. Some intermediate schools also teach civics in grade eight.
[557] Human Rights Watch interview with Said Barghouti, Inspector of History for Arab Schools, Ministry of Education, Nazareth, December 9, 2000. According to Barghouti, a

Other educators still have criticized the recent reforms for failing to address the issue of Palestinian Arab identity adequately in Arab schools and for failing to address it at all in Jewish schools. It must be underlined that all of the changes discussed above refer to changes in Arab schools only. Professor Majid Al Haj, a noted expert on Arab education in Israel based at Haifa University, commented:

> The issue of the Palestinian identity is not really addressed in Arab books and certainly not in the books for Hebrew schools. . . . The syllabus ignores the major issue of citizenship of Arab students. . . . The issue should not be to identify the self as Palestinian but to assess whether one has full citizenship rights. Are we full citizens or not? It's asymmetric education, one-sided multiculturalism, where Arab students are educated for control and Jewish students for ethnocentric rule.[558]

Indeed, a primary focus of Limor Livnat, Minister of Education appointed in 2001, has been to increase the curricula's focus on Jewish values and culture. "What I would like to see is that there is not a single child in Israel who doesn't learn the basics of Jewish and Zionist knowledge and values," she told a journalist.[559] Beginning in the fall of 2001, middle school students will take a course entitled "Jewish heritage," at an annual cost to the state of NIS 30 million ($7.5 million).[560] While Livnat explained that Palestinian Arab students will not be required to take the course and referred to the most recent five-year plan discussed above, she did not outline plans for additional funding for Arab education. These developments illustrate the Ministry of Education's overwhelming emphasis on Jewish education and Jewish children, with Palestinian Arab children as an afterthought.

Conclusion

The Israeli government has made some positive changes in curricula for Arab schools, principally in the few subjects that are specially adapted for Arab

---

curriculum on "homeland and society" is also currently being developed for Jewish and Arab schools to address issues of Zionism and the Palestinian Arab nation.

[558] Human Rights Watch interview with Professor Majid Al-Haj, Haifa University, Haifa, December 5, 2000.

[559] Fisher-Ilan, "Livnat's Lessons."

[560] Relly Sa'ar, "Livnat Announces New Jewish Heritage Course for Schools," *Ha'aretz Daily Newspaper (English Edition)* (Israel), May 14, 2001.

schools. Still, further changes are needed, not only in the special subjects for Arab schools, but in the system as a whole. Barghouti commented:

> In history, geography, and civics, we are trying to deal with it, but that is not enough. It needs to be more comprehensive. There is a need to decide the main objectives of Arab education in Israel and to try to apply them using materials aimed at developing a person to be aware of his identity and his national identity, and the dilemma between both, and how to deal with that.[561]

Part of allowing and enabling children to reconcile difference requires recognition and respect for difference, rather than denial and erasure of it. The Committee on the Rights of the Child has stressed the importance of the aims of education as a means of "reconciling diverse values through dialogues and respect for difference. Moreover children are capable of playing a unique role in bridging many of the differences that have historically separated groups of people from another."[562] Greater consideration and recognition of the unique identity of Palestinian Arab children in curricula and teaching materials in both Jewish and Arab schools can serve to bridge the gap between Palestinian Arab and Jewish children, rather than drive them apart. Only by allowing Palestinian Arab children the right to enjoy their culture, history, and values alongside state national values will children learn by example how to reconcile difference, through tolerance and mutual respect.

---

[561] Human Rights Watch interview with Said Barghouti, Inspector of History for Arab Schools, Ministry of Education, Nazareth, December 9, 2000.

[562] *General Comment 1, The Aims of Education (Article 29(1))*, Committee on the Rights of the Child, para 4.

XIII. ISRAEL'S OBLIGATIONS UNDER INTERNATIONAL AND NATIONAL LAW

> The right to education straddles the division of human rights into civil and political, on one hand, and economic, social and cultural, on the other hand, thereby affirming the conceptual universality of human rights. Both the right to education and rights in education thus ought to be recognized and protected. Moreover, many human rights can only be accessed through education.
>
> –K. Tomaševski, U.N. Special Rapporteur on the Right to Education[563]

International Law

Education is one of the most protected rights in international law. Fundamental to the right to education is the state's obligation to provide it in a non-discriminatory manner. The Universal Declaration of Human Rights, which establishes a right to education, explicitly prohibits discrimination and provides all persons equal protection under the law.[564] Israel is a party to the International Covenant on Civil and Political Rights (ICCPR),[565] the International Covenant on Economic, Social, and Cultural Rights (ICESCR),[566] the Convention on the Rights of the Child (CRC),[567] the Convention against Discrimination in Education,[568] the International Convention on the Elimination

---

[563] Tomaševski, "Removing Obstacles in the Way of the Right to Education," p. 9.

[564] UDHR, arts. 2, 7, 26.

[565] International Covenant on Civil and Political Rights (ICCPR). arts. 2(1), 26, *adopted* December 16, 1966, G.A. Res. 2200A (XXI), 999 U.N.T.S. 171 (entered into force March 23, 1976, and ratified by Israel October 3, 1991). Although the ICCPR does not list primary education as a core civil and political right, article 24 guarantees each child "the right to such measures of protection as are required by his status as a minor on the part of his family society and the State." This provision of article 24 has been interpreted to include education sufficient to enable each child to develop his or her capacities and enjoy civil and political rights as a measure of protection. *General Comment 17, Rights of the Child*, U.N. Human Rights Committee, 35th sess., (April 7, 1989), paras. 3, 5, in *Compilation of General Comments and General Recommendations Adopted by Human Rights Treaty Bodies*, U.N. Doc. HRI\GEN\1\Rev.1 (1994), p. 23. On the right to education in international law, see, generally, Manfred Nowak, 'The Right to Education,' in *Economic, Social, and Cultural Rights*, eds. Asbjorn Eide, et al. (Boston: M. Nijhoff Publishers, 1995), pp. 189-211.

[566] ICESCR, arts. 2(2), 13.

[567] Convention on the Rights of the Child. arts. 2, 13.

[568] Convention against Discrimination in Education. art. 2(b).

of All Forms of Racial Discrimination (CERD),[569] and the Convention on the Elimination of All Forms of Discrimination against Women (CEDAW),[570] which contain similar provisions.

The Right to Education

Everyone has the right to education.
—Universal Declaration of Human Rights, article 26

The right to education is set forth in the Universal Declaration of Human Rights, the ICESCR, and the Convention on the Rights of the Child.[571] Each of these documents specifies that primary education must be "compulsory and available free to all." Secondary education, including vocational education, must be "available and accessible to every child," with the progressive introduction of free secondary education.[572] The Convention on the Rights of the Child further specifies that states must "make educational and vocational information and guidance available and accessible to all children" and "take measures to encourage regular attendance and the reduction of drop-out rates."[573]

The U.N. Committee on Economic, Social, and Cultural Rights has interpreted what is required to fulfill the right to education in a General Comment on article 13 of the ICESCR.[574] According to the committee, educational institutions must be both available in sufficient quantity and physically accessible, that is, "within safe physical reach, either by attendance at some reasonably convenient geographic location (e.g. a neighbourhood school) or via modern technology (e.g. access to a 'distance learning' programme)."[575]

---

[569] The Convention on the Elimination of All Forms of Racial Discrimination obligates Israel to "guarantee the right of everyone, without distinction as to race, colour, or national or ethnic origin, to equality before the law, notably in the enjoyment of . . . [t]he right to education." Convention on the Elimination of All Forms of Racial Discrimination (CERD), art. 5(e)(v), *adopted* December 21, 1965, G.A. Res. 2106 (XX), 660 U.N.T.S. 195 (entered into force January 4, 1969, and ratified by Israel January 3, 1979).

[570] CEDAW, art. 10.

[571] UDHR, art. 26; ICESCR, art. 13; Convention on the Rights of the Child, art. 28.

[572] Convention on the Rights of the Child, art. 28(1); ICESCR, art. 13(2); see UDHR, art. 26(1).

[573] Convention on the Rights of the Child, art. 28(1)(d), (e).

[574] *General Comment 13, The Right to Education,* Committee on Economic, Social and Cultural Rights, para. 6.

[575] Ibid.

The Right to Freedom from Discrimination in Education

Because different states have different levels of resources, international law does not mandate exactly what kind of education must be provided, beyond certain minimum standards. Accordingly, the right to education is considered a "progressive right": by becoming party to the international agreements, a state agrees "to take steps . . . to the maximum of its available resources" to the full realization of the right to education.[576] But although the right to education is a right of progressive implementation, the prohibition on discrimination is not. The Committee on Economic, Social and Cultural Rights has stated: "The prohibition against discrimination enshrined in article 2 (2) of the [International Covenant on Economic, Social and Cultural Rights] is subject to neither progressive realization nor the availability of resources; it applies fully and immediately to all aspects of education and encompasses all internationally prohibited grounds of discrimination."[577]

Thus, regardless of its resources, the state must provide education "on the basis of equal opportunity," "without discrimination of any kind irrespective of the child's race, colour, sex, language, religion, political or other opinion, national ethnic or social origin, property, disability, birth or other status."[578] In addition, the guarantees of equality before the law and the equal protection of law prevent a government from arbitrarily making distinctions among classes of persons in promulgating and enforcing its laws. A state will violate the prohibition on discrimination in education both with direct action, such as

---

[576] ICESCR, art. 2(1). See Convention on the Rights of the Child, art. 28. But see *General Comment 13, The Right to Education,* Committee on Economic, Social and Cultural Rights, para. 44: "The realization of the right to education over time, that is 'progressively', should not be interpreted as depriving States parties' obligations of all meaningful content. Progressive realization means that States parties have a specific and continuing obligation 'to move as expeditiously and effectively as possible' towards the full realization of article 13"; and *General Comment 3, The Nature of States Parties Obligations,* Committee on Economic, Social and Cultural Rights, 5th sess., (December 14, 1990), para. 2: "Such steps should be deliberate, concrete and targeted as clearly as possible towards meeting the obligations recognized in the Covenant."

[577] *General Comment 13, The Right to Education,* Committee on Economic, Social and Cultural Rights, para. 31. See also, *General Comment 11, Plans of Action for Primary Education,* Committee on Economic, Social and Cultural Rights, 20th sess., U.N. Doc. E/C.12/1999/4 (May 10, 1999), para. 10; and *General Comment 3, The Nature of States Parties Obligations,* Committee on Economic, Social and Cultural Rights, para. 2 (stating that the obligation to guarantee the exercise of rights in the International Covenant on Economic, Social and Cultural Rights without discrimination is "of immediate effect").

[578] Convention on the Rights of the Child, arts. 28(1), 2(1).

introducing or failing to repeal discriminatory laws, as well as when it fails to take measures "which address de facto educational discrimination."[579] States must ensure that their domestic legal systems provide "appropriate means of redress, or remedies, . . . to any aggrieved individual or groups," including judicial remedies.[580]

The Convention against Discrimination in Education, ratified by Israel in 1961, spells out what constitutes discrimination in education. The convention defines "discrimination" as:

> any distinction, exclusion, limitation or preference which, being based on race, colour, sex, language, religion, political or other opinion, national or social origin, economic condition or birth, has the purpose or effect of nullifying or impairing equality of treatment in education and in particular . . . [o]f limiting any person or group of persons to education of an inferior standard.[581]

Specifically, the convention prohibits:

---

[579] *General Comment 13, The Right to Education,* Committee on Economic, Social and Cultural Rights, para. 59.

[580] *General Comment 9, The Domestic Application of the Covenant,* Committee on Economic, Social and Cultural Rights, 19th sess., U.N. Doc. E/C.12/1998/24 (December 3, 1998), paras. 2, 9. See also, *General Comment 3, The Nature of States Parties Obligations,* Committee on Economic, Social and Cultural Rights, para. 5.

[581] Convention against Discrimination in Education, art. 1. This convention was adopted by the General Conference of the United Nations Educational, Scientific and Cultural Organization (UNESCO) on December 14, 1960 and entered into force on May 22, 1962. The full text is reprinted in the appendix. The Convention against Discrimination in Education and the subsequent Protocol Instituting a Conciliation and Good Offices Commission established a mechanism for states parties to enforce the convention against other states parties, but these provisions have never been used. Despite this relative lack of use, the convention remains an important source of international law on education, as attested to by recent references to it in the UNESCO Executive Board Decisions adopted at the 152nd session, Paris, October 16-17, 1997; at the Committee on Economic, Social and Cultural Rights, 21st session, November 15-December 3, 1999; and in the nine new signatories to the CDE since 1993, bringing the total number of states parties to ninety. In addition, the Committee on Economic, Social and Cultural Rights has interpreted the prohibition on discrimination and the rights to education in article 2(2) and 13 of the ICESCR in accord with the Convention against Discrimination in Education. *General Comment 13: The Right to Education,* Committee on Economic, Social, and Cultural Rights, paras. 31, 33, 34.

any differences of treatment by the public authorities between
nationals, except on the basis of merit or need . . . [and] in any form
of assistance granted by the public authorities to educational
institutions, any restrictions or preference based solely on the ground
that pupils belong to a particular group.[582]

While the Convention against Discrimination in Education permits the
establishment and maintenance of separate educational systems for religious or
linguistic reasons, participation in these systems must be optional, the education
offered must be "in keeping with the wishes of the pupil's parents or legal
guardians," and the education provided must conform to standards for
"education of the same level."[583] Moreover, as a party to the convention, Israel
has agreed to develop and apply a national policy that "ensure[s] that the
standards of education are equivalent in all public education institutions of the
same level, and that the conditions relating to the quality of education provided
are also equivalent."[584]

International law also explicitly guarantees the right to education without
discrimination for disabled children.[585]

The prohibition on all forms of discrimination does not mean that every
distinction is impermissible.   The U.N. Human Rights Committee has
interpreted the ICCPR to mean that "not every differentiation of treatment will
constitute discrimination, if the criteria for such differentiation are reasonable
and objective and if the aim is to achieve a purpose which is legitimate under the
Covenant."[586] Indeed, the principal of equality sometimes requires states "to
take affirmative action in order to diminish or eliminate conditions which cause
or help to perpetuate discrimination prohibited by the Convention."[587]

---

[582] Ibid., arts. 3(c), (d).
[583] Ibid., art. 2(b). See *General Comment 13, The Right to Education*, Committee on
Economic, Social and Cultural Rights, para. 33 (affirming article 2 of the Convention
against Discrimination in Education).
[584] Convention against Discrimination in Education, art. 4(b).
[585] Convention on the Rights of the Child, arts. 2, 23(3); Declaration on the Rights of
Disabled Persons, paras. 2, 6, 10.
[586] *General Comment 18, Non-Discrimination*, U.N. Human Rights Committee, 37th sess.,
(November 10, 1989), para. 13, in *Compilation of General Comments and General
Recommendations Adopted by Human Rights Treaty Bodies*, p. 26.
[587] Ibid., para. 10.

The Status of International Law in Israeli Law

Israel is legally bound by the treaties that it has ratified. However, these treaties generally will not have the status of law in Israeli courts until the Knesset passes additional, enacting legislation. Nevertheless, the courts have cited international treaties, including the Convention on the Rights of the Child, in their rulings as having interpretive authority. The December 2000 Pupils' Rights Law, states that the law's aim is to determine the "principles for the rights of the student in the spirit of human dignity and the principles of the U.N. Convention on the Rights of the Child."[588]

Israeli Law

Israel lacks an effective domestic legal framework for protecting all children from discrimination in education. Although many, including the Israeli government, argue that Israeli law as it currently exists should protect the right to education and freedom from discrimination, these rights are not being enforced for Palestinian Arab children.

Sources of Law

The state of Israel may use both constitutional law and ordinary statutes to protect children's rights. Israel has no formal constitution and no bill of rights. Rather, the Knesset (Israel's parliament) has enacted a series of Basic Laws that define the government's forms and powers.[589] Only two Basic Laws address civil liberties expressly: the 1992 Basic Law: Freedom of Occupation, which establishes the right to choose one's occupation,[590] and the 1992 Basic Law: Human Dignity and Freedom, which provides that "[a]ll persons are entitled to protection of their life, body and dignity."[591]

The Basic Laws, together with the decisions of the Israeli High Court, form

---

[588] Pupils' Rights Law, art. 1 (2000) (English translation by Human Rights Watch).

[589] The Knesset originally intended the Basic Laws to be the basis of a constitution, but this has never occurred. See "The Harari Resolution," 5 *Knesset Protocols* 1743 (1950). The failure to enact a formal constitution is due, at least in part, to opposition from Jewish religious parties, who have opposed laws regarding civil liberties and human rights that might invalidate certain religious laws.

[590] Basic Law: Freedom of Occupation, sec. 3 (1992).

[591] Basic Law: Human Dignity and Freedom, sec. 4 (1992). The law also prohibits the "the violation of the property of a person," and the deprivation of or restrictions on liberty; provides for a general right to leave Israel and for citizens' rights to re-enter; and establishes a right of privacy. Ibid., secs. 3, 5-7.

a kind of unwritten constitution and are considered constitutional law.[592] The High Court in a series of decisions has singled out and enforced certain basic civil rights in limited contexts, including the freedom of speech, the right to demonstrate, and the principle of equality. While these judicially recognized principles guide the Court's own decisions, the Court cannot use them to strike down primary legislation.[593]

Similarly, the extent of the Court's power to invalidate ordinary statutes on the grounds that they violate a Basic Law is not entirely clear. Before 1992, the High Court would only strike down legislation that violated the few provisions of the Basic Laws that it considered "entrenched," none of which contained civil rights. Following the passage of the 1992 Basic Laws, which contained provisions that appeared to limit the Knesset's power to infringe upon the rights the Basic Laws protect, the Court suggested that in some circumstances it could strike down laws that violate individual rights.[594]

Right to Education

The Basic Laws do not expressly mention the right to education, and the High Court has ruled that the right to human dignity does not encompass it.[595] However, ordinary statutes mandate some basic requirements. Under the Compulsory Education Law, the state is responsible for providing free education.[596] School attendance between the ages of three (kindergarten) and

---

[592] For more information generally, see Kretzmer, *The Legal Status of the Arabs in Israel,* pp. 7-8; and Daphne Barak-Erez, "From an Unwritten to a Written Constitution: The Israeli Challenge in American Perspective," *Columbia Human Rights Law Review,* vol. 26, pp. 312-317.

[593] Kretzmer, *The Legal Status of the Arabs in Israel,* pp. 8, 11.

[594] See *Adalah, et. al., v. The Minister of Religious Affairs, et. al.,* H.C. 240/98 (1998).

[595] *Shocharei G.I.L.A.T. Association v. Minister of Education, Culture and Sport,* 50(3) P.D. 2, 24-26 (1996). The Israeli government reported to the Committee on Economic, Social and Cultural Rights in 1998:

> While it is impossible to contest the legal existence of the right to education, the scope of constitutional protection accorded to it has not yet been defined by the courts of Israel. On one occasion, a Supreme Court judge held that the right to education is not a constitutional right, citing the absence of a positive constitutional rule to that effect. However, the President of the Supreme Court in a recent case expressed the opinion that the matter is not yet settled and that the above-mentioned judicial opinion is not binding upon the full court.

Committee on Economic, Social and Cultural Rights, *Initial Report: Israel,* U.N. Doc. E/1990/5/Add.39(3) (January 20, 1998), para. 609.

[596] Compulsory Education Law, part III, 7A (1949).

fifteen (grade ten) is compulsory and free for all. Grades eleven and twelve are also free by law,[597] and "schools are obligated by the policy of the Ministry of Education to enable [pupils in grades 11 and 12] to study and encourage them to continue their schooling."[598] The Pupils' Rights Law, passed by the Knesset in December 2000, also stipulates that "every child and youth in the State of Israel has the right to an education according to all instructions of the law."[599]

Nondiscrimination/The Principle of Equality

Israel does not categorize its citizens consistently. Frequently the government divides them into "Jews" and "Arabs." Sometimes it breaks them down on the basis of religion–"Jewish," "Muslim," Christian," and "Druze," or, simply, "non-Jewish." Other times it categorizes them by what appears to be ethnicity–Arab, Bedouin, Ashkenazi, and Sephardic (or Mizrahi). The education system is divided by language–Hebrew and Arabic. Regardless of how Palestinian Arab citizens of Israel are categorized–by race, religion, language, nationality, or ethnicity–international law protects them from discrimination on any of these and other grounds.

Of the ordinary law relating to education, Part II of the Compulsory Education Law prohibits local educational authorities from discriminating on the basis of ethnicity in the registration and admission of students, and in tracking or creating separate classrooms for students within a school.[600] The Pupils Rights Law contains a similar provision.[601] However, these laws apply only to local authorities or the schools themselves, and not to the central government.

---

[597] Ibid., part I (1949).
[598] Economics and Budgeting Administration, Ministry of Education, *Facts and Figures About Education and Culture in Israel*, p. 80.
[599] Pupils' Rights Law, art. 3 (2000).
[600] The Compulsory Education Law specifies:

The local education authority and an education institution will not discriminate on the basis of ethnicity in any of the following areas:

1) registration and admission of students;

2) designation of separate educational programs and paths for advancement in the same educational institution;

3) creation of separate classrooms within the same institute.

Compulsory Education Law, part II, 3B(a) (1949) (English translation by Human Rights Watch). The provision resulted from an amendment to the law passed in May 1991 following a lawsuit brought by Mizrahi parents from B'nai Brak whose children had not been admitted to a local Orthodox parochial school due to a quota of 30 percent for Mizrahi children. See Adva Center, *Israel Equality Monitor*, no. 1, September 1991, p. 4.
[601] Article 5(a) of the Pupils' Rights Law states:

There is no general prohibition of discrimination or guarantee of equality in any of Israel's Basic Laws. Indeed, equality was explicitly excluded from the Basic Law: Human Freedom and Dignity when it was drafted.[602] Despite this, some argue that the Basic Law: Human Freedom and Dignity does create a constitutional right to equality.[603] The Israeli High Court of Justice has specifically declined to address this argument.[604]

The High Court has recognized equality as a judicial principle and has declared that administrative discretion may not be used to discriminate on the grounds of religion or race.[605] However, with the exception of a few cases, which are limited in scope, it has dismissed petitions dealing with equal rights for Palestinian Arab citizens.

Local education, the education institution or its functionary, shall not discriminate against a student on the basis of ethnicity, on the basis of socioeconomic background, or on the basis of political affiliation of the child or of his parents in each of the following:

1) student registration, acceptance into, or rejection from the education institution;

2) determination of separate curricula and teaching methods within the same education institution;

3) establishment of separated classes within the same education institution;

4) rights and duties of students in the enforcement of discipline.

Pupils' Rights Law, art. 5(a) (2000) (English translation by Human Rights Watch).

[602] The religious lobby in Israel opposed the inclusion of a principle of equality in the Basic Law because it might have invalidated religious law, particularly in the area of family law. Generally speaking, Israeli citizens are subject to the family law of their own religion. See U.N. Human Rights Committee, *Initial Report of States Parties Due in 1993: Israel*, para. 823.

[603] Although the High Court held in 1948 that the Declaration of Independence by itself is not "constitutional law which determines the validity or invalidity of ordinances and statutes" (*Zeev v. Gubernik* 1 P.D. 85, 89 (1948)), the 1994 amendment to the Basic Law: Human Dignity and Freedom states that fundamental human rights "shall be upheld in the spirit of the principles set forth on the Declaration of the Establishment of the State of Israel," which states that the "State of Israel will ensure complete equality of social and political rights to all its inhabitants irrespective of religion, race or sex; it will guarantee freedom of religion, conscience, language, education and culture; . . . and it will be faithful to the principles of the Charter of the United Nations." 1 Laws of the State of Israel (L.S.I.) 3, 4 (1948).

[604] In the first case to raise the issue, the High Court declined to address it. *Adalah, et. al., v. The Minister of Religious Affairs, et. al.*, H.C. 240/98 (1998).

[605] *Registrar of Companies v. Kardosh*, 16 P.D. 1209, 1224 (1961). See *Peretz v. Kfar Shmaryahu Local Council*, 16 P.D. 2101 (1962).

In three recent cases, the High Court for the first time addressed in its rulings the unequal treatment of Palestinian Arab citizens. In the *Qa'dan* case, brought by Palestinian Arab citizens of Israel who were barred from purchasing a home in a cooperative Jewish community built on state lands, the Court stated that the principle of equality prohibits the state from distinguishing among its citizens on the basis of religion or nationality. Confining its decision to the facts of the case, it ruled that the authorities could not allocate land to citizens solely on the basis of their religion, though it noted that discrimination between Jews and non-Jews might be acceptable under unspecified "special circumstances." The Court then ordered the government to take such "special circumstances" into account when it determined whether it would allow the family to settle in the neighborhood; it did not rule that the family could move into the Jewish community.[606]

In *Adalah v. The Minister of Religious Affairs* ("Ministry of Religious Affairs case"), the Court found that the ministry's 1998 budget discriminated against Palestinian Arab religious communities:

> We can say, unfortunately, that today there is no equality for Arab religious communities in budget allocations of the Ministry of Religious Affairs. This conclusion is evident in the gap between the percentage of resources allocated to the non-Jewish and Jewish sectors. . . . Thus, the Arab religious communities that comprise 20 percent of the state's population are allocated only 2 percent of the budget of the Ministry of Religious Affairs. This gap speaks for itself.

Despite its finding, the Court refused to invalidate the provisions of the Budget Law at issue:

> [I]t is not enough to argue that the Arab community does not receive a portion of the budget of the Ministry of Religious Affairs which is proportional to this community's percentage in the population. Even if this is the case, it does not mean that substantive inequality exists. To establish the existence of substantive inequality, it is necessary to examine the religious needs of each religious community. Only after such an examination can we conclude that substantive inequality exists.

---

[606] *Qa'dan v. Israel Lands Administration*. 54(1) P.D. 258 (2000). The decision did not invalidate past discriminatory land allocations.

The Court found that the petitioner's requests were too general for the Court to give a "concrete and specific remedy."[607]

Adalah subsequently petitioned the High Court against the Minister of Religious Affairs to distribute funds for religious cemeteries equally to Jewish and Arab religious communities, and the Court ruled that the ministry should allocate the monies on an equal basis.[608]

The High Court of Justice has never ruled on whether the general education budget discriminates against Palestinian Arabs. Indeed, if the 1998 Ministry of Religious Affairs case is any indication, the Court might well find such a petition too general to provide a remedy. Discrimination cases are difficult to prove, in part because the Ministry of Education controls national education data and does not release budgets disaggregated by sector.[609] Where parties have petitioned the High Court regarding a particular ministry policy, the Education Ministry typically corrects or promises to correct the inequality, and the Court accepts the ministry's promise without ruling that the change is legally required. For example, in the *Shahar* case, discussed above, the Ministry of Education conceded that it had not provided Shahar academic enrichment programs to the Palestinian Arab sector and promised to allocate 20 percent of that budget for the Palestinian Arab sector within five years. The High Court in its decision explicitly declined to consider "whether the state has a duty to include the Arab sector in the special programs that are part of the educational and welfare services that the Ministry of Education provides." The Court concluded that "it is superfluous, of course, to discuss in principle the question of the duty of the state to ensure parity in educational allocations for the Arab sector."[610]

Similarly, in *The Parents Committee in Segev Shalom v. The Government-Appointed Council in Segev Shalom*, the local Parents Committee sued to compel the establishment of kindergartens for all four hundred kindergarten-aged Bedouin children in the locality. The Court dismissed the case when the council and the Ministry of Education agreed to reopen kindergartens for two

---

[607] *Adalah, et. al., v. The Minister of Religious Affairs, et. al.*. H.C. 240/98 (1998), secs. 18, 19, 24 (English translation by Adalah).

[608] *Adalah, et. al. v. Minister of Religious Affairs, et. al.*, H.C. 1113/99 (2000).

[609] Human Rights Watch telephone interview with Yousef Taiseer Jabareen, formerly an attorney for the Association for Civil Rights in Israel (ACRI), Washington, D.C., July 17, 2001. For information about the difficulties in proving discrimination under Israeli law, see Kretzmer, *The Legal Status of the Arabs in Israel*. pp. 128-29.

[610] *Follow-Up Committee on Arab Education, et. al. v. The Ministry of Education, et. al.* ("The Shahar Case"). H.C. 2814/97 (2000).

hundred children. Thus, the Court did not rule that the government was legally bound to provide kindergarten for the children.[611]

Moreover, when the High Court finds that differences between Palestinian Arabs and Jews justify certain privileges, it rules that government policies are not invalid because they further legitimate distinctions.[612] In *Agbaria v. The Minister of Education*, the High Court considered a challenge to the government policy of implementing the Long School Day law in development areas which, at the time, included only Jewish localities. The Court upheld the policy on the grounds that providing benefits to those towns only was a legitimate distinction because educational support to development areas met national needs; it was not, therefore, discriminatory.[613]

Thus, the High Court, as well as the Israeli government, has recognized the legality and value of affirmative action.[614] According to Judge Eliahu Matza:

Whether caused by discriminatory laws which existed in the past and are no longer valid, or whether through faulty perceptions which have become engrained in society, a gap is evident in the equality of opportunity, which increases the chances of the stronger groups and decreases those of the weaker ones. Balance can be effected on this gap by affirmative action. It is based on the precept that certain members of society are in an inferior position and providing equal

[611] *The Parents Committee in Segev Shalom, et. al. v. The Government-Appointed Council in Segev Shalom, et. al.*, H.C. 8534/99 (2000).

[612] For cases upholding differential treatment, see *Bourkan v. Minister of Finance*, 32(2) P.D. 800 (1978) (upholding the restriction of sales of apartments in the Jewish Quarter of the Old City of Jerusalem to Jews); *Wattad v. Minister of Finance*, 38(3) P.D. 113 (1983) (upholding a government policy of paying extra child allowances to Jewish religious students who had not served in the army despite a provision in the law that payments be made only to students who had completed army service, which, thus, excluded Palestinian Arab students); and *Avitan v. Israel Lands Administration*, H.C. 528/88 (unreported judgment) (October 25, 1989) (upholding the Israel Lands Administration's refusal to lease to a Jewish citizen property in a Bedouin settlement set up by the government on the grounds the government policy was legitimate, that it was justifiable for government to offer special terms to Bedouin, and that there was no discrimination based on ethnic or national group because the Bedouin were favored not because they were Arab but because of their nomadic lifestyle).

[613] *Agbaria v. The Minister of Education*, 45 P.D. 222 (1990). In 1991 government renewed the program, the petitioners re-filed, and the Court again dismissed the case. *Agbaria v. The Minister of Education*, 45(5) P.D. 742 (1991).

[614] See, for example, U.N. Human Rights Committee, *Initial Report of States Parties Due in 1993: Israel*, paras. 829-830.

opportunity will no longer be sufficient to close the gap. Providing equal opportunity under these circumstances will only fulfill a formal theory of equality but will not afford the underprivileged groups a viable change to receive their portion of society's resources. Long-term implementation of formal equality only increases the danger that human nature and character will result in the perpetuation of discrimination. Remedying the inequities of the past and attaining actual equality can, therefore, be accomplished only by giving preference to the weaker group.[615]

However, as the above chapters demonstrate, while Israel pursues policies of affirmative action in education, these policies have been applied primarily to benefit particular Jewish groups and to further discriminate against Palestinian Arab students.

---

[615] Judge Eliahu Matza, *Israeli Women's Lobby v. The Government*, 48(5) P.D. 529 (1994), quoted in *Sikkuy's Report on Equality and integration of the Arab Citizens in Israel 1999-2000*, (Israel: Sikkuy, June 2000), p. 8.

APPENDIX A: CALCULATION OF THE DISTRIBUTION OF TEACHING HOURS

Table 23: Calculation of the Distribution of Teaching Hours 1999-2000

	Full-time equivalents (work units)[616]		Hours[617]		Students		Hours/student	
	Jewish schools	Arab schools	Jewish schools	Arab schools	Jewish students	Palestinian Arab students	Jewish students	Palestinian Arab students
Total	80,023	18,046	2,176,128	496,254	1,180,905	328,418	1.84	1.51
Kindergarten (official)	8,600	1,119	258,000	33,570	170,360	43,920	1.51	0.76
Primary	33,996	9,406	1,019,880	282,180	563,839	182,519	1.81	1.55
Intermediate	13,951	3,268	334,824	78,432	188,122	53,708	1.78	1.46
Secondary	23,476	4,253	563,424	102,072	258,584	48,271	2.18	2.11

Sources: CBS, *Statistical Abstract of Israel 2000*, no. 51, tables 22.10, 22.27; Yosef Gidanian, Central Bureau of Statistics, e-mails to Human Rights Watch, June 18, 2001 and July 31, 2001; and Ministry of Education, *Proposed Budget for the Ministry of Education 2001 and Explanations as Presented to the Fifteenth Knesset*, no. 11, October 2000, p. 144.

[616] A full-time equivalent is the "number of hours constituting a full teaching post." CBS, *Statistical Abstract of Israel 2000*, p. (104). This data is consistent with that presented in Ministry of Education, *Proposed Budget for the Ministry of Education 2000*, pp. 157, 168, 179.
[617] In kindergarten and primary education, thirty hours per week constituted a full teaching post; in intermediate and secondary education, a full teaching post was twenty-four hours per week. CBS, *Statistical Abstract of Israel 2000*, p. (104); Yosef Gidanian, Central Bureau of Statistics, e-mail to Human Rights Watch, July 31, 2001.

Table 24: Numerical Comparison of Jewish and Arab Education in Israel

	Jewish education	Arab education
Enrolled students (2000-2001) (total number)	77.8% (1,250,000)	22.2% (356,000)
Allocation of teaching hours (1999-2000) (average weekly teaching hours/student)	81.6% (1.84)	18.4% (1.51)
Schools		
Average pupils/class (1998-1999)	26	30
Average children/teacher (1999-2000)	15.5	18.7
Distribution of classrooms (1998) (total number)	80.5% (34,747)	19.5% (8,423)
Schools with libraries (1994-1996)	80.7%	64.4%
Schools with educational counseling (1994-1996)	78.7%	36.2%
Schools with psychological counseling (1994-1996)	83.2%	40.0%
Schools with counseling by a social worker (1994-1996)	64.4%	53.7%
Schools with truant officers (1994-1996)	65.1%	53.7%
Teachers		
Teachers with an academic degree (1997-1998)	59.5%	39.7%
Teachers rated "not qualified"	4.1%	7.9%
Primary schools with voluntary in-service training (1994-1995)	87.9%	60.1%
Primary schools with no programs to improve teaching (1994-1995)	6.4%	21.5%
Kindergarten (ages 3-5)		
Kindergarten attendance (private, municipal, and state) (1998-1999)		
age 3	89.3%	22.5%
age 4	92.9%	33.5%
age 5	94.0%	80.7%
Pupils/teaching staff: government kindergartens (1999-2000)	19.8	39.3
Special Education		

Distribution of teaching hours (total) (1999-2000)	85.9%	14.1%
Teaching hours for integration (mainstreaming) (1998-1999)	91.6%	8.4%
Special education kindergartens (1998-1999)	484 (91.5%)	45 (8.5%)
Integrated kindergartens (1998-1999)	61 (100%)	0 (0%)
Special education schools (excluding kindergartens) (1998-1999)	222 (83.5%)	44 (16.5%)
Students in primary schools for "handicapped children" (1999-2000)	13,165 (85.4%)	2,253 (14.6%)
Performance		
Drop-out rates by age seventeen (1998-1999)	10.4%	31.7%
Bagrut pass rate among all seventeen-year-olds (1999-2000)	45.6%	27.5%
Bagrut pass rate among examinees	63.0%	43.4%
Qualification rate for university admission among all seventeen-year-olds (1999-2000)	40.4%	18.4%
University applicants who were rejected (1998-1999)	16.7%	44.7%
University students studying for first (undergraduate) degree (1998-1999)	91.3%	8.7%
University first degree recipients (1998-1999)	94.3%	5.7%

Sources: Ministry of Education, "Statistics of the Matriculation Examination (*Bagrut*) 2000 Report," http://www.netvision.net.il/bagrut/netunim2000.htm (accessed on May 10, 2001), pp. 5, 7, 45; State of Israel Ministry of Justice, Ministry of Foreign Affairs, *Initial Periodic Report of the State of Israel Concerning the Implementation of the Convention on the Rights of the Child (CRC)*, February 20, 2001, p. 307; Daphna Golan, Chair, Committee for Closing the Gap, Pedagogical Secretariat, Ministry of Education, *Closing the Gaps in Arab Education in Israel: Data About Hebrew-Arab Education; Recommendations of the Committee for Closing the Gap; Protocol of the Meeting of the Directorship, December 13, 2000*, December 2000, p. 3; Ministry of Education, *Proposed Budget for the Ministry of Education 2001 and Explanations as Presented to the Fifteenth Knesset*, no. 11, October 2000, pp. 144, 158; CBS, *Survey of Education and Welfare Services 1995/1996: Secondary Schools, Hebrew and Arab Education*, (Jerusalem: CBS, May 1999); CBS, *Statistical Abstract of Israel 2000*, no. 51; and CBS, *Survey of Education and Welfare Services 1994/1995: Primary and Intermediate Schools, Hebrew and Arab Education*, (Jerusalem: CBS, October 1997).

APPENDIX C: EXCERPTS FROM THE INTERNATIONAL COVENANT ON CIVIL AND POLITICAL RIGHTS

Preamble

The States Parties to the present Covenant,

Considering that, in accordance with the principles proclaimed in the Charter of the United Nations, recognition of the inherent dignity and of the equal and inalienable rights of all members of the human family is the foundation of freedom, justice and peace in the world,

Recognizing that these rights derive from the inherent dignity of the human person,

Recognizing that, in accordance with the Universal Declaration of Human Rights, the ideal of free human beings enjoying civil and political freedom and freedom from fear and want can only be achieved if conditions are created whereby everyone may enjoy his civil and political rights, as well as his economic, social and cultural rights,

Considering the obligation of States under the Charter of the United Nations to promote universal respect for, and observance of, human rights and freedoms,

Realizing that the individual, having duties to other individuals and to the community to which he belongs, is under a responsibility to strive for the promotion and observance of the rights recognized in the present Covenant,

Agree upon the following articles:

Article 2

1. Each State Party to the present Covenant undertakes to respect and to ensure to all individuals within its territory and subject to its jurisdiction the rights recognized in the present Covenant, without distinction of any kind, such as race, colour, sex, language, religion, political or other opinion, national or social origin, property, birth or other status.

APPENDIX D: EXCERPTS FROM THE INTERNATIONAL COVENANT ON ECONOMIC, SOCIAL AND CULTURAL RIGHTS

Preamble

The States Parties to the present Covenant, Considering that, in accordance with the principles proclaimed in the Charter of the United Nations, recognition of the inherent dignity and of the equal and inalienable rights of all members of the human family is the foundation of freedom, justice and peace in the world,

Recognizing that these rights derive from the inherent dignity of the human person,

Recognizing that, in accordance with the Universal Declaration of Human Rights, the ideal of free human beings enjoying freedom from fear and want can only be achieved if conditions are created whereby everyone may enjoy his economic, social and cultural rights, as well as his civil and political rights,

Considering the obligation of States under the Charter of the United Nations to promote universal respect for, and observance of, human rights and freedoms,

Realizing that the individual, having duties to other individuals and to the community to which he belongs, is under a responsibility to strive for the promotion and observance of the rights recognized in the present Covenant,

Agree upon the following articles:

Article 2

2. The States Parties to the present Covenant undertake to guarantee that the rights enunciated in the present Covenant will be exercised without discrimination of any kind as to race, colour, sex, language, religion, political or other opinion, national or social origin, property, birth or other status.

Article 13

1. The States Parties to the present Covenant recognize the right of everyone to education. They agree that education shall be directed to the full development of the human personality and the sense of its dignity, and shall strengthen the respect for human rights and fundamental freedoms. They further agree that education shall enable all persons to participate effectively in a free society, promote understanding, tolerance and friendship among all nations and all racial, ethnic or religious groups, and further the activities of the United Nations for the maintenance of peace.

2. The States Parties to the present Covenant recognize that, with a view to achieving the full realization of this right:

(a) Primary education shall be compulsory and available free to all;

(b) Secondary education in its different forms, including technical and vocational secondary education, shall be made generally available and accessible to all by every appropriate means, and in particular by the progressive introduction of free education;

(c) Higher education shall be made equally accessible to all, on the basis of capacity, by every appropriate means, and in particular by the progressive introduction of free education;

(d) Fundamental education shall be encouraged or intensified as far as possible for those persons who have not received or completed the whole period of their primary education;

(e) The development of a system of schools at all levels shall be actively pursued, an adequate fellowship system shall be established, and the material conditions of teaching staff shall be continuously improved.

3. The States Parties to the present Covenant undertake to have respect for the liberty of parents and, when applicable, legal guardians to choose for their children schools, other than those established by the public authorities, which conform to such minimum educational standards as may be laid down or approved by the State and to ensure the religious and moral education of their children in conformity with their own convictions.

4. No part of this article shall be construed so as to interfere with the liberty of individuals and bodies to establish and direct educational institutions, subject always to the observance of the principles set forth in paragraph I of this article and to the requirement that the education given in such institutions shall conform to such minimum standards as may be laid down by the State.

APPENDIX E: EXCERPTS FROM THE CONVENTION ON THE RIGHTS OF THE CHILD

Article 2

1. States Parties shall respect and ensure the rights set forth in the present Convention to each child within their jurisdiction without discrimination of any kind, irrespective of the child's or his or her parent's or legal guardian's race, colour, sex, language, religion, political or other opinion, national, ethnic or social origin, property, disability, birth or other status.

2. States Parties shall take all appropriate measures to ensure that the child is protected against all forms of discrimination or punishment on the basis of the status, activities, expressed opinions, or beliefs of the child's parents, legal guardians, or family members.

Article 28

1. States Parties recognize the right of the child to education, and with a view to achieving this right progressively and on the basis of equal opportunity, they shall, in particular:

(a) Make primary education compulsory and available free to all;

(b) Encourage the development of different forms of secondary education, including general and vocational education, make them available and accessible to every child, and take appropriate measures such as the introduction of free education and offering financial assistance in case of need;

(c) Make higher education accessible to all on the basis of capacity by every appropriate means;

(d) Make educational and vocational information and guidance available and accessible to all children;

(e) Take measures to encourage regular attendance at schools and the reduction of drop-out rates.

2. States Parties shall take all appropriate measures to ensure that school discipline is administered in a manner consistent with the child's human dignity and in conformity with the present Convention.

3. States Parties shall promote and encourage international cooperation in matters relating to education, in particular with a view to contributing to the elimination of ignorance and illiteracy throughout the world and facilitating access to scientific and technical knowledge

179

and modern teaching methods. In this regard, particular account shall be taken of the needs of developing countries.

Article 29

1. States Parties agree that the education of the child shall be directed to:

(a) The development of the child's personality, talents and mental and physical abilities to their fullest potential;

(b) The development of respect for human rights and fundamental freedoms, and for the principles enshrined in the Charter of the United Nations;

(c) The development of respect for the child's parents, his or her own cultural identity, language and values, for the national values of the country in which the child is living, the country from which he or she may originate, and for

civilizations different from his or her own;

(d) The preparation of the child for responsible life in a free society, in the spirit of understanding, peace, tolerance, equality of sexes, and friendship among all peoples, ethnic, national and religious groups and persons of indigenous origin;

(e) The development of respect for the natural environment.

2. No part of the present article or article 28 shall be construed so as to interfere with the liberty of individuals and bodies to establish and direct educational institutions, subject always to the observance of the principle set forth in paragraph 1 of the present article and to the requirements that the education given in such institutions shall conform to such minimum standards as may be laid down by the State.

APPENDIX F: THE CONVENTION AGAINST DISCRIMINATION IN EDUCATION

The General Conference of the United Nations Educational, Scientific and Cultural Organization, meeting in Paris from 14 November to 15 December 1960, at its eleventh session,

Recalling that the Universal Declaration of Human Rights asserts the principle of non-discrimination and proclaims that every person has the right to education,

Considering that discrimination in education is a violation of rights enunciated in that Declaration,

Considering that, under the terms of its Constitution, the United Nations Educational, Scientific and Cultural Organization has the purpose of instituting collaboration among the nations with a view to furthering for all universal respect for human rights and equality of educational opportunity,

Recognizing that, consequently, the United Nations Educational, Scientific and Cultural Organization, while respecting the diversity of national educational systems, has the duty not only to proscribe any form of discrimination in education but also to promote equality of opportunity and treatment for all in education,

Having before it proposals concerning the different aspects of discrimination in education, constituting item 17.1.4 of the agenda of the session,

Having decided at its tenth session that this question should be made the subject of an international convention as well as of recommendations to Member States,

Adopts this Convention on the fourteenth day of December 1960.

Article 1

1. For the purpose of this Convention, the term "discrimination" includes any distinction, exclusion, limitation or preference which, being based on race, colour, sex, language, religion, political or other opinion, national or social origin, economic condition or birth, has the purpose or effect of nullifying or impairing equality of treatment in education and in particular:

(a) Of depriving any person or group of persons of access to education of any type or at any level;

(b) Of limiting any person or group of persons to education of an inferior standard;

(c) Subject to the provisions of article 2 of this Convention, of establishing or maintaining separate educational systems or

181

institutions for persons or groups of persons; or

(d) Of inflicting on any person or group of persons conditions which are incompatible with the dignity of man.

2. For the purposes of this Convention, the term "education" refers to all types and levels of education, and includes access to education, the standard and quality of education, and the conditions under which it is given.

Article 2

When permitted in a State, the following situations shall not be deemed to constitute discrimination, within the meaning of article 1 of this Convention:

(a) The establishment or maintenance of separate educational systems or institutions for pupils of the two sexes, if these systems or institutions offer equivalent access to education, provide a teaching staff with qualifications of the same standard as well as school premises and equipment of the same quality, and afford the opportunity to take the same or equivalent courses of study;

(b) The establishment or maintenance, for religious or linguistic reasons, of separate educational systems or institutions offering an education which is in keeping with the wishes of the pupil's parents or legal guardians, if

participation in such systems or attendance at such institutions is optional and if the education provided conforms to such standards as may be laid down or approved by the competent authorities, in particular for education of the same level;

(c) The establishment or maintenance of private educational institutions, if the object of the institutions is not to secure the exclusion of any group but to provide educational facilities in addition to those provided by the public authorities, if the institutions are conducted in accordance with that object, and if the education provided conforms with such standards as may be laid down or approved by the competent authorities, in particular for education of the same level.

Article 3

In order to eliminate and prevent discrimination within the meaning of this Convention, the States Parties thereto undertake:

(a) To abrogate any statutory provisions and any administrative instructions and to discontinue any administrative practices which involve discrimination in education;

(b) To ensure, by legislation where necessary, that there is no discrimination in the admission of pupils to educational institutions;

(c) Not to allow any differences of treatment by the public authorities between nationals, except on the basis of merit or need, in the matter of school fees and the grant of scholarships or other forms of assistance to pupils and necessary permits and facilities for the pursuit of studies in foreign countries;

(d) Not to allow, in any form of assistance granted by the public authorities to educational institutions, any restrictions or preference based solely on the ground that pupils belong to a particular group;

(e) To give foreign nationals resident within their territory the same access to education as that given to their own nationals.

Article 4

The States Parties to this Convention undertake furthermore to formulate, develop and apply a national policy which, by methods appropriate to the circumstances and to national usage, will tend to promote equality of opportunity and of treatment in the matter of education and in particular:

(a) To make primary education free and compulsory; make secondary education in its different forms generally available and accessible to all; make higher education equally accessible to all on the basis of individual capacity; assure compliance by all with the obligation to attend school prescribed by law;

(b) To ensure that the standards of education are equivalent in all public education institutions of the same level, and that the conditions relating to the quality of education provided are also equivalent;

(c) To encourage and intensify by appropriate methods the education of persons who have not received any primary education or who have not completed the entire primary education course and the continuation of their education on the basis of individual capacity;

(d) To provide training for the teaching profession without discrimination.

Article 5

1. The States Parties to this Convention agree that:

(a) Education shall be directed to the full development of the human personality an d to the strengthening of respect for human rights and fundamental freedoms; it shall promote understanding, tolerance and friendship among all nations, racial or religious groups, and shall further the activities of the United Nations for the maintenance of peace;

(b) It is essential to respect the liberty of parents and, where applicable, of legal guardians, firstly to choose for their children institutions other than those maintained by the public authorities but conforming to such minimum educational standards as may be laid down or approved by the competent authorities and, secondly, to ensure in a manner consistent with the procedures followed in the State for the application of its legislation, the religious and moral education of the children in conformity with their own convictions; and no person or group of persons should be compelled to receive religious instruction inconsistent with his or their conviction;

(c) It is essential to recognize the right of members of national minorities to carry on their own educational activities, including the maintenance of schools and, depending on the educational policy of each State, the use or the teaching of their own language, provided however:

(i) That this right is not exercised in a manner which prevents the members of these minorities from understanding the culture and language of the community as a whole and from participating in its - activities, or which prejudices national sovereignty;

(ii) That the standard of education is not lower than the general standard laid down or approved by the competent authorities; and

(iii) That attendance at such schools is optional.

2. The States Parties to this Convention undertake to take all necessary measures to ensure the application of the principles enunciated in paragraph 1 of this article.

Article 6

In the application of this Convention, the States Parties to it undertake to pay the greatest attention to any recommendations hereafter adopted by the General Conference of the United Nations Educational, Scientific and Cultural Organization defining the measures to be taken against the different forms of discrimination in education and for the purpose of ensuring equality of opportunity and treatment in education.

Article 7

The States Parties to this Convention shall in their periodic reports submitted to the General Conference of the United Nations Educational, Scientific and Cultural Organization on dates and in a manner to be determined by it, give information on the legislative and administrative provisions which they have adopted and other action which they have taken for the application of this Convention, including that taken for the formulation and the development of the national policy defined in article 4 as well as the results achieved and the obstacles encountered in the application of that policy.

Article 8

Any dispute which may arise between any two or more States Parties to this Convention concerning the interpretation or application of this Convention which is not settled by negotiations shall at the request of the parties to the dispute be referred, failing other means of settling the dispute, to the International Court of Justice for decision.

Article 9

Reservations to this Convention shall not be permitted.

Article 10

This Convention shall not have the effect of diminishing the rights which individuals or groups may enjoy by virtue of agreements concluded between two or more States, where such rights are not contrary to the letter or spirit of this Convention.

Article 11

This Convention is drawn up in English, French, Russian and Spanish, the four texts being equally authoritative.

Article 12

1. This Convention shall be subject to ratification or acceptance by States Members of the United Nations Educational, Scientific and Cultural Organization in accordance with their respective constitutional procedures.

2. The instruments of ratification or acceptance shall be deposited with the Director-General of the United Nations Educational, Scientific and Cultural Organization.

Article 13

1. This Convention shall be open to accession by all States not Members of the United Nations Educational, Scientific and Cultural Organization which are invited to do so by the Executive Board of the Organization.

2. Accession shall be effected by the deposit of an instrument of accession with the Director-General of the United Nations Educational, Scientific and Cultural Organization.

Article 14

This Convention shall enter into force three months after the date of the deposit of the third instrument of ratification, acceptance or accession, but only with respect to those States which have deposited their respective instruments on or before that date. It shall enter into force with respect to any other State three months after the deposit of its instrument of ratification, acceptance or accession.

Article 15

The States Parties to this Convention recognize that the Convention is applicable not only to their metropolitan territory but also to all non-self-governing, trust, colonial and other territories for the international relations of which they are responsible; they undertake to consult, if necessary, the governments or other competent authorities of these territories on or before ratification, acceptance or accession with a view to securing the application of the Convention to those territories, and to notify the Director-General of the United Nations Educational, Scientific and Cultural Organization of the territories to which it is accordingly applied, the notification to take effect three months after the date of its receipt.

Article 16

1. Each State Party to this Convention may denounce the Convention on its own behalf or on behalf of any territory for whose international relations it is responsible.

2. The denunciation shall be notified by an instrument in writing, deposited with the Director-General of the United

Nations Educational, Scientific and Cultural Organization.

3. The denunciation shall take effect twelve months after the receipt of the instrument of denunciation.

Article 17

The Director-General of the United Nations Educational, Scientific and Cultural Organization shall inform the States Members of the Organization, the States not members of the Organization which are referred to in article 13, as well as the United Nations, of the deposit of all the instruments of ratification, acceptance and accession provided for in articles 12 and 13, and of notifications and denunciations provided for in articles 15 and 16 respectively.

Article 18

1. This Convention may be revised by the General Conference of the United Nations Educational, Scientific and Cultural Organization. Any such revision shall, however, bind only the States which shall become Parties to the revising convention.

2. If the General Conference should adopt a new convention revising this Convention in whole or in part, then, unless the new convention otherwise provides, this Convention shall cease to be open to ratification, acceptance or

accession as from the date on which the new revising convention enters into force.

Article 19

In conformity with Article 102 of the Charter of the United Nations, this Convention shall be registered with the Secretariat of the United Nations at the request of the Director-General of the United Nations Educational, Scientific and Cultural Organization.

DONE in Paris, this fifteenth day of December 1960, in two authentic copies bearing the signatures of the President of the eleventh session of the General Conference and of the Director-General of the United Nations Educational, Scientific and Cultural Organization, which shall be deposited in the archives of the United Nations Educational, Scientific and Cultural Organization, and certified true copies of which shall be delivered to all the States referred to in articles 12 and 13 as well as to the United Nations.

The foregoing is the authentic text of the Convention duly adopted by the General Conference of the United Nations Educational, Scientific and Cultural Organization during its eleventh session, which was held in Paris and declared closed the fifteenth day of December 1960.

IN FAITH WHEREOF we have appended our signatures this fifteenth day of December 1960.